THE NEW BOOK OF OPERA ANECDOTES

Date: 12/28/20

782.1 MOR
Mordden, Ethan,
The new book of opera
anecdotes /

3650 SUMMIT BLVD.
WEST PALM BEACH, FL 33406

THE NEW BOOK OF OPERA
ANECDOTES

Ethan Mordden

OXFORD
UNIVERSITY PRESS

OXFORD
UNIVERSITY PRESS

Oxford University Press is a department of the University of Oxford.
It furthers the University's objective of excellence in research, scholarship,
and education by publishing worldwide. Oxford is a registered trade mark of
Oxford University Press in the UK and certain other countries.

Published in the United States of America by Oxford University Press
198 Madison Avenue, New York, NY 10016, United States of America.

© Ethan Mordden 2020

All rights reserved. No part of this publication may be reproduced,
stored in a retrieval system, or transmitted, in any form or by any means,
without the prior permission in writing of Oxford University Press,
or as expressly permitted by law, by license, or under terms agreed with
the appropriate reproduction rights organization. Inquiries concerning
reproduction outside the scope of the above should be sent to the
Rights Department, Oxford University Press, at the address above.

You must not circulate this work in any other form
and you must impose this same condition on any acquirer.

Library of Congress Cataloging-in-Publication Data
Names: Mordden, Ethan, author.
Title: The new book of opera anecdotes / Ethan Mordden.
Description: New York : Oxford University Press, 2020. | Includes index. |
Identifiers: LCCN 2019046465 (print) | LCCN 2019046466 (ebook)
| ISBN 9780190877682 (paperback) | ISBN 9780190877699 (pdf)
| ISBN 9780190877705 (epub)
Subjects: LCSH: Opera—Anecdotes.
Classification: LCC ML1700 .M718 2020 (print) | LCC ML1700 (ebook)
| DDC 782.1—dc23
LC record available at https://lccn.loc.gov/2019046465
LC ebook record available at https://lccn.loc.gov/2019046466

1 3 5 7 9 8 6 4 2

Printed by Sheridan Books, Inc.
United States of America

CONTENTS

ACKNOWLEDGMENTS

To my longtime friend and, incidentally, agent, Joe Spieler; to Matthew Epstein, Sheri Greenawald, Ken Mandelbaum, Peter McClintock, Erick Neher, Neil Rosenshein; at Oxford, to my trusty superintendent, Joellyn Ausanka, performer and advisor Benjamin Sears, and my fine editor-in-chief, Norman Hirschy.

INTRODUCTION

This is not an updating or expansion of my earlier *Opera Anecdotes* of thirty-five years ago. Instead, this is a brand-new book with new stories. A tiny bit of the original work has been carried over (amounting to less than three per cent of the new work's content), simply because some of opera's lore is the cement that holds everything together—the inevitable "What time's the next swan?" Leo Slezak story, for instance: it's what the opera buff flashes on when he hears the words "opera anecdotes." Even so, the material repeated here appears in different form than before. Even the little introductory essays on outstanding figures such as Maria Callas and Arturo Toscanini have been newly written.

Also, as before, these stories are my retellings in my own voice, and I have taken liberties in dramatizing a tale, beefing up the characterization, adding in background material, and so on. Most of the anecdotes are amusing or enlightening, but there are dark accounts as well, as when Dmitri Shostakovich shows up for his interrogation, which in Soviet Russia meant being beaten to death. But then, luckily, something happened instead.

And that really could be the motto of any collection of opera tales: something happens instead.

THE NEW BOOK OF OPERA ANECDOTES

It Ain't Over Till the Fat Lady Sings

There Are No Fat Ladies In Opera Anymore; Or, Deborah Voigt and the Little Black Dress

"Why are you so fat?" Georg Solti asked Deborah Voigt as she was auditioning to sing Wagner's Isolde. In an interview with Voigt in *The Guardian*, Ed Pilkington recounts that Solti gave her an ultimatum: when he and Voigt met again, for a performance of Beethoven's Ninth Symphony, if she had slimmed down she could be his Isolde. Yet, as Pilkington reveals, this Isolde was for a CD recording, not a stage performance. So what difference did it make how she looked?

But that's opera today. Once, it was all about the voice. Now it's about looks, acting, and age. Oh, yes: and voice, too.

"I was completely stunned that he said it," Voigt told Pilkington. Yet there was more humiliation to come. Eight years after this, in 2004, Covent Garden hired Voigt to sing Strauss' *Ariadne auf Naxos*, then changed its mind and fired her, in front of the entire opera world, because she couldn't fit into a "little black dress"—that chic invention of Coco Chanel that was designed to take a lady anywhere, from a cocktail party with le tout Paris to lonely exile on the island of Naxos. Worse than the personal slight, to Voigt's mind, was the public's lack of understanding about how much sheer work and dedication go into creating a singer's career: "They think [we] sit on clouds all day and eat bon bons before [we] float down to the stage to sing."

Voigt didn't submit to the insult without seeking a solution: gastric bypass surgery to reduce her food intake. Eating less and thereby redeeming herself in the eye of opera management the world over, Voigt saw her career prosper. She doesn't float; she's down to earth. If there's a problem, effect a solution. But, she warns, this surgery is not to be taken lightly.

"And," she told Pilkington, "I still want cookies tonight."

Before getting into the chapters on specific subjects, let's enjoy an impromptu tour through the years to get into an anecdote mood . . .

Knock Me Over With a Feather

Anton Seidl, one of the great Wagner conductors in the late 1800s, liked to tell of the *Lohengrin* helmet in the property room of the Metropolitan Opera. It was a typical *Lohengrin* helmet until Italo Campanini assumed the role of the Swan Knight, for Campanini added a blue plume to his headgear that rose some three feet into the air.

"And that, my friends," Seidl would say in conclusion, "is Italian opera."

Dance, Little Lady

Geraldine Farrar was only twenty-three (but already a major star in Berlin) when Richard Strauss tried to talk her into singing Salome. Though the opera had just been unveiled, its heroine was known throughout the opera world as a killer of a part, a veritable voice-eater, especially of sopranos with light instruments. (The first Salome, Marie Wittich, was a Bayreuth Kundry and Isolde.) Farrar declined.

Strauss was always trying to cajole lyric voices into trying the role, it seems. Though he wrote it for a dramatic voice, to stand up to the huge orchestration, it needed the look that came with lyric sopranos, svelte and as sinuous as possible.

"You have such theatrical possibilities, Farrar," Strauss told her. "You can dance half-naked. No one will care if you can sing or not."

The Best-Dressed List

Baritone Victor Maurel, Verdi's original Iago and Falstaff, was complimenting Lilli Lehmann on her Donna Anna. Her musicality, her high notes, her classical aplomb! Lehmann is basking in the thrill of it all when he adds, "But for God's sake, burn those ghastly costumes!"

Here's one of the many Met folklore stories told and retold over the years:

Amonasro's Daughter

Zinka Milanov and George London are in the middle of *Aida*'s Nile Scene, when he curses her as "the slave of Pharoahs!" and hurls her to the ground in fury.

Actually, London does little more than gesture ferociously as Milanov sinks to the floor, facing upstage at him. "Pietà!" she cries. "Pietà! Pietà!"

As the strings begin their repeated A Flats, pianissimo con espressione, Milanov whispers, "George, I've been meaning to ask, how's the new baby? They say she's a darling."

She Lives For Art

Arriving at Idlewild (now Kennedy) Airport for her first Met season, Maria Callas is met by the usual pride of reporters, and one calls out, "Madame Callas, you were born in America, raised in Greece, and now you live in Italy. But what language do you speak?

And Callas replies, "I count in English."

The following was a popular tale in the 1960s, when the very self-important Herbert von Karajan was known jocularly as the "Generalmusikdirektor von Europa":

Resurrection

Von Karajan's favorite stage designer at the Salzburg Festival was Günter Schneider-Siemssen, who worked out the intricate scenery for the von Karajan *Ring*. Its special effects were many, as when Hunding's house could turn into a forest verdant with spring simply through adjustments in the lighting.

The story goes that von Karajan gives Schneider-Siemssen a special commission: he wants the designer to lay out the blueprints for von Karajan's tomb.

"Ja, Karajan," comes the reply. "I give you the most splendid mausoleum since Halicarnassus."

"But, Siemssen, don't make it too elaborate, ja? You know, I'll only be there for three days."

She'd Make a Great Aunt Eller

Eva Turner was one of the foremost dramatic sopranos in the 1930s and 1940s, especially famous for Turandot. Perhaps no one else has managed to mix the Chinese princess' cold rage and hidden warmth as well as Turner.

By the late 1940s, just as Rodgers and Hammerstein's *Oklahoma!* opened at Drury Lane, to amaze Londoners with the searching character content that was to revolutionize the musical as a form (and to achieve a run of four years in a huge theatre), Turner found her career winding down. So when the University of Oklahoma invited her to join the faculty, Turner accepted, temporarily leaving the stage.

As Nigel Douglas relates the story in *Legendary Voices*—and Turner herself told it to him—the pianist Myra Hess ran into a friend of Turner's and asked what the singer was up to. "Really," said Hess, "I haven't seen her in ages."

"Oh, Eva's in Oklahoma," came the reply.

A little startled, Hess said, "Really? In which role?"

Confession

Lotte Lehmann and Elisabeth Schwarzkopf, two immortal Marschallins, were out walking, talking shop, and Schwarzkopf observed, "You sing as if you really enjoyed it."

Lehmann stopped walking, turning to Schwarzkopf with "Of course I enjoy it. Don't you?"

"No."

Stunned by the answer, Lehmann went on walking, saying, "And it sounds like that, too."

Met baritone William Walker, a frequent guest on *The Tonight Show* during the Johnny Carson era, told this tale on the air:

Colleagues

Playing Silvio in *Pagliacci* in the regions when he was just starting out in opera, Walker was in his dressing room before cutain time when the soprano playing Nedda (whom he didn't name) paid a visit.

She was not in good voice, she told him, and while she wanted to give everything she had in their big duet, she feared she would have nothing left for the long-held note at the end, when the tempo goes into Largo (very grand and slow) and she has to hit an F in her lower range while he sits on a comfortable A Flat.

"I'll squeeze your hand," she said, "and we'll both cut off and let the orchestra take over for us. Agreed?"

Walker was a good guy, and he assented. When the moment arrived, she squeezed his hand, he cut off his note . . . and she held on to hers, swelling it and then letting it die away with a bit of play with her hands, to steal the moment for her own.

During the intermission, Walker went to her dressing room and asked why she had tricked him.

At her dressing table, calmly seeing to her makeup to turn into Colombina in the commedia dell'arte play-within-the-play, the soprano told him, "You have just learned a valuable lesson, my lad. In this business, it's every man for himself."

A Tale Of Two Operas

Hans Knappertsbusch, who had led so many Wagner performances that he was oracular on the subject, took a busman's holiday to attend a performance of *Tristan Und Isolde* in Vienna.

The next day, the conductor came up to him and, with a recklessly smug grin, asked the great maestro, "Well, Herr Professor, what did you think of my *Tristan*?"

"Gott im Himmel!" Knappertsbusch replied. "You wrote one, too?"

And We Have a Winner

In Puccini's *Turandot*, the princess' suitors don't just have to answer three riddles correctly—they have to answer three very creative and rather abstract riddles correctly. This is way beyond "What's black and white and red all over?" The first riddle, for instance, begins, "In dark night flies a multi-colored phantom..." and the answer is "Hope."

So, as Jane Eaglen told interviewer Helena Matheopoulos, when Eaglen's family planned to take in the singer's Turandot at the Met, she thought it would be fun to try the riddles on the Eaglens the night before.

The second riddle begins with "It sparks like a flame yet is not a flame," and goes on to "It's a fever of intensity and heat" and "It has the vivid glow of the setting sun."

And Mrs. Eaglen asked, "Is it mustard?"

The actual answer is "Blood." And what's black and white and *read* all over is a newspaper.

Sharing the Wealth

Adelina Patti got $5,000 a performance, a vast sum for the nine-teenth century—and she had to be paid in advance in gold, not banknotes.

On one of her various Absolutely Guaranteed Last Farewell Tours, someone chided her greed. Why, she was taking in even more than the President of the United States!

"Then let *him* sing," said Patti.

Larger Than Life

In 1969, in New York for Met gigs as Santuzza and Musetta, Marie Collier took time off to visit a clothing boutique in the Lincoln Center area. Physically imposing and generous of temperament, Collier was as vital in life as on stage, and the sales clerk had to move quickly to keep up with Collier's stream-of-consciousness tour through the store's inventory.

"Now this one," she would say. "No, I think...is there a hat with this? Oh, these *gloves*! If only I had a ball to go to!"

Spotting a dark number with red polka dots, she held it against herself.

"Who am I? It's Minnie [of the golden west, in Puccini's opera]. You know—the Polka Saloon!"

Suddenly, referencing the Poker Scene at the end of Act II, she mimed presenting her cards to Sheriff Rance: "Tre assi e un paio!" she cried triumphantly, not forgetting to add Rance's furious exit line: "Buona notte!"

And the salesgirl piped up with "Are you in show business?"

Erich Spielt Auf

Conductor Erich Kleiber began his career at twenty-two in Darmstadt in 1912, backing up the more senior conductors and leading the operettas. During one of them, he got distracted in a lengthy dialogue scene and forgot to start the orchestra when the comic was due to begin his number.

Stepping downstage, the comic called out, "Ei, fang schon an, Mascagni!," a sarcastic way of saying, "Come on and start the music, Mr. Know-it-all!"

Elvis Has Entered the Building

Régine Crespin is at the Met to hear Leonie Rysanek in *Der Fliegende Holländer*. As she and her husband go down the orchestra aisle to their seats, applause breaks out, and Crespin looks around to learn who the V.I.P. may be. Everyone is standing and clapping, so she can't see much of the orchestra, but an elderly man nearby says with a smile, "Madame…it's for you!"

A Dream Siegfried

After the great success of Decca's *Das Rheingold*, the firm decided to pursue its complete *Ring* with *Siegfried*. Brünnhilde would of course be Birgit Nilsson, but for the hero Decca discovered a youngish Heldentenor with a more glamorous voice than the reigning Siegfried, Wolfgang Windgassen. The new guy was especially enticing for his tremendous *ping!* on the high notes, but he would have to learn the role of Siegfried from scratch.

There was time enough for that, and Decca hired him a coach and even went ahead recording the third-act duet with Wotan (Hans Hotter). In several tries, the scene simply didn't go well, and finally Decca gave up and signed Windgassen, who turned out just fine despite his less brilliant instrument.

For years, Wagner buffs wondered who the cast-off tenor was, as the story was passed around without a name in it. In fact, he was Ernst Kozub, and the reason he didn't bother learning his music was a horribly debilitating disease that he was keeping secret. His "good" (i.e., healthy) time was spent traveling from house to house singing roles he already knew, building up a fund to support his family after his death. He lived just about ten years after his Siegfried would have been released, then succumbed to his illness.

Singing Lessons

Niccolò Porpora, one of the greatest teachers of the early 1700s, took as a pupil a young castrato on a unique plan. No arias. No songs. Just vocal exercises over and over for five years.

Finally, Porpora turned to his student with "Go, my child. You are now the finest singer in all of Europe."

That young castrato was Gaetano Majorano, known as Cafarelli—arguably the most accomplished singer of his age.

Choose

"Who would you rather be," the Duchess of somewhere or other asks Nellie Melba, "a noblewoman like me or a mere singer of tunes?"

"Ha!" the soprano replies. "There are many duchesses. But there is only one Melba!"

Rossini's Model For a Great Singer

"Voce, voce, e voce."

Master Class

Grace Moore was Dorothy Kirsten's mentor, but it was Mary Garden who taught Kirsten how to Make an Entrance: "Dorothy, that first impression is very important. Exude confidence and let your bosoms lead you."

Oh, Yeah?

Football player Red Grange was one of the sport's greatest athletes, but someone once told Grange's coach that Grange couldn't throw or catch.

"All that guy can do is run," he concluded.

The coach snapped back, "And all Galli-Curci can do is sing!"

Amelita Galli-Curci was the most famous coloratura soprano between Luisa Tetrazzini and Lily Pons. In America, her main stamping ground, she became a kind of brand name for "opera soprano"—the Kleenex and Frigidaire of big-deal music theatre.

Laddy, Come Home

Conductor Riccardo Muti was raised in Molfetta, in Italy's Apulia province, but he was born in Naples because his mother, a Napoletana, insisted on bringing each of her five children into the world in her hometown. Naples was all the way on the other side of the boot from Molfetta, and this was during World War II. It was not, to say the least, an easy trip.

Asked why it had to be Naples, Signora Muti would answer, "One day, someone will wonder where you are from, and you will reply, 'Naples.' They will know this great city, so much older than those upstart places in the north. But if you say, 'I was born in Molfetta,' it will take an hour to explain where it is."

And she would conclude with "This way saves time."

Period Setting

Late in her career, Joan Sutherland agreed to record Handel's *Athalia*. When told it would be an authentic traversal of the score using old instruments, she said, "That's fine, I'm a bit of an old instrument myself."

Hold My Beer

Herbert von Karajan was forever trying to lure lyric voices into trying titanic roles, causing them to risk vocal decline. It was hard to say no to the imperious conductor, but Christa Ludwig did so when he tempted her with Isolde.

A mezzo with an expansive top, she did in fact sing a few soprano parts, most notably the Dyer's Wife in *Die Frau Ohne Schatten*. But Isolde, biggest of the big?

When she told Karl Böhm about it, he said, "Karajan pushing you into that voice killer? Donnerwetter, this is *criminal!*"

Two beats. Then: "But with me, you could do it."

St. Patrick Knows Why

In her autobiography, Mary Garden recalls a critic likening her high notes to "the snakes in Ireland."

What did that mean? Were her high notes long and scaly? Biting, perhaps?

She asked her father what he thought, and got this reply: "Mary, there aren't any snakes in Ireland."

Set 'Em Up, Joe

Fresh from the conservatory, Régine Crespin failed in her audition for the Paris Opéra. But they let her watch a performance of *Tristan und Isolde* from the wings.

Kirsten Flagstad was the Isolde, and Crespin was amused to see her sip from a little bottle of something throughout the show. Ah: so that's how these Wagnerian heroines survive!

Actually, Flagstad reveals the secret of singing Wagner a bit later in this book, but for now, when Crespin was introduced to Flagstad, the youngster mentioned the bottle and asked, "Water?"

"Water?" said Flagstad. "*Cognac!*"

Children Will Listen

Jonathan Miller's 1998 Met production of *Le Nozze Di Figaro* sought to naturalize the action, for instance with a gang of petitioners outside the doors of the first-act set, all fighting to get inside to request a favor of the Count—just what one would have seen in any Spanish nobleman's household back in the day.

And, Miller wondered, wouldn't the Count (Dwayne Croft) and Countess (Renée Fleming) have children? Miller envisioned a daughter of about... oh, say six years—exactly the age of Fleming's own daughter, Amelia. In her memoirs, Fleming says she thought the idea "exploitative" at first. But then she asked Amelia, who declared herself "thrilled," and ready to make her Met debut.

So Amelia appeared in *Le Nozze Di Figaro*, albeit in a silent role... until the fourth-act finale, when Miller ranged the principals downstage in a line to sing the joyous chorus "Ah! Tutti contenti saremo così" (We'll all be happy thus). Fleming was thrilled herself when she realized that Amelia was singing right along with everyone else. She didn't know the words and she didn't know the music, but she knew what the feeling was about. Sometimes that's all that matters.

And mother and daughter both were happy thus.

Sands Of Time

Walter Felsenstein, who ran the Komische Oper in Soviet-occupied East Berlin, was a perfectionist who took forever—not weeks, months—to stage a new production.

Otto Klemperer had been engaged to conduct one of these Felsenstein specials, and when an official of the theatre contacted him with "We have a date! It's March 17!" Klemperer said, "Excellent! What year?"

Just Married

Karl Böhm kept telling Leonie Rysanek to stop dragging out her high notes, but her upper register was so big and brilliant that she couldn't resist showing it off.

Then Rysanek remarried, and suddenly she wasn't dragging anymore.

Böhm explained it to Rudolf Bing: "It's the new husband. She can't get back to him fast enough."

The Gods Look Down

For many years, the central staircase in the lobby of Covent Garden was so to say guarded by busts of two of its most celebrated prima donnas, Adelina Patti on one side and Nellie Melba on the other.

One day, a woman of some social standing was in the house on some errand and paused to gaze at the two busts. She thought she ought to recognize them, and, yes, perhaps they were...or could they be...?

Turning to a cleaning woman working nearby, she asked who the two subjects were.

"I don't know, I'm sure, mum," the charwoman replied. "We calls 'em Gert and Daisy."

He's Cute, Anyway

Grace Bumbry's former husband was a tenor who was very easy on the eye though not in great demand for his singing. So he tended to tag along with his wife on her jobs, sitting on the sidelines while she worked.

One day, rehearsing onstage, Bumbry stopped singing and indicated her husband in the auditorium. "Will you look at that good-for-nothing? He's sound asleep!"

Later, someone asked Bumbry why she married him in the first place.

"Honey," she replied, "he looks great carrying my luggage."

Love Song

Planning the gala for the last night of the Old Met, Rudolf Bing wanted Birgit Nilsson for the big closing scene from *Salome*, when the Princess of Judea makes love to the severed head of John the Baptist. She has had him decapitated for just this purpose, so it's quite a moment.

There were plenty of Met names to sing an aria or duet, but the evening needed one really grand selection, and the dramatic soprano of the age in the showpiece of the repertory would set off the gala like the Hope Diamond in a tiara.

To induce Nilsson to agree, Bing told her, "I promise you that it will be my head on that tray."

"That won't be necessary," Nilsson told him. "Every time I sing that music, I imagine it's your head I'm singing to.

A little nonplussed, Bing recovered with "Don't you ever think of someone else's head? Herr von Karajan's, perhaps? Not even once?"

Nilsson smiled. "No," she said tenderly. "It's always you."

Singers

ENRICO CARUSO

Even now, in the time of Jonas Kaufmann and Juan Diego Flórez, when most of the prominent classical-vocal Names of the early twentieth century are forgotten by all but the cognoscenti, Caruso remains a household word, the summoning term for "great opera singer." He was a spinto (that is, a lyric with reserves of power), an exciting Fach that blends command with delicacy, a viscerally exciting sound comparable to what we heard more recently from Luciano Pavarotti, though Caruso's repertory included heroic roles: Radames, Samson, Eléazar, and especially Canio. The famous photograph of Caruso in the *Pagliacci* pajamas and Conehead hat, overweight with too many chins, grinning as he beats a bass drum, is iconic. This, everyone believes, is what opera used to be like.

Nowadays, opera stars are trim and pretty. But there's a surprising shot of Caruso very early in his career, published in some of the many Caruso books, and instead we see a strikingly handsome youngster draped in a bedspread because his one shirt had been laundered and was still drying.

Caruso surprises us generally. He was the least "tenorish" of all the famous tenors, collegial and generous enough to sing "down" if a co-star was in poor voice; almost recklessly unconcerned about his fees and eager to perform for no payment in a good cause; a gifted cartoonist; and even a prankster, as when he surreptitiously squeezed a rubber squeaky toy into Nellie Melba's ear while she was trying to die with dignity in the last act of *La Bohème*. One imagines Melba impatiently whispering, "Stop that infernal merry-making. Tableau! Tableau!"

Stories like that one tell us why Caruso is one of the few singers of the Golden Age who can fairly be called "legendary"—and the legend began with the first "Caruso records," those 78s that became major operatic and record-industry infrastructure. Fred Gaisberg initiated the whole thing when he was an advance scout for the Gramophone and Typewriter Company. Gaisberg heard Caruso at La Scala in 1902 and made a deal to record him in Gaisberg's rooms at the Grand Hotel di Milano: ten arias from what was then the standard repertory (along with Osaka's serenade from Mascagni's *Iris* and two solos from Caruso's La Scala success, Franchetti's *Germania*), to piano accompaniment.

The fee was £10 an aria. Informed of the deal, headquarters immediately cabled back, FEE EXORBITANT FORBID YOU TO RECORD, but Gaisberg went ahead. In *The Music Goes Round*, Gaisberg's memoirs, he recalls the tenor "debonair and fresh" as he "sauntered in" and dispatched the commission "in exactly two hours" without the slightest hiccup.

Further G and T discs, a few for Zonophone and Pathé and, in America, some two hundred ten sides for Victor, made a vast fortune, not only because Caruso was The Tenor Of All Time but because the fragile technology of recorded sound loved Caruso's voice. The acoustic horn found sopranos too shrill and basses too cavernous, but Caruso's tenor was like the third bowl of Goldilocks' porridge: just right. Further, Caruso's Victors came out when the Victrola was becoming a status symbol among the middle class. Earlier, they had to own a grand piano; now they needed the hardware for

Victor's twelve-inch "red seal" vocal singles. Wives were notoriously unhappy with the way the Victrola spoiled the look of the living room; Victor's advertising constantly addressed concerns about the floor model's drab design. And of course one had to crank up the spring that ran the turntable every time one played the thing. Still, everyone bought those Carusos, and they still sell today on CD.

As for Caruso's voice per se, it really was astonishing, and Caruso used it with sublime espressività. His reign as the biggest draw of the Metropolitan Opera, from 1903 to 1920, with an opening night in almost every year, is without parallel in opera history; even Maria Callas's stay as La Scala's Queen of the Lot lasted less than ten years. Further, it was contested by some of the Scala public. No one at the Met contested Caruso. As a critic said of his first Met Radames, "His fire is unbounded. He hurls his heart at his listeners."

Welcome To the Monkey House

A New York police officer named Kane was a dirty cop who ran a scam in the Central Park Zoo. His confederate, a woman named Graham, would approach a single man and engage him in innocent conversation, whereupon Kane would materialize with "Was this gentleman bothering you, Ma'am?"

Graham would reply in the affirmative. She had been molested, she would say, and Kane would arrest the "culprit" and haul him off to jail.

The pair had been working this con for quite some time, always on men of no great social presence—so of course they were getting away with it.

But one day, in 1906, these two pulled their swindle on Caruso in the zoo's monkey house. It was only three years after his Met debut, but he was already so celebrated—and so often photographed—that it's surprising that Graham and Kane hadn't recognized him and steered clear. Somehow, while being booked at the cop shop, Caruso got word to the Met, and Heinrich Conried, the general manager, bailed Caruso out personally.

One would think that Caruso's very public persona and the might of the Met would have killed the case against him instantly, especially as Graham took one look at the headlines and vanished. Shockingly, the case proceeded. Caruso was found guilty, though his penalty was no more than a $10 fine. It is possible that prejudice against Italians (who, like Irish, Jewish, and black people, stood under popular suspicions of various kinds) was at work here, for his conviction was upheld on appeal.

Luckily, Caruso's reputation as everybody's friend defended him in the opera world, and when he made his next appearance at the Met, in *La Bohème*, the audience roared with welcome when the curtain rose on the familiar artists' garret. It helped, too, that Marcella Sembrich—a diva of famous ethical sobriety—was singing Mimì that night. Her very appearance, later in the act, gave Caruso the Good Housekeeping Seal Of Approval.

The Bite That Failed

In a 1916 Met *Carmen*, with Geraldine Farrar in the title role and Caruso her Don José, Farrar decided to apply the techniques she had acquired the previous summer in Hollywood, where she had filmed a silent *Carmen* with reckless verisimilitude.

Now at the Metropolitan, Farrar reached the third act as a seething tigress, and she and the startled Caruso got into it, as they say. He grabbed her, she fought back, he intensified his hold, and she bit his hand, drawing blood.

Caruso threw her off him, and she landed on the stage floor—
"smack on her bottom," as Frances Alda, the Micaëla of the evening,
later recalled.

When the curtain fell and it was time for the bows, Farrar flew at
Caruso with a fury, and we can imagine the scene:

"How dare you?" Farrar cries. "You…you Neapolitan
scoundrel!"

"Careful-a you, Farrar, or I—"

"Please, please, everyone," the stage manager cautions them.
"The audience awaits you before the curtain!"

Pacing back and forth, Farrar tells him, "We're not ready! Send
out little Alda!"

"I *beg* your humble—"

"Please, please, the artists!" the stage manager goes on. "We
must show them the happy Met family!"

Farrar and Caruso go on arguing as Alda takes her solo call,
whereupon Carmen and her Don José, hand in hand despite it all,
go out to acknowledge the ovation with tense smiles.

Back behind the curtain, however, they begin shouting anew.

"And another thing," Farrar starts to say.

"Helluva Carmen! Not to forgive!"

"Then you can find yourself another Carmen!"

"Sì, we get another José, too!"

"Please, another bow, signora, signore! Hear the public
calling for you!"

"*Little Alda*? I'll have you know—"

And so it went, more or less. But Farrar and Caruso were the
kind who make up as easily as they quarrel, and in a few days they
were back singing Bizet.

Some of the public may have been hoping for further hostilities,
but this night, after the Flower Song, in Act Two, the pair embraced

with the mutual respect and even love that one expects from the most remarkable artists the Met had then on offer.

This Gun For Hire

Caruso's second wife, Dorothy, loved to tell the Story of the Gun in the first scene of *La Forza Del Destino*. This happened during a spring season in Havana. There they are: the impetuous young suitor (Caruso, of course) and his timid would-be bride, about to elope. Her maid is there, too. Suddenly her father storms in.

"Vile seducer!" he cries. "Infamous daughter!"

It goes on like that for a bit, but when the father orders his men to arrest the suitor, he draws his pistol—not to fight, but to demonstrate his good faith. He throws it down—and it discharges, the bullet dealing the father a mortal wound.

Or, rather, that's what's supposed to happen. On this night, the sound-effects man backstage failed to provide the gunshot.

Not to worry. "I make-a big noise with my mouth, like this," Caruso told his wife. "BUUUM!"

So the father died and his daughter fainted and the public was thrilled. They gave Caruso six curtain calls for his trouble.

Caruso's Model For a Great Opera Singer

"A big chest, a big mouth, ninety per cent memory and ten per cent intelligence, plenty of hard work, and something from the heart."

This chapter starts with a tour of unique singers, each of a different kind. Caruso was our greatest tenor of all time—and now we have Shalyapin, the first great stage animal of the modern era. The father, one might say, of naturalistic acting in opera...

FYODOR SHALYAPIN

He was a bass specializing in outsized figures—the devil in *Faust*, *Mefistofele*, and *Robert le Diable*; Verdi's King Philip; Massenet's Don Quixote; and of course the great Russian leads, especially Boris Godunof. He was as well the first Russian singer to have a tremendous impact in the West. His years of work ran from 1890 almost to his death, in 1938, by which time he had revolutionized acting in opera to make it realistic above all, even if it offended sensitive souls.

Thus, early on, singing Ivan in Glinka's *A Life For the Tsar* at a provincial Russian theatre, Shalyapin objected to the rather high-style costume he was to wear.

"This man is a peasant, like me," he told the dresser. "He is a child of the wild places—the tundra, the steppes. You want me looking like a princeling. Look at this banquet tunic, these toe slippers! This is not Ivan!"

"But the director hates that Mongolian stuff," the dresser replied. "He says every time we put on a Russian opera, the whole theatre stinks of cabbage and vodka."

But cabbage and vodka was what Ivan is made of. Shalyapin didn't want to be true to the audience: he wanted to be true to the character. Photographs of the real-life Shalyapin show a big, handsome fellow—but every shot of him in costume and makeup gives us a different figure, nothing like his studio portraits and nothing like one another. His *Faust* devil is spruced up in fine feathers and a flourish of manners, because he's in disguise. But Shalyapin's *Mefistofele* devil looks as if he just stepped out of hell, not in the traditional drapery but half-naked, primitive, mad.

Even Don Basilio, the music master of *The Barber Of Seville*, invariably played at the time as a silly old pedant, bore a jaunty and youthful air in Shalyapin's hands: a dirty dog, picking his nose and scratching himself. Nor did he "rest" between his lines. He would become so engaged in reacting to what was happening that one forgot the music and just watched him.

Shocking. But he got away with it because he was such a marvelous singer. Yet as time went on, his portrayals started to overwhelm his vocal style; he would take great liberties with note values and even pitches. True, it suited his more radical creations, and later basses in the same roles, from Boris Christoff to Nicolai Ghiaurov, have treated comparable roles in similar fashion, as if Shalyapin had unleashed a turbulence in these parts that defies the printed score. Big and Crazy characters need Big and Crazy performances. Luckily, when Shalyapin worked with the literalist Toscanini, he was still observing the written music with care. As we'll see below.

The Eccentric General

In Tiflis, at the start of Shalyapin's career, an operagoing army general insisted on lending Shalyapin a star and cross to wear on his costume as Prince Gryemin in *Eugene Onyegin*. "But don't forget to return them," the general said. "We had another Gryemin here. Beastly fellow. Got drunk and pawned my medals."

The general was an unusual fellow, but no one could doubt his love of country. Whenever his wife felt he was getting tyrannical, she would play the Russian national anthem on the piano, which forced the commandant to stand at attention till she stopped.

Calling the Sommelier

One night, singing a Russian opera to an audience that didn't understand the language, Shalyapin suddenly realized that he needed to get a message to his manservant, standing attentively in the wings. Improvising new words to the set music, Shalyapin sang to him, "Go back to the hotel and get the wine bottles I left in my room, as we're moving on as soon as this ridiculous opera is over."

Method Actor

One night, singing Boris Godunof, Shalyapin was in the middle of the Clock Scene (when a terrified Boris sees the ghost of the murdered tsaryevich) and heard stirrings in the auditorium. Looking out of the corner of his eye, he realized that some of the spectators were on their feet, even standing on their chairs: he had been so persuasive that they were looking for the ghost, too.

Come Back, Shane!

Fleeing Soviet Russia, Shalyapin settled in the West, though like many Russians he never felt comfortable cut off from his native culture.

Knowing this, the Soviets tried to cajole Shalyapin into returning. He was one of the most famous Russians alive, and it would give the Communist state prestige to claim him. They tried to bribe him with offers of a house in Moscow and a dacha in the country, all his own—no mean lure given the acute housing shortage in the Soviet capital and Shalyapin's sizeable family of a wife and five children.

"So, Comrade Stalin wants to give me a house and dacha?" said Shalyapin. "He'll give these to me? Yes, and will he give me back my soul that he stole from me? My Russia? Will he give that back, too?"

> Now for the most beautiful voice of all the big Wagner ladies. Astrid Varnay was a better actress and Birgit Nilsson had more reliable top notes. But Flagstad was in a class by herself...

KIRSTEN FLAGSTAD

In the hypertronic world of opera, we expect all the star personalities to be creatures of the wild, clawing their way to the top and eating their young. The feuds! The wars for supremacy in this role, that opera house! Flagstad rose above it all, or so it seemed. She was...serene. Her stage presence was serene and her majestically luminous instrument was serene. Even her life looked serene: out of nowhere, a Norwegian with a background in lyric roles and a bit of this and that at Bayreuth (but also Sieglinde), she arrived at the Metropolitan in the middle of the Depression, took over all the leading Wagner heroines and Beethoven's Leonore, and within just a few years became the hottest ticket in opera.

Flagstad's backstage, too, was serene, that of the no-nonsense performer who spends her dressing-room time looking over the score of the day; she said she could always find some new detail with which to perfect her interpretation. True, she would spend the long Isolde break after Act Two and before her re-entrance for the

Liebestod playing an ornate Solitaire using several decks of cards under rules known only to herself.

So she was methodical—and private. She didn't like American strangers coming up to shake hands on the street or tell her their life story. What was all that to her? And if they asked her what was the secret to singing Wagner heroines, she would answer and then turn and walk away.

Yet they couldn't help wanting to speak to her, because she was so magical. Her Met debut, as Sieglinde, on February 2, 1935, was not only sudden but a sensation. Moreover, it was a broadcast matinee, so the entire nation of opera listeners got to hear her. Diva emerita Geraldine Farrar, hosting an intermission feature on the air, gave up her prepared script to rave over the newcomer, and four days later Flagstad sang an Isolde that all but shook the house. Her Tristan, Lauritz Melchior, became her inseparable singing partner (though they cordially detested each other), and the pair became symbols of the magnificence of the Met.

So Flagstad was on top of the music world—or so it did indeed appear. In fact, her life was about to become the opposite of serene. The trouble began before all this, in a failed lawsuit against Flagstad's husband, Henry Johansen. The attorney for the losing side, Ingolf Sundför, became Johansen's implacable enemy, waiting year after year for an opportunity to get his revenge, like someone out of a Norse saga.

Then war broke out in Europe, and Flagstad, after six years of being an American national treasure, decided to go back to Norway. Charles O'Connell, the Artists and Repertoire man for Victor, who produced Flagstad's recordings, put it this way: "She was tired of singing, tired of Wagner, tired of the Metropolitan, and she longed to settle down quietly with her husband in her own land."[1]

---

1. Flagstad had step-children in Norway as well; her biological daughter lived in Montana.

And then the trouble began. Because—as some said—why would Flagstad risk the dangers of traveling through war-torn Europe to reach Nazi-occupied Norway unless she was a Nazi herself? No less a personage than ex-president Herbert Hoover tried to talk her out of it; he had directed the feeding of Europe after the previous war, and thus had authority on the matter of the complications of wartime.

But Flagstad was stubborn. She underwent quite some ordeal in a trek through Portugal, Spain, France, and Germany, each stop requiring a bureaucratic explosion of documents. Passport, visas, references. Then, back in Norway, there was Ingolf Sundför, now a public prosecutor. And when the war ended, he had Henry Johansen tight in the trap, for Johansen had belonged to Vidkun Quisling's Nasjonal Samling (National Unity) Party, an anti-Communist group. It held together both fascist and, oddly, anti-fascist elements, but Quisling was the Nazis' man in Norway, so even though Johansen had left the party when the Nazis invaded Norway, he had no defense against Sundför's vindictive attack. His health now broken, Johansen died in prison.

Flagstad decided to return to singing, but she, too, had enemies now, spreading false reports as enemies love to do. The smear is heaven to the wicked. In one fantasy, when Flagstad's plane landed in Berlin on her return to her homeland, Hitler himself met her with an armful of flowers. "Where that tender little fabrication originated," she later wrote, "I have no idea." Many in the music world defended her as innocent of collaboration with the Nazis; others didn't know what to think. As the saying runs, A lie goes halfway around the world before the truth ties its shoelaces.

What hurt Flagstad most was not the terrible booing and shouting during her Philadelphia concert (as we learn below), but the way the Met general manager Edward Johnson closed the house to her—the house she (and Melchior) had saved during the Depression.

When Johnson retired, Rudolf Bing welcomed Flagstad back. Then, too, she led a tremendous *Ring* cycle at La Scala under Wilhelm Furtwängler in 1950, and John Culshaw of Decca Records planned to record the first complete *Die Walküre* to preserve Flagstad's Brünnhilde.

And she said no.

She did record most of the role—Act Three and the Todes-verkündigung. And, in a surprisingly sporty move, she learned the part of Fricka in *Das Rheingold* for Culshaw's *Ring*. But a complete Brünnhilde meant facing the high Bs and Cs of the famous Battle Cry, and by the mid-1950s Flagstad had lost her top notes. She was adamant on this point, and had broken off relations with EMI when it was reported—correctly—that on Flagstad's recording of *Tristan und Isolde* Elisabeth Schwarzkopf had slipped in the topmost notes, shading her timbre to match Flagstad exactly.

This is one of opera's great controversies, famous yet today. In *On and Off the Record*, Walter Legge, who produced this unani-mously admired *Tristan*, says it was made possible only when Schwarzkopf (his wife) "promised to sing the top B flats, Bs and Cs for her friend, as she had done in earlier Flagstad duets with [Set] Svanholm."

True, by 1952, when the *Tristan* was taken down, Flagstad's C was all but departed and her B moribund. However, the B flat was still trusty and remained so for years afterward. Which notes were Schwarzkopf's interpolations Legge doesn't specify, but it is safe to say that the younger singer supplied the two Cs in the Love Duet for certain, and the two Bs in the Narration are so grand and exposed that they, too, must have been emendations. But the B flats would have been Flagstad's own.

In any case, when the story got out, the press treated it as an exposé of some grisly atrocity. Sensitive about the power she had lost, now publicly exposed, Flagstad withdrew into herself and vowed never to sing in public again, though ultimately she changed her mind.

So that is how Flagstad ended up: hurt and weary and very disappointed in human nature. John Culshaw's *Ring Resounding* emphasizes this; between the lines, we infer that he saw her as a very great artist brought low by not age but the evil ways of the Sundförs of the world. Lanfranco Rasponi, who interviewed her for *The Last Prima Donnas*, caught Flagstad in a Wagnerian mood: "I want to spend my remaining years quietly on the North Sea," she told him, "ever so dramatic and mysterious, even terrifying at times, always hauntingly beautiful."

And Flagstad's secret to singing Wagnerian heroines was "Always wear comfortable shoes."

That's All You Have To Say?

Met soprano Frances Alda and Met general manager Giulio Gatti-Casazza made an odd pair, as she was flighty and impetuous and he was saturnine, a man of very few words. Still, they married. Then Gatti fell wildly in love with the Met's star dancer, Rosina Galli, and, said Alda, "The two most grievous errors I [ever] made were when I married him—and when I divorced him."

Nevertheless, they remained on at least professional terms. So, listening to a Saturday afternoon broadcast of *Die Walküre* in 1935, Alda was struck by the beauty and dramatic grandeur of the Sieglinde's voice. It seems that Alda had tuned in a bit late rather than sit through that Storm Prelude again, and thus missed Milton Cross' announcement of the cast. Hearing this wonderful singer with the most extraordinary attack on the first syllable of each phrase, Alda became transfixed, and at the intermission she telephoned her ex-husband in his office.

"Gatti, that incredible singer on the air just now—the Sieglinde. Who on earth *is* that?"

And the ever imperturbable Gatti responded, "Una certa Flagstad," meaning, roughly, "Some woman named Flagstad."

The understatement of the century.

The Tenor Is In

Archetypal tenors are hysterics about The Voice. Oh, that draft! My scarf, my scarf! My lozenges! My secret sponge!

But Lauritz Melchior, despite specializing in the biggest roles in the repertory, was of the fearless, rough and ready sort. Charles O'Connell recalled a typical recording date for Flagstad and Melchior on an album of Wagner excerpts: she was in the studio ready to sing—but where was Melchior? Flagstad was generally pleasant, except when she felt she was being taken for granted, not least when Melchior was involved. It gave her, as O'Connell put it, "another opportunity to get balky."

Then, *one second* before they were supposed to start, Melchior staggered in, smoking one of his filthy cigars and looking like someone who had been out duck hunting in the reeds all morning with nothing to eat.

"Where on earth have you been?" a bewildered O'Connell asked him, as Flagstad took it all in with a beady eye. And Melchior blithely told them where he had been: out duck hunting in the reeds all morning with nothing to eat.

Well! How could he possibly get through a big Wagnerian duet now?

Very easily, it turned out. Melchior cleared his throat a few times and said, "Let's go."

And, says O'Connell, "He never in his life sang better."

Welcome Back, Flagstad

"Remember, if there's any trouble, just leave the stage. As soon as it starts, that very second."

So pianist Edwin McArthur advised Flagstad as they stood in the wings waiting to go on in Philadelphia's Academy Of Music, during the singer's first postwar American tour, in 1947.

"I'm not a bit afraid," Flagstad replied. "I'm not going to let them win, whoever they are."

"They" were packs of troublemakers sitting in seats artfully staggered throughout the auditorium, a rent-a-mob paid for by some wealthy slimebag hiding behind the scenes.

No sooner did Flagstad appear than the screams of "*Na-zi!*" and the booing commenced. The noise stopped when Flagstad began to sing and started up again as soon as she finished, and the incessant interference was decorated with what sounded like scripted insults. Yet the more they tried to drive her from the stage, the more firmly she held her ground. She gave absolutely no indication that she even heard them. She just stood there and made music.

"You know how stubborn a Norwegian can get," she later explained.

One wonders what she was thinking of during the noise—the Nazis' brutal occupation of her homeland during the war, of her husband hounded to death in a personal vendetta? After the first set of songs, as Flagstad walked calmly into the wings, a police guard standing backstage told her, "You sure got guts, lady."

Flagstad Returns To the Met

There was resistance in some quarters to Rudolf Bing's engaging Flagstad now that she was back in America, but Bing loved resistance; it brought out the winner in him. Besides, he had *Tristan Und Isolde* and *Fidelio* to put on (and Gluck's *Alceste* in mind as well), and no one in the Met company could equal Flagstad in these works.

As Bing explained it, "The world's greatest soprano should sing in the world's greatest opera house."

The Goddess Revealed

While Decca failed to capture Flagstad in a complete *Walküre*, at least the label did get her for Fricka in *Das Rheingold*—a last new role for Flagstad and thus something of a historical event. It's not clear what anyone was expecting as the recording sessions began, but when Flagstad sang her first words, the somewhat majestic "Wotan, Gemahl! Erwache!" (Wotan, my husband! Awaken!), she brought such command and brilliance to the line that, says John Culshaw, who tells the tale in *Ring Resounding*, "the entire orchestra turned round to gape in amazement."

Culshaw says as well that two of the cast, young and self-important, regarded Flagstad as a has-been till they heard her sing. One of them accosted her in the control room during a playback with "How are things in Sweden?"

Flagstad was of course quick to correct him. Norway, young man, not Sweden!

"Same thing, isn't it?" he replied—and Culshaw made for the exit. "There are times in life," he explains, "when it is necessary to be somewhere else."

From the Brünnhilde of her era, we move to the Wotan of his...

HANS HOTTER

Often cited as the outstanding Wagnerian bass-baritone of the middle of the twentieth century, Hotter made his debut in 1929 and rose to prominence in Germany and Austria in the 1930s, but he did not achieve international fame till the 1950s, when he was already middle-aged. This is the peak time for a Wotan, Gurnemanz, and Hans Sachs—Hotter's signature roles—but it meant that he had scarcely ten good years left before the voice grew tired and wobbly. Still, he virtually never retired, moving into "speaking" roles like *Lulu*'s dirty old Schigolch and the Sprecher in Schoenberg's vast cantata *Gurre-Lieder*. By the time Hotter died, at ninety-four, it seemed incredible not that he had lived so long but that he had *worked* so long.

He was tall and commanding, ideal for his parts, and his singing had an inner intensity perfect for the psychologically vexed characters he usually sang. On Hotter's Met debut, in 1950, Olin Downes of the *New York Times* claimed that Hotter "creates the most impressive and stirring...Dutchman that we have seen. A figure out of legend, a tragedian of the first quality."

Hotter's other roles took in a wonderfully haunted Boris Godunof and Cardinal Borromeo in Pfitzner's endless doze of an opera, the dreaded *Palestrina*, and he sang leads in three Richard Strauss premieres, though the last, *Die Liebe der Danae*, got only a dress rehearsal because of the closing of the theatres in 1944 for the Nazis' Total War.

Typical of Hotter's musicality was his expertise in Lieder, even the songs of Hugo Wolf, a true test of the singer's expressive arts. Yet for all these solemn responsibilities, Hotter was a lively character offstage, a good colleague and, recklessly, openly anti-Nazi in a regime that punished the telling of Hitler jokes with the guillotine.

Silence Is Golden

It was the final dress rehearsal of Richard Strauss' *Friedenstag* (Day Of Peace) at the Vienna State Opera in 1939, and Hotter, in the lead role of the commandant of a fortress, was suffering an attack of hay fever and couldn't sing a note. The opera is an hour-long one-act, and Hotter played the entire performance mute, acting his way through it in mime.

After, the composer burst into Hotter's dressing room, crying, "Wonderful! My congratulations! You were in excellent voice!"

"But, Doctor Strauss," Hotter protested, "I didn't sing a single line."

"Yes, yes, of course," Strauss replied. "But I heard how well it will sound tomorrow when we open."

Krauss Spielt Auf

Hotter was known for humorless grandees, yet he sang also the mercurial Don Giovanni. In 1941, he opened the season in Munich in a new production of Mozart's dark comedy with an impressive cast including Viorica Ursuleac as Anna, Hilde Gueden as Zerlina, and Julius Patzak as Ottavio.

Clemens Krauss (Ursuleac's husband), conducting the first dress rehearsal, thought everyone was too sluggish, especially Hotter. Worse, he was taking too long to change his costume after Act One. Eager to enliven the proceedings, Krauss suddenly told everyone he was starting Act Two, strode to the podium, and struck up the band with Hotter nowhere in sight, though after only four chords from the orchestra Giovanni opens the act, in a duet with Leporello.

Hearing his music go off without him over the backstage loud-speaker, Hotter furiously rushed out on stage and stopped the performance, reproaching Krauss for starting without him.

"Curtain down, bitte," Krauss called out to the company, "Mozart. Second act. Once more from the double bar."

As the dress started up again, this time with Hotter in place, Krauss turned to his assistant, sitting just behind him, and said, "Well, that finally woke him up!"

Record Collectors

After the war, German musicians had to obtain a certificate of exoneration from any possible collaboration with the Nazi regime, jokingly referred to as one's *Persilschein*, after a brand of laundry detergent. Hotter had little trouble, as it was on record that the Nazis had rated him as "politically unreliable," but his interrogator pointed out that Hitler had owned some of Hotter's 78s. Didn't that suggest that Hotter had a Nazi affiliation?

"I hear the Pope has some of my records, too," Hotter told the man. "But that doesn't make me a priest."

Welcome Wagon

On his first visit to London, to sing Wotan at Covent Garden, Hotter passed a newsstand and noticed the headline HOTTER IN LONDON. Thrilled to be so singled out, he proudly took a look at the article.

And promptly felt deflated: it was about a change in the weather.

You Have To Know Wagner's *Ring* To Get This Story

There was a bit of a mishap in Hotter's London *Ring*, though. At the end of *Die Walküre*, having deposited his daughter, Kirsten Flagstad, high up on her rock, kissed her to sleep, and called upon Loge to encircle her with fire, a spotlight blinded Hotter and, missing his footing, he fell some five feet to the stage with a crash, winged helmet, spear, and all. To phrase it in Wagnerian terms, Wotan fell on his *Arsch*.

The audience let out a collective gasp as Hotter struggled to his feet, and as the music flamed on to the final bars, he sought to reassure everyone by striking a commanding pose, with his arms outthrust: the mighty warrior-god. He swung his spear: master of the world. Brünnhilde has paid her penalty and the Wälsung line will prove fruitful when Sieglinde gives birth to Siegfried. All this Hotter somehow conveyed with his body language before striding off to take up his new role as the Wanderer of the earth.

The accident made the papers, and a few days later someone on Covent Garden's governing board asked the house's intendant, David Webster, if Hotter was all right—"Because I heard him as Wotan and I noticed he had some sort of bandage over his eye."

That "bandage" is the famous eye-patch that Wotan wears, having traded half his vision for all-encompassing world-knowledge.

He made the deal with the giant Mimir, master of the spring of wisdom at the foot of Yggdrasil, the World Ash Tree. All educated people in Central and Northern Europe knew the legend, so when Wagner had Wotan tell his wife, Fricka, that he traded his eye to win her, the audience would sense that the King Of the Gods is dishonest and manipulative, thus setting up the fall of Wotan's regime. Later in the *Ring*, the First Norn recounts the legend more faithfully—but elliptically, leaving out important details. Norns are like that.

But let us now consider a second Russian, this one who did it the hard way, living under Soviet rule...

GALINA VISHNYEFSKAYA

We speak of people being "on the wrong side of history," but Vishnyefskaya was born right in the middle of history, having lived through the Nazis' two-year siege of Lyeningrad, when a starving population began simply to drop dead on the street, in the office, or at home even as life went on around it.

Then, after the war, Vishnyefskaya had to live in the Stalinist slave state, with—as we'll see—police spies even among one's colleagues in music. This was especially perilous for an outspoken personality like Vishnyefskaya. "I am capable of anything!" she wrote in her autobiography, *Galina*. She might easily have been arrested but for her reputation as the outstanding Russian soprano of her time, for the Soviets were very eager to maintain cultural prestige. Then too, in their greed for Western currency they pocketed the fees Russian artists collected when performing in the West.

Nowadays, Russian singers work everywhere. But in the 1950s and 1960s, few individuals were allowed to leave the country even temporarily. As Vishnyefskaya's third (and only successful) marriage united her with the famous 'cellist and conductor Mstislaf Rostropovich (Slava to his friends), it was easy for the authorities to let one of the pair out while holding the other as hostage. But the couple liked to concertize together, and Vishnyefskaya was not shy about confronting the commissars about these sabotages of her career.

A devotee of the Russian song literature from Glinka to Shostakovich and especially renowned for her *Onyegin* Tatyana, Vishnyefskaya would also turn up in Western opera houses in Italian roles—a Met Aida, Liù at La Scala. We can hear the latter on a broadcast with Birgit Nilsson and Franco Corelli before a very keen house, bringing us close to a typical Vishnyefskaya story: La Scala's rehearsal pianist advised her to close Liù's first aria, "Signore, ascolta," with a piano on the high B Flat as marked, then crescendo to a fortissimo and suddenly cut it off.

No, no, ridiculous. Why should I?

The pianist told her the public would eat it up, conferring glory on La Scala, honor to Puccini, and so on.

But Vishnyefskaya, as always, resists. Liù is a slave girl, not a drama queen. Finessing the high note would distract from her essentially simple nature.

The pianist insists. This is the way that passage always goes at La Scala. If you don't do it, the audience will think you *can't* do it.

Who cares what they think? I am Galina, I am opera truth, I am capable of anything and I will never surrender!

But once on stage, because she's so stubborn she defies even herself, she gives the note the fortissimo crescendo and the cut-off, and we hear the public react with excited approval.

That was Vishnyefskaya: technically secure and always surprising—but also headstrong, as when she cut the Bolshoi's weekly propaganda meetings. She was to have joined Slava for music-making in the West, but now the Soviets blocked her. And when Slava called the Soviet Embassy in D.C., threatening to cancel his dates and tell the *New York Times* his wife was a prisoner in Russia, there was tremendous upheaval among the commissars. It virtually came down to Vishnyefskaya's having to ask Yekatyerina Furtseva, the duplicitous Minister of Culture, the equivalent of "*Do you know who I am?*"

All this came to the tipping point in 1974, when the Rostropoviches supported Soviet dissidents and were blacklisted. Vishnyefskaya was too valuable to the Bolshoi to be sidelined, but all her recordings suddenly vanished from stores and her performances were ignored in the press.

Slava had it worse, demoted to bookings in far-off, dingy places. Simultaneously, five of the Bolshoi's most famous singers eagerly denounced Vishnyefskaya to the Soviet Central Committee. One of them was a soprano who shared Vishnyefskaya's roles and wasn't remotely as interesting in them, but the others—Vishnyefskaya had thought—had nothing against her, and one had been her pupil. Not surprisingly, Furtseva was unavailable for a meeting—"probably in her usual drunken stupor," Vishnyefskaya notes in her book.

At length, the Soviets threw the Rostropoviches out of the country. They settled in the West, returning to their homeland only after the collapse of the U.S.S.R.

The self-serving attack on Vishnyefskaya by the Bolshoi's Gang Of Five was so shocking that, during a magazine interview with the Rostropoviches that I conducted, the normally unflappable translator was so startled that she questioned Vishnyefskaya's statement. But the singer persisted. The pupil who denounced her was the famous mezzo Yelyena Obraztsova.

Face the Muzhik

Recording Benjamin Britten's *War Requiem* in London's Kingsway Hall in 1963, Vishnyefskaya was alarmed when she was told the other two soloists, Peter Pears and Dietrich Fischer-Dieskau, would stand up front with the orchestra while Vishnyefskaya would be with the chorus at the back of the hall, for an arresting aural effect in which she would enter the ambient angelically, as if from on high.

Perhaps because of a language problem—Vishnyefskaya spoke no English and there seems to have been no translator handy—Vishnyefskaya thought she was being relegated to a supplementary role, though Britten had written her music specifically for her voice. As the recording producer, John Culshaw, kept trying to make Vishnyefskaya understand that she was being favored rather than demoted, she finally threw herself onto the floor, banging her feet and screaming. Some of this was accidentally preserved on a special tape Decca was preparing for Britten (as mentioned elsewhere in this book), and the tantrum makes an odd fit with the pacifist nature of the *War Requiem* itself.

Inaction Figure

The La Scala company occasionally goes out on tour, and in 1974 it was in Moscow with, among other productions, *Tosca*. Then Raina Kabaivanska fell ill without a cover, and the Cavaradossi, Plácido Domingo, told management to get Galina Vishnyefskaya.

When the Scala people broached the matter with the usual Soviet bureaucrats, the answer was no: "Galina Pavlovna isn't in Moscow."

"I just talked to her on the telephone," Domingo told the Scala side. "I'm having dinner with her tomorrow."

Back to the bureaucrats, who now came up with "Galina Pavlovna doesn't sing Tosca in Italian. Only Russian."

"Oh, but she does," said Domingo. "I sang it with her last year in Vienna. In Italian."

The bureaucrats again. Now they had a hot one: "We have spoken to Galina Pavlovna, and she refuses to sing Tosca with your company."

And that was that. The next evening, over dinner, Domingo shared the tale with Vishnyefskaya and asked why she had refused.

"I didn't refuse," she said. "They never told me about it."

To Domingo's bewildered expression, which Vishnyefskaya read as something like *But why did they lie to us?*, she answered, *"This is Russia!"*

Take It Away

Critic David Patrick Stearns tells the tale of meeting Vishnyefskaya after a performance of Shostakovich's Fourteenth Symphony, made of eleven songs for soprano and bass with chamber orchestra, all on the subject of death. The poets range from García Lorca to Guillaume Apollinaire, on prisoners, suicides, Death himself listening to guitar music in the tavern, or "The Zaporizhye Cossacks' Answer To the Sultan Of Constantinople."

Vishnyefskaya was in splendid voice, yet she had retired from opera, and Stearns asked why.

"Oh, opera," he recalls her saying, avoiding his gaze "with mild exasperation." She adds, "All that scenery. All those costumes…"

It's phony, she seems to be saying. It's gaudy and dishonest. "This," she cries, grabbing the program of that evening's concert, the very Russianness of Shostakovich, "is the *real* music!"

Here now is a classic tenor of the Italian type, an exponent of what is called divismo: temperament, feuds, pettiness, and a competitive nature about one, other tenors and, two, everyone else as well...

FRANCO CORELLI

Tall and handsome to a fault, this tenore robusto had a glow that made him unique in his class, partway between suave lyric serenaders such as Cesare Valetti and Giuseppe di Stefano and cannons such as Mario Del Monaco. The latter sailed through Otello countless times while Corelli ultimately set Verdi's score aside as unreachable, after years of study. Yet Corelli was a matchless Calaf—a voice-killer to ambitious lyrics—and he did share most of Del Monaco's roles, from Pollione to Andrea Chenier. Better, Corelli developed subtle touches well beyond Del Monaco's blustering style, enabling Corelli to rival even the deftest of lyrics, as in Gounod's *Roméo et Juliette*, in a luscious diminuendo on the high B Flat at the end of "Ah! lève-toi soleil!"

Detractors claimed the recording technicians had simply turned knobs in the studio when Corelli recorded Gounod's opera, with Mirella Freni. However, many heard him sing that diminuendo in the theatre. It was perhaps a rare vindication, for the Legend Of Corelli is filled with the turmoil of the professional hysteric, forever at odds with everyone about the nature of his greatness. Thus, he executed those Big Sing roles—Ernani, Manrico, Don José, Turiddu—only with the aid of his wife, Loretta, flourishing a cross in the wings to call upon heaven to get him through the evening (even as she shouted criticisms of his performance). And woe betide the singer who dared to challenge Corelli's house-proud stage placement, as Boris Christoff did during a *Don Carlos* dress rehearsal that nearly ended in a sword fight.

On another occasion, a fan in a stage box at a Corelli *Trovatore* shouted, "[Fedora] Barbieri sola! Va via, Corelli!" (Only Barbieri! Get lost, Corelli!) during the applause after the duet in the gypsy camp. Corelli immediately tore offstage into the passage leading to the boxes, to confront his critic, and there was quite a to-do, complicated by a horde of cast members and house staff, who rushed onto the scene to serve as hall monitors, in the helpful Italian manner.

Then there were the Corelli whims, such as his insistence on traveling with his pet poodle, a logistical headache the Corellis were always happy to pass on to opera-house management. Or Franco would give the press a bold announcement such as...he's going to play Billy Bigelow in a revival of *Carousel*. He actually said so, in a magazine interview. After all, Ezio Pinza, Lawrence Tibbett, Giorgio Tozzi, Robert Weede, and Cesare Siepi had all sung on Broadway by then. However, they were either native speakers of English or fluent in it; Corelli really wasn't, not Rodgers and Hammerstein fluent. Corelli waved this away. "It's all arranged," he said, with a merry smile. And of course it never happened.

But there is this: he was a spectacular singer, blessed with a full and gorgeous instrument and extremely expressive in his use of it. The passion that he brought to his 1961 La Scala Raoul (in Meyerbeer's *Les Huguenots*, albeit in the Italian verismo version) was extraordinary, and Corelli's big duet with Giulietta Simionato was hair-raising in a way that, we feel, no other pair, ever, could outdo.

Then, too, though he was something like a self-taught primitive, Corelli worked hard to develop his gifts. It was ego; but it was art. And at six feet two inches, with an athletic physique (he had been a champion swimmer in his youth) he looked wonderful in those period costumes, and his entrance as a cowboy in Puccini's *La Fanciulla Del West* invariably provoked little gasps from the unprepared.

It's also worth noting that Corelli learned roles quickly. In the ten years after his debut, in 1951, he sang a wide assortment of parts, even in music he wasn't right for, as with Handel's *Hercules*, at La Scala, or as Pierre in Prokofyef's *War and Peace*, at the Florence May Festival. Even after he had established himself, rather than coast on specialties he sought new adventures—Zandonai's *Giulietta e Romeo*, Mussorksky's *Khovanshchina* (in the thankless role of Andryey, while Boris Christoff ate up the stage as his wild and crazy father), Bellini's *Il Pirata*, and Donizetti's *Poliuto*, the last two at La Scala with Callas and Ettore Bastianini. It was in all an astonishing career, with a cute footnote: many a soprano recalled performances with Corelli as the most marvelous of her life.

Who Steals My Sponge Steals Trash

On one of the Met's spring tours, Birgit Nilsson, singing in *Aida* opposite Corelli, noted with amusement that he hid wet sponges around the stage to moisten his throat before a tricky high note. As Nilsson herself habitually parked glasses of ginger ale in the Met's multi-level *Elektra* set, filled with handy nooks and crannies, she knew how useful it could be to avoid "dry mouth."

Nevertheless, she thought it would prove a great joke to move Corelli's sponges so he couldn't find them. He countered by slipping one into his trousers in an intimate spot. Then, according to Nilsson, just before Franco had to sing a high C, he pulled out his sponge, sucked up the water in it, tossed it aside, and hit his money note.

Says Nilsson in conclusion, "I almost fell flat for laughing."

Nilsson told the tale thus to Corelli biographer René Seghers, but Radames has no high C anywhere in the opera. Verdi scarcely ever gave that note to a tenor in his Italian works, because, as a practical man of the theatre, he knew the C would make any tenor anxious throughout the preceding scene, ruining his concentration. (French tenors were different, as most of them still sang the highest notes in falsetto at the time.) True, there is a high C in the *Trovatore* aria known by Italians as "la 'pira,'" this being "Di quella pira," the rousing bolero Manrico sings at the end of the opera's Part Three. But Verdi wrote a G there; the high note is an interpolation. Further, many tenors take the number down a half-step or even a whole step, so they have to reach only a B or B Flat.

The Greatest "Vittoria!" Ever Heard

Temperamental Franco made the mistake of talking politics with the conductor of that evening's *Tosca*, Carlo Felice Cillario, and now the maestro was out to get him. He urged the orchestra to play forte on the most ordinary plot lines, drowning Corelli out, and after "Recondita armonia" (Secret harmony), instead of the traditional halt while the audience applauds, Cillario drove his players on, infuriating Corelli. The Sacristan then says, "Eccellenza, vado" (I'm going, excellency), to which the tenor replies, "Fa'il tuo piacere!" (Do as you please!). Corelli all but shouted the words in Cillario's face.

After the intermission, the two continued their battle on Cavaradossi's cries of "Vittoria!," always a moment for the tenor to go wild on F Sharp and then A Sharp, and Corelli had never been wilder in his life. The very house shook. Cillario rebounded by taking the ensuing Allegro Concitato too fast for Corelli to breathe properly, but he held up under the onslaught—and by now the audience had realized that something was going on between pit and stage, and it sided entirely with Corelli, giving him an ovation.

A breather: the tenor is out of the story for the rest of the act. After the intermission, however, the battle returned at "E lucevan le stelle" (The stars were shining). Again, Cillario ignored the public's applause and kept right on playing Puccini. Corelli bit his thumb at Cillario...and stormed offstage just as Dorothy Kirsten was making her entrance for their big duet.

Met general manager Schuyler Chapin pushed Corelli back onstage, and the opera proceeded to its finish. But then, paying no heed to the stage manager, who was arranging the bows, Corelli ran down to where the conductor exits the pit and threw himself upon Cillario. With stagehands and staff trying to keep the two from killing each other, the group somehow found itself back on the stage, and as Kirsten came off from her call, everyone pointed Corelli through the curtains to accept his applause. Oh, my curtain call? Don't mind if I do.

Of course the public went wild: their man had won.

And that's when Chapin turned to Cillario and said, "Maybe this isn't a good night for the conductor to take a solo bow."

From Italy, Russia, Norway, and Germany, we move to Australia...

JOAN SUTHERLAND

When she arrived in London, in 1951, with Muriel, her battleaxe of a mother, young Joan cut an unimpressive figure. At twenty-four, she was strikingly tall and awkward, with a self-deprecating air that suggested a born third-rater. Nor did the fledgling command any stage presence—and she didn't yet claim a distinct Fach. Many took her for a budding Wagnerian soprano. Some thought her a mezzo. No one could have guesssed that she had it in her to astonish and overwhelm in a Fach all her own: the bel canto coloratura with a gigantic voice and, under the right director, even a magnetic presence created out of a complete inability to act. One was mesmerized waiting to see what she wouldn't do next.

She got to Covent Garden quickly enough, with a Rhine Maiden here and one of Carmen's sidekicks there; now grand Amelia and then wispy Gilda; Weber, Mozart, Offenbach, Poulenc (the New Prioress in *Dialogues Des Carmelites*); even modern English works, from Britten (Lady Rich in *Gloriana*) and Tippett (Jenifer in *The Midsummer Marriage*).

Little of this anticipated Sutherland's future in Bellini and Donizetti, yet one person knew exactly what Sutherland should be singing—and it wasn't *The Midsummer Marriage*, even if her part was filled with flighty vocal decoration. No, what Sutherland's fellow Australian Richard Bonynge saw in her was the next great Norma, Elvira, Alcina, Semiramide. Step by step, Bonynge coached Sutherland in technique, line, espressività. So it seemed logical for Sutherland and Bonynge to marry and become a cultural package, for he nourished conducting ambitions.

Critics at first scorned him as a vanity add-on, but in time he proved himself a stylish interpreter. He was as well the solution to the problems Sutherland was having with certain Italian conductors who fought her on tempo and other matters. "Son io il maestro qui!" (I'm in charge here!), Nello Santi told her when they were preparing *La Sonnambula* at La Fenice and she found his conducting leaden. Eventually she walked out on the production, making international headlines and prompted her Auntie Blos (short for Blossom), to reprove her with "You did a Callas."

So she had temperament, Sutherland. Her image was that of the uncomplaining trouper, placid of character and never having to cancel. In fact, Sutherland battled chronic medical woes, from sinusitis to ear abscesses to back trouble. And when she felt oppressed, she did push back, not least when the aggressive Australian press waxed unpleasant on the first Sutherland-Bonynge tour of her homeland.

"Orang-utans," the Bonynges called them. How they throng one! What silly questions they ask! "How does it feel to be back in Australia?" Oh, come on, how is it supposed to feel?

One reporter, long before, asked Thomas Beecham, ending *his* tour to go back to England, "When will you be returning to Australia, Sir Thomas?"

And the conductor replied, "Does anyone ever *return* to Australia?"

Take My Mother-in-Law. Please.

For years, Joan's mother—a singer herself—fought with Bonynge over his leading Joan into the coloratura repertory. As Muriel Sutherland saw it, Joan was a dramatic soprano, or even a mezzo like herself. What an Amneris Joan would make! A Laura! An Eboli!

Even after Joan became Mrs. Bonynge, in 1954, the fighting went on, till Bonynge finally challenged his mother-in-law. What made her such an authority, when he had been studying Golden Age vocalism all his adult life? Really, what did she know about singing opera in the first place?

The two of them happened to be at the piano, and Muriel planted her feet, assumed a pose, and motioned Bonynge to the keyboard with a peremptory wave of her hand.

"Verdi," she said. "*Don Carlo*. 'O don fatale.' You'll play it and I'll sing it."

It sounded a little like a Deanna Durbin movie, but play it Bonynge did. And, to his shock, Muriel sang Eboli's big dramatic solo superbly.

"Now," she said, after the last thundering chord. "Do I know singing or don't I?"

Yes, she knew singing. But she didn't know Joan.

The Covent Garden Lucia

The many inappropriate casting gigs Covent Garden imposed on Joan during the 1950s delayed the start of The Real Joan Sutherland to 1957. It was then that the BBC broadcast about forty-five minutes of an extremely unknown Donizetti work, *Emilia di Liverpool*, which gave Joan a showpiece finale scene typical of bel canto.

"When we heard Sutherland do this," said *Emilia*'s conductor, John Pritchard, it was unmistakeable: "This is a voice that is going to take over in the Bellini and Donizetti operas with a vengeance." Then Sutherland got a chance to sing comparably florid music at Covent Garden, as the Israelite Woman in Handel's *Samson*, with a "Let the bright seraphim" that dazzled the public with its trumpet solo and Joan's vocal fireworks rushing at last up to a glittering high D, first at the Leeds festival and then, back in London, in house.

This was in the fall of 1958, just after Sutherland had been, once more, workhorse Joan, wasted in two *Ring* cycles as Woglinde and the Woodbird. But Covent Garden's chief, David Webster, knew what a prize he had, and he sent Joan to Italy to study *Lucia di Lammermoor* with one of the great coach-conductors, Tullio Serafin, who would be in the pit for Joan's Lucias. As stage director, Webster hired Franco Zeffirelli, who had a knack for bringing out the best in the inexperienced. (One of his miracles was the reinvention of Maria Callas, who had no sense of humor whatsoever, as a comedienne in Rossini's *Il Turco In Italia*; later, he made a Shakespearean out of Elizabeth Taylor in his film of *The Taming Of the Shrew*.)

Working around Sutherland's lack of dramatic flair, Zeffirelli assigned her physical things to do in the Mad Scene: suddenly staring upward when she heard the famous flute cadenza as if it were the cry of the man she has just murdered and then singing her echo "at" it as if chasing his ghost; cowering and flinching and looking obsessively at nothing; running around and among the wedding guests *while she sang*. Here was a mad scene that really was mad: and Sutherland played it in a gruesomely blood-stained nightgown (a departure from British etiquette that infuriated Serafin). After all, if you stab your husband to death in the first moments of the honeymoon, there's going to be a bit of a mess.

Above all, there was the singing; the Covent Garden public on that first night, February 17, 1959, was stunned. Two acts before the mad scene, after Lucia's first solos, the ovation seemed as if it would never end. "My God," said Geraint Evans, standing backstage, "how far can this go?"

Even though Sutherland was a singer rather than a singing actor, her instrument lent a certain drama to everything all on its own. Lucia had been a canary's favorite role, but Sutherland wasn't a dainty miss: she was vast, and opera isn't about modest talent (as Leontyne Price explains, in one of the final stories in this book). True, Sutherland was emerging in territory already mapped out by Maria Callas, the first to kill off the canaries. But Callas' short prime was ending, and the Norma-Lucia-Amina catalogue was up for the taking.

On February 17, 1959, Joan Sutherland took it.

Let the Florid Music Sound

Nowadays, the Handel Authenticity Revival is in full swing, but in 1961, when Sutherland joined Grace Bumbry, Kenneth McKellar, and David Ward in recording *Messiah*, the work was still being sung "straight," without much of the embellishment technique of Handel's time. In fact, Sutherland had started work on an earlier *Messiah* album superintended by Thomas Beecham and had to quit when Beecham grew impatient with her decorating of the vocal line.

At that, Joan's new conductor, Adrian Boult, felt bemused at the Sutherland-Bonynge version of Handel, though Boult did go along with it, making his performance far more stylish than Beecham's, anachronistically anti-Baroque even for its day.

Still, Boult had to have his joke. He dubbed the recording *Mad Scene From Messiah*.

The Young Person's Guide To Lucia

Joan's interpretation of *The Bride of Lammermoor* (to use Sir Walter Scott's novel's title) became what Germans call her Paraderolle, the part she took with her everywhere as her calling card: in Palermo, Genoa, Paris, Venice, Milan, San Francisco, Los Angeles, Dallas, New York, Barcelona, even Miami Beach. And of course everyone fell in love with Sutherland and even with *Lucia* itself. One holdout was the Bonynges' little boy, Adam, who was treated to a dress rehearsal at the Met, his father explaining the story to him scene by scene.

"Why is Mummy going to marry the bad man?" Adam asked in Act Two. And when the chorus women showed up in tartans and caps smartly trimmed with big green feathers, Adam asked if they were American Indians. Then the tenor and baritone pulled out their swords on each other, and Adam got thrilled: "Daddy, shouldn't they kill each other now?"

Bonynge had warned the boy about the murder, to preclude his being frightened when Joan entered in the bloody nightgown, but Adam took it in stride.

"Now Mummy's cutting him up," he noted, with an air of satisfaction.

Sutherland In Charge

One day, during a full-cast rehearsal of *La Sonnambula* not long before opening night—a time when even gallant nerves are apt to fray— somebody irritated Sutherland. This was at the San Francisco Opera, and the offender was the company's general manager, Kurt Herbert Adler. Smoking his pipe, he came bustling in while director Lotfi Mansouri was trying to sort out a big scene. Worse, Adler started interfering with Mansouri's staging, and Sutherland went into defiance mode.

"Mr. Adler," she began, in tones only the greatest singer in the business dares use, "this happens to be Mr. Mansouri's production, so kindly leave us to get on with it!"

Stunned at first (they were in his house, after all), Adler chose discretion over valor, and began to withdraw.

"And no smoking on the stage!" Sutherland added, as Adler tactfully disappeared.

What Do You Mean "We"?

Sutherland was a big girl, tall and stately—"Junoesque" used to be the applicable term. She was not overweight, just ... grand.

Once, Luciano Pavarotti, having just sung a rehearsal with Sutherland, came over to her, huffing and puffing and quite out of breath.

Wiping his brow with his eternal handkerchief, Pavarotti said to her, "We fat people know how difficult it is."

"Luciano," said Sutherland, forthright as ever, "we are not fat. *You* are fat. *I* am big.

Do You Ever Miss the Midsummer Marriage?

In Norma Major's biography of Sutherland, the soprano is asked if she would ever sing a modern work again, and Sutherland answers,

"Yes, with a gun at my head."

Aged In Wood

Not till 1985 did Sutherland tackle the classic nineteenth-century coloratura role of Ophélie in Ambroise Thomas' *Hamlet*, in Toronto. It was to be her last new role on stage, and at sixty she was a little long in the tooth for Shakespeare's hapless maiden.

But Joan found a way. "I shall be hidden by veils," she vowed.

Speaking of Pavarotti, let us close this calendar of great singers with the "modern Caruso"…

LUCIANO PAVAROTTI

He was maddening. When he began, in 1961, as Rodolfo, he was an ingratiating stage personality with the most adept instrument of all the tenors of his day, in a boyish splendor that was lyric yet sturdy, with an assured command of the high C that, for many others, is a note of noisy desperation.

Further, though not an actor in the psychologically nuanced sense, Pavarotti played persuasively as Nemorino and Cavaradossi, justifying character and working well with colleagues. True, he reacted to music rather than to words. Once, as Tebaldo in Bellini's *I Capuleti e i Montecchi* (The Capulets and the Montagues), Pavarotti fudged a cue at "Stolto! A un sol mio grido" (Fool! At one cry from me), the duet with Romeo, because (Pavarotti later admitted) "I was so caught up in the beauty of Giacomo Aragall's voice."

Yet our memory of Pavarotti is ruined by his later years, when he had given up maintaining even a semblance of the singer-actor and took next to no interest in what was happening onstage or what the other singers were doing. Often, he would not even trouble to enter at the indicated moment in the action, preferring to be discovered from the start sitting at a table as if for a store CD signing. And there he would perform his part, while treating himself to libations.

Then, too, Pavarotti became known for his absurd behavior offstage—the entourage and the traveling personal kitchen, reminiscent of the antics of eighteenth-century opera stars. Nevertheless, Pavarotti's many recordings tell of Golden Age singing. In his complete set of *La Favorita* with Fiorenza Cossotto, Pavarotti climaxes the first aria, "Una vergine, un'angel di Dio," just as it stands in the Italian score, on a scale rising to a high C Sharp, then, with a graceful glissando-like portamento, dropping to an E. It's lovely, but also hair-raising. It reminds us that opera is, at its core, not about anything but—as Rossini tells us—voice, more voice, most voice.

Hungry Baby

Pavarotti and Mirella Freni are The Kids From Modena, born the same year and raised in the same neighborhood. Their mothers knew each other from work, in a tobacco factory, but the tobacco tends to taint breast milk, and the two infants had to share a wet nurse.

"It's obvious," says Freni, "who got all the milk."

Renata Scotto, who came to loathe Pavarotti (as we'll learn a few stories hence) so much that she brought him up in her memoirs without uttering his name, told this tale on him in those pages...

Ghost Story

Pavarotti was singing Oronte in Verdi's *I Lombardi alla Prima Crociata* (The Lombards On the First Crusade) in Rome near the start of his career. As the fourth act opens, the soprano, in a cavern near Jerusalem, hears a heavenly choir and sees a vision of her beloved— this same Oronte—who has died at the end of the third act.

It's a major scene, with just a few telling phrases for the soprano that conclude in two tricky cadenzas, followed by the tenor's solo, "In cielo benedetto" (In blessed heaven).

Unfortunately, Pavarotti couldn't read music and thus depended on coaches when he learned new roles. They would play out his parts on the piano over and over till he had memorized them. Seeing that he died in Act Three, Pavarotti apparently didn't bother returning for any further *Lombardi* coaching, so he had no idea about his role in Act Four.

Thus, when a *Lombardi* rehearsal reached Pavarotti's entrance in Act Four, he didn't come in, and the conductor, Gianandrea Gavazzeni, asked what was wrong.

"What is this music?" Pavarotti asked, bewildered. "Didn't I die already?"

"This is your apotheosis as a voice from on high."

"Well, nobody told me about it," Pavarotti replied, snapping his score shut. "Now I will have to go somewhere and learn it." As he departed, the tenor added, "If Verdi wanted me to sing in Act Four, he shouldn't have killed me off in Act Three."

The Love Call

Throughout opera's history there have been singer partnerships. The "*Puritani* Quartet" of Giulia Grisi, Giovanni Battista Rubini, Antonio Tamburini, and Luigi Lablache (with the mononymous Mario taking over for Rubini when the quartet created *Don Pasquale*) is the classic example. A more recent one recalls the collaboration of Maria Callas, Giuseppe di Stefano, and Tito Gobbi on EMI's 1950s recordings of Italian opera (though occasionally a more robust tenor would substitute for di Stefano or a more lyrical baritone for Gobbi).

But here we speak of Joan Sutherland, Marilyn Horne, and Luciano Pavarotti, great friends and great colleagues. One time, as Horne recounts in her second volume of memoirs, Sutherland's phone rang: it was Pavarotti, and eventually Horne, who was visiting, got on as well.

Now, Horne was always known to her intimates as Jackie, a childhood nickname, and it was Jackee this, Jackee that, and "Jackee, I saw on the television Joan an' you. Oh, Jackee, you were so wonderful, you sang so beeyootiful, you look so beeyootiful."

And of course Pavarotti always gives a little something extra, so "An' you look so fuckable, too!"

The San Francisco *Gioconda*

After some years, Pavarotti stopped learning new roles, but he did take on Enzo for San Francisco, with Renata Scotto. Her first try at the work, it was to be telecast, and the last thing she wanted was to have to carry her partner along. In fact, the work is so crowded that soprano and tenor scarcely have a chance for a *gran duetto*; besides, he's in love with the mezzo. Still, Scotto was facing a *big* role: roaming throughout Venice from the Doge's Palace to the lonely Giudecca, Gioconda turns up everywhere just in time to avert some crisis or other, and she has interesting encounters with almost everyone. *Aida* is a monodrama by comparison.

And there was that good-for-nothing Pavarotti, never knowing when to come in, never knowing the right words, demanding a rehearsal in his hotel room…and then hogging the curtain calls. These of course are laid out in advance. As Scotto herself said, a set protocol "avoids hurt feelings and trampled feet, and adds order to the backstage chaos." And the protocol in San Francisco was: no solo bows, only group calls.

After Act III—the big act, when five of the six principals, the chorus, and the ballet corps (for "The Dance Of the Hours") go totalist—Pavarotti (in Scotto's words, now) "pushed everyone aside," and took a solo call. Scotto turned to the nearest house official and asked if there were to be such solos for them all. He said no.

After the last act, one dominated by the Gioconda, Pavarotti again barged out alone before the curtain. *What?* "Is there no discipline in this house?" Scotto asked someone important. "Is this a circus?"

"This is his theatre," the man answered, "and he can do as he pleases." In other words: Pavarotti is the king of opera, and you are nothing.

Well, that tore it. Scotto stormed off to her dressing room, tailed by the television camera people, greedy for geschrei. And they got some: fed up with not only Pavarotti's antics but Adler's indulgence, Scotto let loose with some thoughts on the lack of professionalism in the house. As Scotto saw it, these were *gente di merda*. And that's what she called them, on national television.

Shitheads!

Otello On the West Side

This story is hard to believe, but Joseph Volpe, the Met's General Manager, used to tell it himself: Pavarotti was parading along Sixty-fifth Street in full Otello costume and makeup.

Actually, he was chasing after his secretary and alleged girl friend, whom we'll call "Dorinda." She had suddenly decided that she was finished with Pavarotti's quixotic ways and was going home to Europe. In fact, as we speak, she is heading for the airport.

So Pavarotti is running after her, though he is supposed to be onstage singing Act One of *Otello* in a Met gala. And Volpe is running after Pavarotti.

"Dorinda," Volpe cries, when he catches up with them, "you're coming back to the Met. And you, Luciano, are, too."

Apparently Dorinda was satisfied that she had made her point and agreed to return to the house. Her Otello came along as Volpe herded them back inside.

The incident never made the news, and it might have remained no more than a Met house legend but for Volpe's recounting it in *The King and I*, a Pavarotti memoir by his longtime manager, Herbert Breslin.

Pavarotti's Opinion Of Flattery

It is natural to greet opera singers with a bit of praise for whatever music they just performed—their "Nessun dorma," their Rodolfo, their encore of Tosti's "Marechiare." And no doubt Pavarotti was worthy of it.

Still, he found the etiquette tiresome. "Don't always say to me how I'm so great or that I sing well tonight," he would announce. "I know better than you whether or not I sing well."

I Didn't Come Here To Be Insulted

Pavarotti loved to tell how Kurt Herbert Adler invited the tenor to take part in a concert.

Pavarotti said he'd think about it, and Adler snapped back with "You can't think, so just do it."

"I can't think?" Pavarotti asked.

"Tenors are brainless," Adler told him. "Everyone knows that."

Now for a tour through the ages with singers of all kinds...

Pasta Triumphant

It was Maria Callas who was famed for angrily addressing someone in the audience with a line from a role during an actual performance, but it was Giuditta Pasta who did it first, when singing Bellini's *Beatrice Di Tenda* to a raucous audience at Venice's La Fenice. In her first-act duet with her husband in the piece, the baritone role of the Duke Of Milan (who married her only to extend his power and really loves another), Pasta suddenly turned from him on a key line and hurled it into the auditorium: "Se amar non puoi, rispettami. Salvami almen l'onor." Thus, "If you can't love me," she told them all, "respect me. Save for me at least my honor."

It's worth noting that, of all the great singers of bygone eras, the one that historians always compared Callas to was Giuditta Pasta.

BRIEF LIVES: HENRIETTE SONTAG

A genuine beauty, Sontag was born to a theatrical family, with an opera-singer father and an actress mother. At thirteen, their daughter created the title role in Weber's *Euryanthe* in its premiere, in 1823, and, a year later, was the first soprano to be heard in Beethoven's Ninth Symphony.

Sontag was an above all charming performer, habitually winning the intimate admiration of the upper crust everywhere she appeared. In *The Great Singers*, Henry Pleasants tells us that after her first season in London, no less a celebrity than Sir Walter Scott presented her with a commemorative album of signatures of "two dukes, twenty-three lords, eighty-seven earls, a hundred and sixty-eight knights, and hundred and thirteen gentlemen, fifty-nine authors, forty-three musicians, thirty-eight painters and twenty-six ladies, including four duchesses."

Then an Italian count won her heart. But he was a diplomat, and ambassadorial nicety demanded Sontag's instant retirement from the stage. She made her farewell in *Semiramide*, sang a few concerts in Russia, and virtually vanished from the musical scene.

Then Sontag's husband lost his position, and she returned to the stage to support them—after eighteen years! Still in gala voice, she was on tour in North America when she accepted an engagement in Mexico City, though cholera was raging there. She had time for one Lucia before the disease struck her down, at the age of forty-eight.

Name That Tune

At one of Rossini's famous musical soirées, the very young Adelina Patti sang his own "Una voce poco fa," heavily embellished. *Very* heavily.

When she had finished, he asked, "And who wrote that lovely little selection?"

BRIEF LIVES: LEO SLEZAK

Tenor. Born in Moravia in 1853, he was six feet, four inches and barrel-chested, leading him to specialize in the testosterone roles— Manrico, Tannhäuser, Radames, and especially Otello. Slezak looked so formidable onstage that when he planned to learn Rodolfo in *La Bohème*, Puccini said, "That would be like an elephant courting a weasel."

Slezak was a high-spirited actor, famous for the way he literally threw himself upon Antonio Scotti's Iago in their scene after "Ora e per sempre addio" (Now and forever, goodbye). Yet in real life he was a merry fellow, in fact the Loge of the opera world, ever ready for a practical joke.

In one famous tale, after singing the knightly Renaud in Gluck's crusader piece *Armide* at the Met, Slezak grabbed an imposing old man with a beard who happened to be standing around backstage, pulled him on for a curtain call, then solemnly knelt before him. To reporters who crowded him just after this apparently historic moment, Slezak explained, "That was Gluck. He told me that never in his life had he heard his opera sung so magnificently as I have tonight." The story made the papers, though of course Gluck had died over a century before.

Anyway, the story is apocryphal—Slezak never sang *Armide* with the Met—but it typifies a man so full of fun that, when his tenor gave out he started a new career as a movie star in Germany, famous as the sultan in one of the last of the Nazi-era color epics, *Münchausen*.

Slezak died three years later, but he left a son, Walter, to carry on in the American light theatre (he introduced "I've Told Every Little

Star" in Jerome Kern's *Music In the Air*), and Walter's daughter Erika maintained a forty-two-year run on television's *One Life To Live*.

Above all, Leo Slezak takes pride of place in these pages as the begetter of the most famous opera anecdote of all time. While singing Lohengrin one night, waiting backstage to board the swan boat in which he makes his entrance in Act One, Slezak saw the boat suddenly shudder, leap into life, and take off before he could get on: the engineer had jumped his cue.

Turning to whoever was standing near, Slezak asked, "Wann geht der nächste Schwan?"

Or, as everyone puts it, "What time's the next swan?"

Here now are two tales of one of opera's most imperious divas:

Melba Wouldn't Buy Me a Bow-Wow

Was she the most celebrated lyric soprano at the turn of the twentieth century? Nellie Melba, of the perfectly placed "silvery" timbre, was certainly the most insufferable of prima donnas whenever she thought any of her perquisites were under assault.

Thus, at her home base, Covent Garden, when the young John McCormack was about to walk out for a curtain call with the diva, Melba stopped him dead in his tracks with "In this house, nobody takes bows with Melba!"

Always Gracious

Now Melba's singing in a command performance at Windsor Castle, after a state dinner for the King of Greece. The court chamberlain, thanking Melba after the event, commented on how well the music went.

Nonsense! "What a dreary concert this would have been," Melba told him, "if I hadn't come!"

BRIEF LIVES: MARY GARDEN

Born in 1874 in Abderdeen, slim and pretty and an utterly mesmerizing actress, soprano Garden loved the offbeat, and she may have created more leading roles than anyone else of her time, including Debussy's Mélisande. Legend tells us that she wasn't much of a singer per se, but her recordings say otherwise, and she got through Violetta and Salome, parts that no one can play without a voice.

We honor her here for the greatest professional debut in opera history: going on halfway through Charpentier's *Louise* at the Opéra-Comique having never rehearsed it or even getting a warm-up—and her first notes were "Depuis le jour," the work's most expansive lyrical passage. The scheduled Louise, Marthe Rioton, was in poor voice that night, and, after a hair-raising second act, bolted for the stage door and could not be recalled.

So on went Garden, with the one thing she always had in abundance, confidence. The critics scoffed, because how could anyone be good under those conditions? But "I liked it," Garden said, and "My public liked it." Reviews didn't matter, because Garden was going to make her career on what she actually did, not on what somebody or other said about her.

She never took a husband, because she married her art, which "never gave me anything but joy, and what man could give that?" She was smart, too, ever ready with a comeback, as when some stuffed shirt asked what was holding up her décolleté dress. "Your age," she replied, "and my discretion."

She broke new ground, it seemed, everywhere she went, turning the young male protagonist of Massenet's *Le Jongleur De Notre-Dame* into a trouser role and being, to my knowledge, the first woman to run an opera company, in Chicago, and for just one year (by contract). The press said she lost a million dollars, and while she was at it she coined a new term for her position, *directa*. And she sold out again and again in operas that, after she had moved on, were seldom heard from. As the Indian heroine of Victor Herbert's *Natoma* (1911), another of her creations, Garden got to perform a number called the "Dagger Dance" (because she is planning to stab the bad guy when it ends), during which the opera's soubrette is in the process of being abducted.

At rehearsals, Herbert worried that the audience would miss the dance while distracted by the abduction. But Joseph Redding, the librettist of the occasion, reassured him: "Victor, that man could be taking his pants off and nobody would see him while Mary's on the stage."

"I began my career at the top," she concluded. "I stayed at the top, and I left at the top."

She died in 1967, just shy of ninety-three.

Now for a pair of Lotte Lehmann stories...

A Lesson In Manners

In Vienna, they say, you never know who your enemies are, because even those who hate you will seem to go out of their way to charm you.

Then it's the knife in the back—but Lotte Lehmann, singing at the Vienna State Opera early in her career, came from Prussia, in northern Germany, where you said what you meant and meant what you said. There was no "charm" game in Prussia, and Lehmann's blunt manners did not go over well with her colleagues, so Vienna's stage director Wilhelm von Wymetal thought to coach her in the Viennese style.

"For instance," he told Lehmann, "all you ever say is a simple 'Good morning' instead of 'Good morning, Frau Kammersängerin.' Everyone here is touchy about titles, you know. Respect, respect. And couldn't you add a cheery 'And how are you today?' What would that cost you?"

"Nothing," Lehmann admitted. "But why should I ask when I'm not in the least interested in how any of them are?"

Lehmann and the Nazis

Lehmann was no friend of the regime once the Hitler gang came to power, and when Austria, too, fell to the Nazis, Lehmann decided to move to America. Her emigration began with an invitation from the Berlin State Opera to appear *als Gast*, with the warning that Hermann Göring was personally overseeing the matter. This was a serious threat, and he showed up for their interview (she was ordered to attend) brandishing a riding crop and with a blade in his belt.

Prussian to the core, Lehmann began with "I am not in the habit of discussing contracts between a knife and a whip." But Göring was eager to corral all the best artists as a showcase for music in Berlin, and he offered her anything, everything. A fabulous salary. A pension.

A villa. The promise that any critic who slighted her would be shot. And…is there anything in particular Frau Lehmann would like to add?

"A castle on the Rhine," she said. After all, there are a lot of those, most of them probably vacant.

Göring wanted Lehmann to agree to sing only in Germany, which she thought ridiculous—and when she received the contract, none of the wonderful promises Göring had made was to be found therein. So Lehmann refused to sign it, and now she seemed to have some inkling—for the first time—just how the Hitler regime worked, with worthless words and duplicitous actions.

Doesn't it seem odd that Lehmann hadn't known this already? There was plenty of evidence, and of far worse than dishonest opera-singer contracts. Yet she claims—as so many did—that she wasn't political. It reminds one of Lotte Lenya's experience when she first visited Germany after the war and didn't meet a single soul who even knew any Nazis. "It was all a dream," Lenya concluded, sarcastically.

In any case, the stage was now set for Lehmann to plan a new life after putting an ocean between herself and Wilhelm Göring.

And now to England and points east…

Constructive Criticism

The opera was *The Marriage Of Figaro*, back in the day of London's Vic-Wells company, run by the famously outspoken Lilian Baylis. The evening's Cherubino was newcomer Joan Cross, eventually to become a boldface name in the history of English opera.

As Cross came back behind the curtain after her call, Baylis was waiting for her, to say, "You sing nicely, dear. Pity you can't act."

Snake Tartare

During World War II, the Teatro Reale of Rome traveled to Berlin with all its singers, orchestra players, sets, and costumes for a cultural exchange with the Nazi government. The headliners were invited to appear at a reception at the home of the party propaganda chief, Josef Goebbels.

At one point during the party, Tito Gobbi blithely told mezzo Gianna Pederzini that by staring very hard at someone's back, Gobbi could force him to turn around. Pederzini demanded proof, so Gobbi demonstrated on bass Giulio Neri, who did indeed look behind himself.

"That was a fluke," said Pederzini. "Once more, to be sure."

Gobbi repeated the stunt, again successfully. Then Gobbi tried it on another of the singers, again with success. He may have gotten drunk with power, though, because when Pederzini urged him to try it on one of the Nazis, he foolishly took her up on it. She suggested Goebbels himself—and Gobbi's stare once more got a response. Imagine: Dr. Goebbels himself subject to paranormal suggestion. *Stratisferico*!

Now it gets scary. Marveling at Gobbi's power, Pederzini begged for just one more proof, to be absolutely certain. Dr. Goebbels again, please.

So Gobbi stared at Goebbels' back...and this time the Nazi propaganda chief didn't simply glance behind him. He turned completely around, looked fixedly at Gobbi, and then very slowly moved through the room to confront him.

Keep in mind that Goebbels was a man so dangerous he could murder at will. Gobbi and Pederzini stood helplessly rooted to the spot in fear, and when Goebbels reached them Gobbi—thinking fast—asked for his *Autogramm*.

"I will do better than that," Goebbels replied. "I will present you with a signed photograph."

Thanking Goebbels, Gobbi started to say where he was staying in Berlin, but Goebbels coldly interrupted him with "We know everything about you."

And a few days later, frantic hotel staff summoned Gobbi to the hotel lobby, where Goebbels was waiting for him, with his hands behind his back. Was he holding a pistol? A sabre? Affecting an expression of diplomatic serenity, Gobbi approached, whereupon Goebbels handed him the promised photograph, not only signed but framed.

Gobbi thanked him. And Goebbels turned and strode out of his life forever.

The Most Foolish Assessment Of a Singer By an Impresario In the Twentieth Century

Conductor Leo Blech escaped Nazi Germany and, luckily, ended up in Sweden, which was never invaded because it maintained a strict neutrality and the Nazis needed Swedish cooperation in the disposition of their iron ore, the generating source of the ball bearings that were crucial in arms manufacture.

Blech was now running the Stockholm Opera. One of its youngest contractees, a soprano, was never able to land a leading role, and Blech was the reason why. Said he: "She is altogether unmusical, so there is no reason to give her an assignment of importance. She can be the one who brings a message or attends a party."

The singer was Birgit Nilsson.

Nilsson got her break nonetheless, when Fritz Busch was guest-conducting at the Opera, heard her, and insisted she sing Lady Macbeth with him in an upcoming production.

Giuseppe Di Stefano, Comprimario

The smallest singing role in *La Traviata* is that of Flora's servant, whose entire part consists of four words, "La cena è pronta" (Dinner is served). But there's a trick to it, because he appears at the height of a scene bustling with suspenseful worry, for Violetta and her rejected lover are both onstage and fireworks are expected.

So when Riccardo Muti was recording the opera for EMI, he expressed disappointment with the men whom management kept offering him for the role. They were simply singing the words, whereas Muti wanted someone who could echo the intensity of the macabre whirlwind figures Verdi wrote for the scene's orchestral accompaniment.

"We don't have anyone else lined up," EMI's producer told Muti, after he had protested the seventh applicant. "Would the maestro perhaps be willing to supply the four words himself?"

Muti brushed this away; that's not his department. Instead, he agreed to lay down an orchestral track for those few measures only, to be filled in later when the label found someone with a sense of drama.

By chance, Giuseppe di Stefano turned up in London, and, accepting a bottle of champagne as recompense, came to the studio to supply the needed tension in the four words.

It may seem a small point, but in fact di Stefano somehow conveys the drama of the moment while still sounding like a servant announcing dinner.

The Return Of the Native

Giancarlo Del Monaco's Met staging of *Madama Butterfly* emphasized the ardent nature of the first-act love duet. With just moments left, he had the Pinkerton, Richard Leech, take off the tunic of his naval uniform, leaving him in his white undershirt, and, after the singing ended, during the orchestral peroration that closes the act, he and the Butterfly, Catherine Malfitano, kissed as he tugged the top of her kimono down, revealing her bare shoulders.

And that was all that one member of the audience could take. From her seat in the orchestra, former Met Butterfly Licia Albanese let fly with a lusty *Boo!* that became, for a few days, the talk of the opera town.

Jonas Kaufmann's Audition For Giorgio Strehler

Most unusually, the Italian director wouldn't audition one singer at a time. Instead, Strehler would call in a pride of them all at once—five or six tenors, say—to sing the same Mozart arias, one of Don Ottavio's (from *Don Giovanni*) and (from *Così Fan Tutte*) Ferrando's "Un aura amorosa."

Kaufmann, still in his twenties, was all the same confident enough to suggest singing something else. Strehler's assistants all said no at once, but Strehler asked what Kaufmann had in mind.

"Edgardo's aria from *Lucia*, Herr Direktor."

"Fine."

Kaufmann sang it, and Strehler responded with "So now it's Donizetti for Kaufmann? No more Mozart?"

"I never said that," Kaufmann replied, backing it up with a luscious reading of "Un aura amorosa," which Strehler interrupted, asking him to kneel while he sang.

What? But okay, why not?

Kaufmann started again, but again Strehler stopped him, asking if he could close his eyes while he sang.

And again: why not?

So Kaufmann sang a little Mozart on his knees with his eyes closed, and Strehler knew he had found a tenor with a sense of adventure and daring.

"That's it!" he cried to the bewildered Kaufmann. "You're hired!"

Tales Of the Metropolitan

The Met has always comprised two more or less equal power struc-
tures: on one hand money (i.e., the Met Board) and on the other
hand art (the music). From the beginning, there has been a Board
drawn from the one per cent; and there have been creative person-
nel, struggling to make music without interference.[1]

It was post–Civil War parvenu money that founded the Met, the
railroad and war-industry fortunes that rose up to challenge New
York's Knickerbocker aristos whose social clout dated back to old
Nieuw Amsterdam. The Knickerbockers held court in the Academy
Of Music, down on Fourteenth Street, though the fashionable
retail-and-high-life district now ran between Union Square and
Twenty-third Street. Moving into all but uncharted territory, the
Met Maecenases nested (in 1883) on the block between Broadway
and Seventh Avenue and Thirty-Ninth and Fortieth Streets, in
absurdly cramped quarters. There was no lobby, rehearsal space was
limited, and scenery for every production except the one immediately in view had to be ferried back and forth from warehouses.

At that, the neighborhood was dodgy. True, the Casino Theatre—
the first playhouse specifically built for musicals—had gone up

1. True, other companies have Boards, but in the Met's case the Board owned the building
itself. Rather less comparably, after a financial disaster that closed the house for a year, La
Scala in 1898 was reconstituted with a Board, but one made of artistically knowledgeable
souls along with the usual plutocrats. After World War I, the Board was dissolved and La
Scala became the *ente autonomo* (self-governing entity) it so famously has been ever since.

(in 1882) just across Broadway from the Met's future front door. But the area above Forty-Second Street was a place of drifters and ne'er-do-wells, of boarding houses and livery stables, where no one of the genteel community ever set foot.

Nevertheless, the Met prospered, till in 1906 an upstart company opened house at Thirty-Fourth Street and Eighth Avenue, cutting into the operagoing audience with fascinating new singers and wonderful repertory premieres. Tenors Alessandro Bonci, Giovanni Zenatello, and John McCormack came forth. Sopranos Luisa Tetrazzini and Mary Garden dazzled the public with, respectively, madly enthusiastic coloratura and mesmerizing stage presence. The novel titles were *Les Contes d'Hoffmann*, *Elektra*, and *Salome* (banned at the Met after a single performance because it drove J. P. Morgan's daughter straight to her fainting couch, my dear).

This new company was Oscar Hammerstein's Manhattan Opera, noted also for its house conductor, Cleofonte Campanini, and its youthful and ebullient chorus. The Met was *largo*; the Manhattan was *allegro vivace*. An opera fanatic, Hammerstein (grandfather of Richard Rodgers' partner) was prominent for his innovations in cigar manufacture (he held countless patents) and expertise in producing vaudeville. The Met's general manager, Heinrich Conried, referred to Hammerstein's operation as "the so-called opera house on Thirty-Fourth Street." But in his second season, Hammerstein *made* $250,000 while the Met *lost* almost $100,000.

As we'll see below, the Met bought Hammerstein out and surged into the postwar era scooping up the best singers. The roster lost its aces, Geraldine Farrar (to retirement, at her rock-star height) and Enrico Caruso (to death), but it gained Rosa Ponselle (the textbook Norma between Pasta and Callas); lovably tempestuous Maria Jeritza; Kirsten Flagstad, Lauritz Melchior, and Friedrich Schorr for Wagner; Ezio Pinza, who made bass roles as glamorous as those of a tenor; Lawrence Tibbett, a baritone of such dramatic power that a subgenre of new operas built around "Tibbett roles" was created.

This is when the Met's managers first come into focus for us, from the diplomatically remote Giulio Gatti-Casazza to the squishy ex-tenor Edward Johnson (who virtually let his assistant Edward Ziegler run the house) to Rudolf Bing, an anecdote collector's dream for his tyrannical ukases and blistering wit. "I'm awfully sorry, I didn't get that," he told someone during a talk with the stagehands' union. "Would you mind screaming it again?"

Bing was a revolutionary at the Met, trying to bring in brand-name conductors and luring directors from the theatre to enliven the stagings, though as singers came and went even during a production's first season it tended to fall apart quickly. Still, Tyrone Guthrie's *Carmen* in 1952, for Risë Stevens and Richard Tucker, was very atmospheric, especially in Guthrie's handling of the chorus as individuals rather than a static mob and his placing the final duet in a room where the torero and his friends are partying before the bullfight, then emptying it of all but Carmen and the stalking Don José. Virgil Thomson, in the *Herald-Tribune*, liked the cast and hoped "they will be kept together." But by the third performance there was a new bullfighter and the next time a new Don José.

Perhaps Bing's most crucial renovation lay in supervising the move to a better infrastructural layout. Everyone loved the old Met for its historical associations, and everyone agreed that the Met had to relocate. "La Scala and Covent Garden are old, too," said a disagreeing James McCracken. "But no one wants to tear *them* down." On the other hand, "This is farewell only to bricks and mortar," Bing declared. "The Met itself goes on."

Yes: but elsewhere, and the plans were already half a century old. The Met's unofficial CEO, financier Otto H. Kahn, had been agitating for a new house as far back as 1908. Kahn even bought a plot at Ninth Avenue and Fifty-Seventh Street and then took a huge loss when the Board decided against a move. Many other locations were scouted over the years, and it was almost a shock when it was suddenly announced that a slum-clearance project in the West Sixties was going to create the Lincoln Center arts complex. (Those wondering what the neighborhood looked like before demolition began can look up the original 1957 poster art for the musical *West Side Story*, in which the two romantic leads are seen running blissfully down a street right in the middle of it all.)

The Met made the move in 1966, Bing retired in 1972, and for a long while the company was more or less directionless, as the designated new manager, Goeran Gentele, was killed while trying to pass a car on the open road, running head-on into a truck. (Two of his daughters were killed as well.) At times it seemed that the Board—or someone more or less representing it—was in charge; at other times it seemed that an impresario of artists was. Who was minding the store—music or Wall Street?

Worse, for the first time in its history the Met began to cast its second- and third-line singers in leading roles, giving the opera house the feel of a Staattheater, the German term (roughly meaning "the building shared by the opera, ballet, and drama ensembles") for a provincial outfit utilizing workmanlike, often sparkless talent. This was an existential catastrophe after Bing, whose agenda centered on assembling starry casts. Bing bettered even the Salzburg Festival for the von Karajan *Ring* by using the conductor's people *and* Birgit Nilsson, the greatest Brünnhilde of the age. And when Bing himself came before the curtain to announce that a *Tosca* with Renata Tebaldi, Barry Morell, and Tito Gobbi had suffered a cancelation, he offered a solution that no other house could have rivaled: "Madame Tebaldi is fine," he said, silencing the murmurs of anger. "So is Signor

Gobbi. But Mister Morell is unfortunately indisposed...and Signor Franco Corelli will sing in his place."

Typical of the new Met's problems was the *Tristan* disaster of 1973, which started when one of Gentele's few acts as the incoming manager was to bypass the house Isolde—Nilsson, of course—for Catarina Ligendza, an estimable artist when she actually shows up. This time, as often before, she didn't. The conductor, Erich Leinsdorf, protested Ligendza's cover, Doris Jung, because she had never sung the part before and Isolde requires a performer who has scaled its heights and thus knows when to save the voice and when to open up.

Meanwhile, the Tristan, Jon Vickers, arrived late for rehearsals, and *he* protested the second substitute, Klara Barlow, who had had success as Isolde but not in a house the size of the Met. Vickers departed (though he later sang in the production, and with Barlow), to be replaced by Jess Thomas.

That should have settled the matter. But Gentele had created another problem when he insisted on appointing a music director, the first ever at the Met. And Gentele's choice was Rafael Kubelik, a wonderful conductor. However, as a music director Kubelik was... a wonderful conductor. He had very odd ideas about casting and repertory, and, incredibly, his contract allowed him to be on site only at the start and end of the season—not in the middle, which was when the *Tristan* brouhaha occurred.

Just to show that opera still matters in America—at least in its cultural capital—the *Tristan* controversy made headlines, not least when Leinsdorf talked to the press about it. He may have resented an outsider's being made music director when he, Leinsdorf, had been at the house since 1938. In any case, he told the *New York Times*, "There seems to be a conspicuous absence of the Metropolitan's much-touted musical direction."

Kubelik resigned. He had never been anything but a figurehead, because a proper music director takes a residential part in a company's day-to-day life. More integral to the Met's post-Bing style was the Director Of Productions (from 1974), John Dexter, grouchy and intimidating but imaginative enough to make operas as varied as *Dialogues Des Carmelites* and *I Vespri Siciliani* resonate on a largely empty stage simply through character interaction. Dexter could even be thought of as a major link between the "all singing, no acting" stars of the Bing era (as in the Margaret Webster story below) and today's thespian stars.

The Met's Dexter years stretched into eras of stability, when the Board, though still heard, was at least not seen. From 1990 to 2006, Joseph Volpe and, from 2006, Peter Gelb, the Met rose above the Board-instituted chaos of the 1970s (including the hiring of a general manager, Hugh Southern, who seemed never to be around and seldom involved in planning or running the one season he spent on the job).

Volpe's background was unique. The Met's very first managers were professional showmen: Gatti came from La Scala, and Herbert Witherspoon and Edward Johnson were singers. Bing had logged a great deal of administrative experience in the music world. Volpe, however, had risen in the ranks of the Met's backstage as a carpenter, which gave him insight into the house's physical operations and, obviously, made union negotiations easier.

Gelb has emphasized Bing's interest in hiring theatre directors, as in Robert Lepage's $16,000,000 *Ring* cycle built on forty-five tons of mobile aluminum beams. Met personnel called it "the machine," and its strenuous fluttering proved a distraction to many in the audience. Still, the use of projections enabled Lepage to give Wagner— for once in the *Ring*'s existence—exactly what he asked for, with the magic and monsters all in place. Never before had the public *seen*

Siegfried's battle with Fafner. Von Karajan's dragon looked like an irate carpet—but then, von Karajan was more concerned with the lighting of his stage than its contents. When he bragged to Rudolf Bing about the number of lighting rehearsals needed to perfect the Karajan *Ring*, Bing dryly replied, "I could have got it that dark in one."

Laughter In the House

In its earliest years, the Old Met was a much more compact outfit than it later became. The 1886–1887 season, for example, ran from November 8 to February 26 (while giving performances only on Monday, Wednesday, Friday, and Saturday afternoon), and the roster took in just thirty-one singers and two conductors. Thus, manager Edmond C. Stanton had at most two people capable in a particular role, including tricky ones such as the tenor leads in *Rienzi* and *Tristan und Isolde*, both of which were given that season.

This could lead to intense rivalries, especially if two singers regarded a certain part as unsharable. It happens that Stanton was giving *Fidelio*, using two outstanding Leonores in Marianne Brandt and Lilli Lehmann—and Lehmann thought of herself as so singular a soprano that no other must dare sing a "Lehmann role." So it was that on January 14, 1887, when Brandt sang the *Fidelio* prima, harsh laughter broke out from a box at the opera's tenderest moment, in the dialogue before "O namenlose Freude," at Leonore's line "Nichts, nichts, mein Florestan." (Nothing, nothing, my Florestan.)

Some 3,500 heads turned to see who had laughed, but whoever it was had hidden deep inside the box. For her part, Brandt was so rattled that she came apart in the ensuing music and the conductor, Anton Seidl, had to stop the orchestra so Brandt could collect herself and carry on.

No one knows for certain who the culprit was, but how could it have been anyone but Lehmann? Who else had the motive to do such a thing and who else was so competitive and spiteful? The event got into the newspapers, and the *Times'* Henry Krehbiel noted that, between the cast's coming out for their calls, "hisses were directed toward the box."

The Fire

Josiah Cady won the contest for the architecture of the Met, and he designed it to make the building as fireproof as possible. He set up a sprinkler system backstage and a giant water tank on high, fixed with pipes stoppered by solder that would melt under heat, causing the tank to empty onto the stage. Further, the deck was held up by four thousand beams made of not wood but iron, and the usual asbestos curtain could be lowered to contain any fire behind the footlights, where virtually all theatre fires started.

Alas. Sometime after the Met opened, the sprinkler system and the tank had ceased to be operational, the metal beams below the stage had been replaced by wooden beams to make room for scenery storage, and the asbestos curtain had been chained up because, in late August of 1892, workmen were painting scenery and the asbestos was locking the fumes within the work area. All it took after that was a careless painter letting his cigarette fall onto canvas. And so the house went up, gutting the building so badly that the Met canceled its 1892–1893 season, not to reopen till November of 1893.

As to the man whose smoking caused the disaster: after his first panicked cries of "Fire!," he began to run and fell through one of the open stage traps, landing forty feet below. The firefighters rescued him, but at Bellevue Hospital he was so out of his head that he could only babble incomprehensibly, and soon died.

He was the sole casualty.

Carmen Doesn't Die In This Version

In its first season after the fire, the Met offered *Carmen* with an eye-opening cast: Jean de Reszke as José, Emma Eames as Micaëla, hulking Jean Lasalle as the torero, and the Carmen of Emma Calvé.

There are Carmens tempestuous and Carmens cool, Carmens erotic and Carmens humorous. After all, *she* doesn't know that the orchestra is stalking her with a Fate Theme. The French style in Carmens is to sing it well but do nothing until the Card Song; some do nothing till the cast party after the last performance.

Emma Calvé was a Carmen tempestuous. At one performance, just as de Reszke was about to launch the Flower Song, she stuck a rose into his mouth. Playful Carmen.

At another performance, possibly on the annual tour, Calvé didn't crumple to the floor after de Reszke stabbed her, but for some reason stormed offstage instead. And de Reszke stormed right after her, brought her back to where he had stabbed her, and forced her down on the deck. Will you please die already?

Calvé wouldn't. And she got her revenge by singing José's remorseful last lines along with de Reszke. Immortal Carmen.

Fiasco

Nellie Melba had always wanted to sing Wagner, and though everyone tried to talk her out of it, she insisted on opening the *Siegfried* in the 1896–1897 season as Brünnhilde. Melba's delicate instrument couldn't have gotten through Elsa or Elisabeth, much less the power role of the valkyrie, and she should have known she was boxing above her weight class from the dress rehearsal.

The prima was a disaster not to be equaled at the house for generations after. Henry Krehbiel in the *New York Post*[2] wrote, "Mme. Melba's share in the performance cannot be discussed even in general terms," which is a nice way of putting it. W. J. Henderson of the *Times* finessed his way around it all with "[Melba's] style of singing [is] not suited to a complete embodiment of Brünnhilde, and…her ambition…was more potent than wise."

Who let her do this? Management, obviously—but some blamed the Siegfried, Jean de Reszke, for encouraging Melba to tackle the opera in the first place. *He* said he had urged it on her to sing not Brünnhilde but the Forest Bird, one of the *Ring*'s few genuinely lyric parts.

One performance of the work was enough for Melba. The remaining Brünnhildes were sung by Felia Litvinne and Georgine von Januschowsky.

Melba's final words on the subject were "I have been a fool."

Reveal the Grail!

Heinrich Conried, the Met's general manager from 1903 to 1908, saw a tremendous opportunity in staging *Parsifal*, as it had been the exclusive property of Bayreuth ever since its 1882 premiere. True,

---

2. Because of their deadlines for the next day's edition, the critics couldn't review Melba on opening night, as Brünnhilde doesn't appear in Siegfried till partway through the third and final act. So the Met made an exception and allowed journalists to attend the rehearsal.

there had been concert performances locally, but they were either abridged (one series even left out all the choral scenes, important parts of each of the three acts) or poorly performed.

Conried knew *Parsifal* would be irresistible for the controversy it would raise, as the Lady Macbeth of Bayreuth—Wagner's widow, Cosima—would erupt in self-righteous fury. Indeed, she exceeded Conried's wildest dreams, drawing all of Western Civ into her tantrum. Even the clergy took part, suggesting it was blasphemy to treat *Parsifal* as entertainment. At Bayreuth, at least, it was a sacrament rather than an opera.

Others simply observed that *Parsifal* was protected by copyright till 1913—but the United States didn't recognize European copyright law, and Conried announced the Met *Parsifal* for Christmas Eve of 1903. The box office had to turn away an immense crowd that night, and all eleven performances sold out, more yet on the post-season tour. Conried then treated himself to a personal benefit performance, taking all the proceeds. The work was the biggest draw in Met history to that point, more popular even than Goldmark's *Die Königin Von Saba* (The Queen Of Sheba) had been, with its spectacle and furtive erotic dalliance.

And *Parsifal* lacked *Sheba*'s sheer lyrical fun. The performance began in the afternoon, to allow for a dinner break of an hour and forty-five minutes later on. Yes, but what dinner? Because the Met had been built so far out of Manhattan's central dining district, there were scarcely any places to eat. The so-called lobster palaces above Forty-Second Street on Broadway were a bit racy for many operagoing couples, though there was a Delmonico's—the last word in "gentle" dining—on Fifth Avenue at Forty-Fifth Street. At that, amid the many articles dealing with the problem, some writers advised Parsifalites to bring along a block of chocolate or even to fast, as befits so spiritual a piece.

Conried cleverly collected a cast that would justify the music without costing a lot, as this was one attraction that would sell no matter who was singing. Alois Burgstaller was the young knight-to-be, Anton Van Rooy the iconically wounded Fisher King, Robert Blass old Gurnemanz, and Milka Ternina the *ewig-weibliche* Kundry, under conductor Alfred Hertz. In an act of scrupulous noblesse oblige, Conried gave his public Louise Homer (a regular Amneris, Azucena, and Ortrud, though she did sing smaller parts, too) as the unseen voice at the end of Act One, a role lasting scarcely fifteen seconds. And the cast held together remarkably over the season, with few alternates.

Cosima promised to close the doors of Bayreuth to all of them, and did so. But it was a great honor to take part in this *Parsifal*, one of the most Wagnerian acts in American opera history. How often is elite art the national talk of the town? A Met usher's wife gave birth the day before the premiere, and the happy pair named their newborn baby boy after this magnificent happening: Parsifal McGillicuddy.

The Fine Print

When the Met's professional éminence grise, Otto Kahn, made the company's official offer of the general manager's post to Giulio Gatti-Casazza (to start in 1908), Gatti was startled to see a clause stating that the Met reserved the right to boot Gatti if it chose to. The term of employment ran for three years, and, at the end of each year, that troublesome Board could cancel the contract.

Yet Gatti was giving up a very successful reign as head of La Scala—and bringing with him Toscanini, by general agreement the best conductor of Italian opera on the planet (not to mention his superb readings of Wagner). Was this the way to treat leaders of the opera world?

"Do not be concerned," Toscanini told him. "You and I are not the sort of men who get fired after a trial period."

Uni-Set

Otto Kahn was so sure he would be able to persuade the Board to ratify a move to a more expansive physical plant that he assured Gatti that three years after he arrived in New York there would be a New Met.

In fact, it took fifty-eight years. But meanwhile Gatti inspected all the company's premises, including the scenery storehouses. Coming upon the set of a piazza with a door in the back giving onto the sea, Gatti was unable to figure out what opera this would be for, as it appeared to marry two incongruent locales.

"What work does this belong to?" he asked a subordinate.

"It depends," came the answer. "Sometimes it's *Mignon* and sometimes it's *Otello*."

The Woman No Man Could Resist

Lina Cavalieri was appreciated as a soprano but famous as an adventuress. Beautiful to the nth, she began by odd-jobbing in her native Rome but got to Paris and the Folies Bergère early on. She married, arranged to become unmarried, then took up the opera, specializing in the more alluring verismo heroines—Manon Lescaut, Fedora, Adriana Lecouvreur, all of which she sang in her two seasons at the Met, from 1906 to 1908.

But the house couldn't keep her, because she had the alarming habit of enchanting young scions of the ruling class, irritating daddy with the possibility of breach-of-promise litigation or, worse, marriage. For a member of the upper crust to wive in the theatre world was absolutely unsuitable—though it did happen, for instance to the original *Florodora* Sextet. There was even a prominent play about it, Clyde Fitch's *Captain Jinks Of the Horse Marines* (1901), which gave Ethel Barrymore her big break, as a soprano pursued by a cavalry officer.

Two years of Cavalieri was all the Met Board could take. Gatti was ordered to let her go, and he was not unhappy to oblige, for while she sold well, her value as a performer was uncertain. True, you couldn't take your eyes off her. But her voice, as W. J. Henderson reported in the *New York Sun*, was "very pretty in quality, but not rich or vibrant."

Oscar Hammerstein of course snapped Cavalieri up, if only to further his war with the Met and the ruling class in general (even though the latter took in his own subscribers). However, Cavalieri ran afoul of Hammerstein's biggest draw, the redoubtable Scot Mary Garden. She had agreed to join the Manhattan Opera on the condition that she be allowed to take along with her the contemporary French works in which she excelled, and she happily made *Pelléas and Mélisande* a great success for Hammerstein.

Yet he blew his top when she told him that Cavalieri must not sing *Thaïs*. This was Massenet, Garden's preserve. She had seen the announcement on a poster outside the opera house, marched into Hammerstein's office, and there the two of them—as she recalled in her memoirs—fought it out.

"You've got nothing to do with my theatre!" he shouted. "I'll do what I goddamn please, and nobody, not you or anybody else, is going to stop me!"

"You can do what *you* please," Garden replied, "and I can do what *I* please."

Whereupon she attended a rehearsal like a pro, signed a letter of resignation, left the premises, and booked passage to return to Europe.

Now even the often irrational Hammerstein knew he was licked. He surrendered, albeit furiously, and when Garden made her entrance in that contested Thaïs, tossing roses at the Alexandrian party guests as she always did, the audience rose to its feet with such an ovation that conductor Campanini had to stop the music. "I never heard so much screaming and yelling and 'Bravas!' in all my life," she says. Apparently they knew about the fracas with Hammerstein. New York was grateful for Hammerstein's opera—but New York was in love with Mary Garden.

Now Lina Cavalieri was out at the Manhattan as well. But she did at least get an Astor out of the whole thing. That marriage didn't last, but along came a French tenor, and the two were living in Florence during World War II when the bombing alarms went off. Instead of running to the shelter, Cavalieri stopped to save her jewelry and died in the raid: like the heroines she had portrayed, glamorous to the end.

Hammerstein Tries To Destroy Himself But the Met Saves Him

For all his superb instincts as an opera impresario, Hammerstein was difficult even when he didn't have to be, because he loved to fight. In 1909, he picked a beauty: he deliberately and pointlessly insulted his biggest supporter, Mrs. Clarence Mackay, wife of one of the richest men in the northeast (and the future father-in-law of Irving Berlin).

The cause of Hammerstein's fight with Mrs. Mackay doesn't matter, because Hammerstein lived to fight and fought to live. But, in brief: he lent Manhattan forces—Campanini and the orchestra—to play Debussy's all but brand new *La Mer* at a wedding reception the Mackays were giving. The hostess was lavish with her thanks—Campanini got an emerald ring—but Hammerstein, who didn't attend, got nothing.

So he was gleefully enraged, and now the fun begins, he thinks. But wait a second, Hammerstein. Mrs. Mackay entreated her Society friends to help her keep your opera house in the black. They obliged. And where Society went, not only did others follow but the press focused attention on your doings, because Society leaders were the rock stars of the day.

Alas, Hammerstein brushed all that aside. Everything for others and nothing for me? he thought. Well, let's see how she likes this: a letter ordering her never to set foot in the Manhattan Opera House again. He gave it to his assistant (his son Arthur), but Arthur tore it up. Hammerstein then wrote another one and delivered it himself.

Immediately, Manhattan subscriptions were canceled, out of loyalty to Mrs. Mackay, and the press went back to ogling Society at the Metropolitan. It was enough to sink Hammerstein's opera within a year or two. But then something else happened.

The Met, at its wit's end enduring Hammerstein's coup after coup of singing sensations and smash-hit opera curiosities, bought him out for $1,250,000, negotiated by Arthur while his father was exiled to Europe to forestall further antagonism. In the final agreement, Hammerstein had to give up producing opera in New York, Boston, Philadelphia, and Chicago for ten years. Further, all artist contracts, stage properties, and orchestral parts under Hammerstein's ownership were to be ceded to the Met. Hammerstein was allowed to keep the Manhattan Opera House itself, along with another opera house in Philadelphia, which nobody wanted, anyway.

Thus, Arthur had pulled off a splendid coup, getting the Met to reward the Hammersteins for giving up a venture that was virtually in ruins in the first place. After cabling his father with the good news, Arthur took the next boat over, and the two met in Paris. There the senior Hammerstein exultantly told Arthur that the family was now the proud owner of prime real estate on the Kingsway in London.

"What?" said Arthur. "You bought property in London?" And now, dreading the answer, he added, perhaps somewhat feebly, plaintively, "*Why*?"

Why else? "To build an opera house, of course!" his father cried. And Arthur replied, "*I'll never speak to you again as long as I live!*"

The Firing Of Fremstad

Was Olive Fremstad a mezzo or a soprano? She started in operetta, went into opera in roles such as Azucena and Venus, and by the time of her Met debut, in 1903, she was becoming a full-fledged Wagnerian soprano, as Sieglinde, Elsa, Isolde, the three Brünnhildes. But was it at the expense of her instrument? After her *Siegfried* Awakening Scene with Heinrich Knote, one critic wrote, "She is lacerating her fine dramatic contralto voice, throwing the shreds at us and calling them Brünnhilde."

Still, Fremstad found the big Wagner heroines irresistible— Brünnhilde so noble, Isolde so fiery. Fremstad was terrific onstage in these parts, so wholly at one with the characters that she swept the audience along with her into a kind of mythopoetic naturalism. When she tried Strauss' Salome, she did her background research in a mortuary, to find out exactly how much death costs in pounds and ounces. So, when the Baptist's head was presented to her, she staggered under its weight.

Fremstad had a passionate following, but Gatti didn't like her. "Very difficult" was his assessment, in his usual conciseness. She was expensive and balked at many things, such as working the day before or after a performance, which vexed the rehearsal schedule.

Finally, in 1914, Gatti had had enough. Other singers could take over Fremstad's roles for less money, and they'd rehearse when they were told to rehearse. Fremstad asked for one last favor—to make her farewell as Isolde, her greatest role and the one that gave her the most to do. It would be a night to immortalize her. But Gatti assigned that performance to Fremstad's hated rival Johanna Gadski, scheduling Elsa as Fremstad's last Met outing.

Lohengrin! It's the tenor's opera, even the mezzo's. Elsa was Fremstad's second least favorite part (after Giulietta in *The Tales Of Hoffmann*), tricky to sing and dramatically thin. Everything that happens in the story is done *to* her; she herself does only one thing—and that by breaking her solemn word. What a squish! Even the chorus has more to do!

Nevertheless, Fremstad's public cheered so much at the end of the opera that Gatti ordered the asbestos curtain lowered, to clear the house. The audience resisted and the asbestos went back up. It was a grand occasion, but it really should have been a *Tristan*. And now Fremstad had to give up singing to her Metropolitan public. "I spring into life when the curtain rises," she once said, "and when it falls I might as well die." Sometime after, Fremstad swallowed her pride and wrote Gatti, begging to come back. He did not answer.

She retired a bit later, and died in 1950, of unemployment.

She Shall Remain Nameless

They tell of a soprano of the old days who was completely terrible but under the protection of someone from the money side of the house. One night, she was singing Micaëla; after her third-act aria, a shot rings out, Micaëla gets scared, and she runs offstage. But this night, somebody in the house called out, "Damn it! He missed!"

I Remember It Well

Right from the start, soprano Geraldine Farrar and conductor Arturo Toscanini made a great team. Of course they tangled at first, not least in an idiotic disagreement over her approach to some detail in *Madama Butterfly*, enshrined in a famous story.

This was in 1908, during the opera's third season in the house, and Farrar had already made Cio-Cio-San her own. Toscanini was new to the production. So Farrar attempted to make it clear that this was her opera—even her house. "Don't forget, maestro," she said. "I am a star."

Oh, for heaven's sake. Toscanini's reply comes in different versions, from "The stars are in the heavens" to "Here we are not stars but artists, and you are a bad artist." Given that, in 1908, Toscanini's command of English was meager, this is fanciful storytelling. At that, Francis Robinson, later the Met's PR man, quotes Farrar with "The public pays to see my face, not your back." Farrar herself, in her second autobiography (of two), leans toward the "stars in the heavens" line. But one way or another, the two made their peace, created some wonderful nights of opera together, and became lovers.

However, Farrar eventually tired of her "back street" status, and demanded that Toscanini divorce his wife and marry Farrar. This, to a socially conservative Italian of Toscanini's generation, was unthinkable. And Toscanini didn't just end the affair: he packed up his family and returned to Italy.

Some years later, when he was back in New York, Farrar had him up for dinner. She went all out on the menu, serving caviar as an hors d'oeuvre.

"So how did it go?" a friend asked him later.

"I slept with that woman for seven years," Toscanini replied. "Wouldn't you think she'd remember that I hate fish?"

Language Lab

Toscanini duly amassed a small English vocabulary, though he couldn't understand anything if you spoke too fast.

One time, he was driving an orchestra rehearsal very hard, till one of the players failed to please him and Toscanini ripped into him in classic Italian invective.

But this player, unlike the others, was not cowed. He immediately fired back at Toscanini in self-defense in vigorous street English.

Waving it all away as he picked up his baton, Toscanini told him, "Too late to apologize."

Crazy Doings At Kahn's Palazzo

Otto Kahn was not only the most powerful man on the Met Board but also its most positive influence, discovering talent that Gatti might have been unaware of. It says much that *The New Yorker* once called Kahn "the Metropolitan Richelieu."

So we owe him a story, even if this one isn't about opera per se. In fact, it's about theatre, for Kahn had been in Paris just before the outbreak of World War I, when Jacques Copeau founded Le Théâtre du Vieux-Colombier on Paris' left bank, far from the Parisian show shops to the north, where artificialty and mannerism held sway.

Fascinated by Copeau's revolutionary artistry, Kahn had Copeau bring his company to Broadway, where Kahn paid for the restoration of the old Garrick Theatre, by then disused in its lonely vigil across Herald Square from Macy's department store. For two seasons, from the fall of 1917 to the spring of 1919, the Vieux-Colombier gave New Yorkers a taste of authentic French drama, from Molière and Marivaux to Copeau's own adaptation of Dostoyefsky, *Les Frères Karamazov*. Two years of mostly unfamiliar works in a foreign language were bound to lose money—all of it Kahn's—but he went through with it out of sheer love of art.

Between the two seasons, in the summer of 1918, Kahn invited the whole troupe to stay at his Morristown estate, where Copeau kept everyone hopping with a rigorous schedule from dawn to dusk: exercises, rehearsals, dance practice, aesthetic discussions, meals, naps, language practice.

Of course, the sudden incursion of these bohemians attracted comment from the locals. When a reporter came out to interview Copeau, the black cab driver who took him to the railroad station asked, "Who's all them people in Mistah Kahn's house?"

"Actors," the reporter answered.

"Uh-huh," said the driver. "I knew *something* was wrong with them."

Sez You

A lover of novelties, Kahn persuaded Gatti to stage Ernst Křenek's *Jonny Spielt Auf* (Johnny Starts the Music), in 1929. The adventures of a lawless black jazzman in Europe, the opera mostly used a con-temporary classical idiom but featured as well pop-music models. One passage was marked *Schnelles-"Grammophon"-Tempo* (Fast, in the style of a 78 dance-band side).

Michael Bohnen and then Lawrence Tibbett played Jonny (in blackface), and the doings in Křenek's mad comedy took in theft and murder, capped by a finale in which Jonny, atop a world globe, led an ecstatic crowd of worshipers eager to see American jazz conquer Western Civilization.

Not everyone found this amusing. After the first performance, as the audience was departing, one of the box holders—either a Board member or the next thing to it, and of course someone Kahn had known for decades—rounded on him in a fury on his way out. "I think this is disgraceful!" he shouted. "You ought to be ashamed of yourself for imposing this five-and dime travesty on the rest of us! Horse-whipped!" And off he went.

Now, how to reply to this burst of criticism? "Who cares what you think?" works well, perhaps with variations built on rude language of the sort the silken Kahn didn't use in his dreams. Instead, he simply turned to someone and asked, mildly, "Who on earth is that?"

The Firing Of Gatti-Casazza

Running the house for twenty-seven years, Giulio Gatti-Casazza was the first Met manager whose name still has ring, because his regime was filled with the fabled great, from Caruso and Farrar to Flagstad and Melchior. As well, Gatti decorated the production calendar with the sumptuous visuals of set designer Joseph Urban, Florenz Ziegfeld's particular favoirite and unrivaled in arting up Broadway musicals with painterly genius.

Gatti was a Character, too. Like Andy Warhol of a later era, he was filled with caustic views of the many demanding personalities he had to deal with while never giving voice to his opinions. As an Italian, Gatti used his native language as a locked portal, to keep people out—and even with Italians he could prove frustratingly mute. Few knew that he spoke French as well as—secretly—English.

He was almost mysterious. Yet his ideal was transparent: to present great singers and conductors in an ever widening repertory. True, he was stingy about giving them rehearsal time, which most impresarios see as an expensive vanity. You're a pro, right? Go out there and do it. To be fair, Gatti did maintain a roster of singers who could. And the radio broadcasts that were to enrich many a Saturday afternoon began on his watch, making the Met a genuinely national institution.

But Gatti had an Achilles heel: he had fallen in love with a Met ballerina, and after his soprano wife, Frances Alda, divorced him, Gatti married the dancer. The difference in their ages was as scandalous as the adultery had been.

Then came the Wall Street Crash, and suddenly the Met's fortunes were in flux, with a new set of Powers That Be behind the scenes. As Gatti wrote at the time, "It is not the quality of the spectacle [i.e., "spettacolo," meaning the performances in general] and of the singers that counts, but the condition of the Stock Exchange. If the stocks go up, then everything is all right; if they go down, good night!"

Further, Otto Kahn, the sympathetic Board member Gatti was used to dealing with, was replaced by Paul Cravath, who thought opera "the last of our Victorian expressions" and seemed blind to its importance as art. Cravath also frowned with maximum prejudice on Gatti's remarriage; wasn't it bad enough that Gatti's first wife had been a company member, too? Weakening Gatti's position even more was the Met's unavoidable loss of income in the Depression. The 1931–1932 season ran half a million dollars in the red.

More: there was a feeling that the Met wasn't *national*. New American operas weren't enough. There had to be more American *singers* in leading roles—and not just Lawrence Tibbett. Maybe the manager himself should be American, too.

When the Board let Gatti know that his contract would not be renewed at its conclusion, he might have fought back. After all, he had been a mainstay in New York culture for twenty-seven years. But he would be sixty-six after what would now be his last season, and he may simply have become exhausted having to deal with that infernal Board and its money men, rather than, as in Europe, more arts-oriented members. Yet there's always a Board of some kind somehow, and it always gets in the way.

Resentful and tired out, Gatti knew it was now time for him to leave. It was generally believed that his successor would be a Met tenor (and a Canadian, which is not American but close enough), Edward Johnson. However, the Board startled one and all in choosing a former Met bass, Herbert Witherspoon (who did, unlike Johnson, have some opera adminstration experience elsewhere). Witherspoon worked in the house during Gatti's final season, that of 1934–1935, then took over as Gatti sailed home on the *Rex*. Just before a Board meeting, Witherspoon was heading to his office when he suddenly dropped dead on the spot.

> Witherspoon had died of a heart attack, at sixty-one. Johnson succeeded him for fifteen years, till the arrival of Rudolf Bing.

Good Career Move

Leonard Warren, one of the Met's outstanding "Verdi baritones," with a voice sized to suit the house and an upper range that would have been the envy of a tenor, won the Met Auditions Of the Air in 1939. He was still so untried that though he knew a few arias, he hadn't learned a single role.

Rather than throw him out on stage to flounder, Edward Johnson told Warren he was sending him to Italy to coach with experts, thus to master Amonasro, Germont, Count Di Luna, Ford, and of course Rigoletto.

"But those are all star roles," Warren pointed out. "Shouldn't I start with supporting bits, like the guys who come on and sing three lines and then go home?"

"With your voice?" Johnson replied. "My boy, you'll be a star or you'll be nothing. And when you come back from Europe, you're going to be a star."

This next slightly off-color tale is Met folklore, told in various versions from the 1950s on.

The Ezio Pinza Story

So there's this guy with a more than passing resemblance to Ezio Pinza. He's a New York garment-center factotum by the name of Sam Goldstein. On a trip to Chicago, he is greeted as "Mr. Pinza"— as he is everywhere he goes—and, as always, he corrects them with "Sam Goldstein is the name. Goldstein."

Of course no one believes him, because his near-twinning of Ezio Pinza is uncanny. When he checks into his hotel in Chicago and corrects the desk clerk, that worthy says, "Oh, of course, Mr. Pin—I mean Mr. Goldstein. I understand. You're incognito, certainly. We aim to please." Ringing the desk bell, he tells the baggage man, "Show Mr. Goldstein to the VIP suite."

On the way up in the elevator, the bellhop says, "I really enjoy your records, Mr. Pinza."

"Sam Goldstein is the name. Goldstein."

"Yes, of course, Mr., uh, Goldstein."

But in the bedroom of the suite, Goldstein encounters a beautiful young woman in the bed. Smiling, she says, "Is there anything I can do to brighten your stay in Chicago, Mr. Pinza?"

"Sam…" and extending his arms out, he sings, "enchawnted eeffning!"

John Briggs, who recounts the tale in rather different form in *Requiem For a Yellow Brick Brewery*, says that someone at the Met dared to tell Pinza the story, and that Pinza, after listening "in absolute stony silence," said, "Do I sound like dot?"

Ethnic Profiling

The autocratic conductor Fritz Reiner was rehearsing the full cast and orchestra in *Salome*, getting extremely irritated with the five men playing the Jews at Herod's court who are squabbling among themselves over the nature of God and His manifestations on earth.

The roles have no names. The are called First Jew, Second Jew, and so on, and Reiner was forcing them to sing their little scene again and again until they got it down to his satisfaction, after which they could leave. It wasn't enough for them to sing through their music perfectly: they had to sing through it perfectly twice in a row.

Finally, they did, and Reiner announced, "That was correct. The Jews can now go home."

Whereupon three-quarters of the orchestra players got up and started packing their instruments away.

Opera Vs. Theatre

Rudolf Bing's first season in the house, that of 1949–1950, when he was observing rather than managing, told him that many changes needed to be made, above all in the almost total lack of dramatic cohesion on stage. The Met had always had *some* acting singers, but it was a singer's house above all, used to stand-and-deliver artists who paid little attention to what their words were conveying, or even to what was occurring in the action in a general way. They weren't singing words: they were singing notes.

Bing knew that most Met singers would regard this as a hateful revolution, so he cast his first sortie—*Don Carlo*, a new production to open the season—with newcomers in three of the leading roles. Jussi Bjoerling, Robert Merrill, and Jerome Hines were Met veterans, but Delia Rigal, Fedora Barbieri, and Cesare Siepi (replacing Boris Christoff, barred from the United States through a political snafu) came to the Met fresh off the boat. Further, Bing brought in a stage director from the world of the spoken theatre, Margaret Webster. Her background was prodigious, with a heavy inlay of Shakespeare (and her actress mother was a British Dame, May Whitty, gazetted as far back as 1918). Webster was, to a point, musical as well, having sung in the school choir. She could even read music.

But she wasn't prepared for how untheatrical her "actors" were. They felt themselves elements in a panorama, a nobility, with a mandate to lift the spirit through music, music, and more music. Not storytelling. Singing. Everyone in the Met family was an adherent of this emphasis on voice, too. "The house," Webster explained in her memoirs, *Don't Put Your Daughter On the Stage,* "ran on zeal"—and it wasn't a zeal to act. For the first time in her career, she was to direct performers who worked from the heart, not the mind. As *Don Carlo*'s conductor, Fritz Stiedry, warned her, "God gave larynxes to stable boys."

The complications were endless. For instance, no matter how many people were on stage at any given moment, everybody had to be able to see the conductor. Then, too, no sooner had the first performances passed than the cast changed. By the third *Don Carlo,* Blanche Thebom had replaced Barbieri; on the fourth and fifth *Don Carlo,* Hans Hotter replaced Jerome Hines. Immediately after that, Eleanor Steber and Richard Tucker replaced Rigal and Bjoerling.

It drove Webster crazy, because she was in charge of putting the new arrivals into the staging, and thus had to start all over, again and again. And there was always that "singer" mentality to deal with, as when Webster told Tucker to take Steber's hand, and he asked Webster when.

"When you say you do," Webster told him.

"When's that?" Tucker asked, and Webster showed him the line in the score, "Io prendo la tua man." (I take your hand.)

"Oh," said Tucker. "Is that what that means?"

Nevertheless, *Don Carlo* came off well, and Bing was to revive the production often over the years. But Webster finally met her match in her next staging for Bing, the following season, for another opening night: *Aida. Don Carlo,* at least, wasn't already routined in the house, with a bunch of veterans used to doing their roles in a certain way. *Aida,* however, brought out the hardened conservatives, unalterably opposed to stage direction. I know what works for me in this part and *that's how I'm going to play it.*

Even so, Webster tried to spark a conversation between the singers and the text. What is the piece about? How do each of you respond to the other principals? Does Radames like Amneris, or does he find her irritating and pushy? Doesn't she have an eerie habit of always showing up at *just* the wrong moment? And now: why don't we read through the text and discover for ourselves what this story tells us about the world?

The Radames, Mario Del Monaco, looked startled, then resentful. He stared at Webster. He shrugged. Okay, lady director. It was the most emotion Webster ever saw from him, including when he was performing on stage. The Aida, Zinka Milanov, didn't like the sound of any of this, and Webster noticed the two of them exchanging a sympathetic glance.

The reading started well, because Jerome Hines, the Ramfis, was up first, and Hines was game. But after his opening line, Del Monaco replied in a monotone. Webster did everything she could to excite the participants, but the well-seasoned Milanov knew exactly how to deal with this interference in the singing of Verdi. When she read the lines of her first aria, "Ritorna vincitor" (Come back victorious), she pronounced them haltingly—"as if," Webster recalled, "she'd never heard the words before."

Now Milanov peered at the text, brought it closer to her eyes, held it far away. "Excuse me," she said, rummaging in her handbag for a pair of eyeglasses. Even then, she read as if confused. She tried a line, looked up, limped through the next line, looked down. She shifted in her chair. "Nu…mi…pie…tà" (Gods, pity me), she got out. She'd sung these words many times before; she was the Aida of the Met. Yet now every phrase seemed incomprehensible to her.

Finally, Milanov paused and took off her eyepiece. She looked at Webster. "Wrong glasses," said Milanov.

And Webster concludes her reminiscence with "I know when I am licked."

George Szell's Tannhäuser

"Today you look like a toilet brush," Szell told pianist Gary Graffman's wife, Naomi, though Szell supposedly liked the Graffmans. Imagine what he was saying to people he didn't care for. One of the most unpleasant conductors ever to achieve a smashing reputation for his musical abilities, Szell was a terror to everyone.

Determined to upgrade the Met's conductor roster, Bing had his heart set on a Szell Met, if only for a single opera. True, Szell had been at the house during the Johnson regime, and he was willing. But as the maestro of the Cleveland orchestra (where he was known as "Dr. Cyclops"), he was not often free to sit in on even a portion of the Met season.

Then Szell accepted a brief engagement guesting with the New York Philharmonic, and Bing was able to slot Szell in for a new *Tannhäuser*, in 1953. Before Bing could celebrate, however, Szell pulled a Szell and announced that he was not happy with the casting. Ramon Vinay and Margaret Harshaw lacked the velvet for Tannhäuser and Elisabeth, or so Szell thought. Nor did he note any spark in Jerome Hines as the Landgrave, a dull role that Hines only made duller. The minnesingers' cohort were inexperienced in these roles and created a ghastly Schmiß[3] in the ensemble at the end of Act One.

After five repetitions, Szell went back to Cleveland, not before writing to the New York *Herald-Tribune* to complain of "present conditions at the Metropolitan" (i.e., under Rudolf Bing) and to announce that he would not be returning for the opera's last two performances.

Bing was beside himself with rage, and one of his assistants observed that Szell was his own worst enemy.

---

3. A Schmiß is opera slang for when singers and orchestra suddenly fall out of sync.

To which Bing snapped back, "Not while I'm alive."

In the Broadway version, George S. Kaufman says it about Jed Harris, a producer and director who, like Szell, alienated everyone he came into contact with.

Beauty Tips

When out for dinner, Zinka Milanov habitually gathered up the unused pats of butter, wrapped them in napkins, and put them into her purse.

"For complexion," she would say. "Botter is badter than cold cream!"

Spiritual Advice

Waiting in the wings to make her entrance in a *Trovatore*, Milanov spotted tenor Kurt Baum deep in religious devotion.

"No, Baum," she told him. "If you don' have it yet already, God ain' gonna give it to you now."

Pay the Man

As if Maria Callas were not a handful by herself, her husband, Giovanni Battista Meneghini, was even worse, forever inventing complications big and small in his business dealings with the Met. One example: he insisted on being paid in cash for each of his wife's performances before the opera started.

At this time, the Met had a set top fee of $1,000 a performance (though travel expenses could be added as a kind of secret bonus, unknown to rival singers), and Bing decided to create a big and small complication of his own: he paid Meneghini in five-dollar bills.

In *My Wife Maria Callas*, Meneghini changed it to one-dollar bills. And, he added proudly, "I counted the money carefully twice" and wouldn't let Callas take the stage "until I had finished."

The Firing Of Callas

It's not that Bing liked to fire people. It's that he had an opera house to run and couldn't allow singers, conductors, agents, and so on, to dictate terms to him. And he did often try his resentful best to give the most interesting artists what they wanted if he possibly could.

But he wasn't able to give Callas what she wanted, because her fondest wish was to break the implied contract of her letter of intent to sing at the Met in the 1958–1959 season in several roles, one of which was Verdi's Lady Macbeth.

Much lay in that part, for the Met had no *Macbeth* production on hand; this would be a new one, no expense spared. Callas had complained to not only Bing but the press as well about the shabby physique and carriage of the *Norma*, *La Traviata*, and *Lucia Di Lammermoor* productions she had sung in her first two Met visits, at a time when she was used to the scintillating creations of Luchino Visconti and Margherita Wallmann at La Scala, including the former's *La Sonnambula* of 1955, in which Callas appeared as a kind of nineteenth-century ballerina, moving with the gracefully affected little steps of the première danseuse, pale and bejewelled, with a wondering air that brought the Romantic Era back alive. This

Sonnambula was one of the most sensational events of the decade, one befitting the greatest of stars, and Callas responded enthusiastically to Bing's offer of a brand-new Callas *Macbeth*.

Oh, but wait. Do I really want to sing that fearsome part? And the clothes are so unglamorous; you spend the whole evening wrapped in a carpet. And it isn't a diva piece, like Norma or Violetta. That baritone keeps pushing his way in—and then Bing demands that I go on that dreary Spring Tour, playing to those nobodies out in the provinces, far from the flashbulbs and cocktails of la dolce vita. Now that I think of it, the whole Met thing just completely lacks chic.

And then an opportunity fell out of the sky: a very high-paying American concert tour which would conflict with the Met dates. To the Met's $1,000 a night, the tour would net $5,000. Later, Callas' husband did admit that the two of them schemed to ditch the Met. "We absolutely must free ourselves from that Metropolitan," he tells her in his aforementioned memoir, and she replies, "If you can manage that, you're good."

He managed it, having Callas refuse to bounce back and forth between the heavy Lady Macbeth and her other Met assignment, the dainty Violetta. In fact, Bing had allowed Callas as much time as she had asked for to balance the two. But now she pretended he hadn't.

Time was pressing; Callas must sign the Met contract. But Callas does not sign. Ultimatum. Silence. Then: BING FIRES CALLAS was the headline read around the world. In Dallas playing Cherubini's Medea when she heard the news, Callas sang as if Rudolf Bing were playing Jason.

Meanwhile, Bing pulled off a coup by replacing Callas in the *Macbeth* with another great singer, Leonie Rysanek. To send her off in style, he hired a fan to take up a position in one of the two standing-room sections down front at the side of the orchestra, to turn his head into the auditorium and shout, "Brava, Callas!" when Rysanek made her first entrance. Legend tells us that she didn't hear him, but the public did, and with the natural American sympathy for the underdog the audience made certain to give Rysanek a generous welcome.

Beat the Clock

While singing in *Aida*, Antonietta Stella enlivened the opera's second intermission by insisting on a solo bow. This was in contravention of the house rules at the time: all of the principals in a given act must bow together.

Stella had her own rules, apparently, and if she wasn't allowed her solo call she said she wouldn't continue with the opera.

Somehow or other, whenever trouble threatened, Bing would show up within fifty seconds; many believed he had the whole place wire-tapped. Apprised of the problem, he turned to Stella and said, "Madame, you have exactly three minutes to change your mind. If not, I will cancel the rest of the performance and go before the curtain to tell the public *why* I am canceling the rest of the performance. I will refund every ticket-holder's admission and sue you for the loss. And I will initiate a case with the American Guild of Musical Artists."

As Stella stood there, incredulous and shocked, Bing looked at his watch and added, "Incidentally, you now have two minutes and a half."

Stella sang the rest of *Aida*.

Send In the Clones

On December 18, 1959, Bing unveiled a new production of *Tristan und Isolde* starring Birgit Nilsson, with Karl Liebl and conductor

Karl Böhm. The scenery was drab and there was little character interaction, but Nilsson was—as Paul Henry Lang of the *New York Times* said—"a true princess, not only in Ireland but in all the world of opera." She was the new Flagstad, they said, though Nilsson lacked Flagstad's warmth, specializing instead in a steely *ping!* that could lay one flat against the back of one's chair. Word went out: you simply had to hear her.

Nilsson blithely poured out a second Met Isolde on December 23, this time opposite Ramon Vinay. Then, for the third *Tristan*, Vinay was indisposed. And his cover, Liebl again, had a cold and couldn't sustain a Wagner marathon. Incredibly, given how hard it is to cast a good Tristan, Bing had a second cover on hand, Albert Da Costa. But he was indisposed as well.

With all three Tristans out of commission, Bing was faced with canceling the show. But to suspend a Nilsson showpiece on a sell-out and extremely eager audience was unthinkable.

So Bing did the impossible: Vinay sang Act One, Liebl sang Act Two, and Da Costa sang Act Three. Bravi, gentlemen—but really, nobody cared. This was a night for Nilsson.

Diplomacy

The Bing era was punctuated by regularly scheduled fights with the unions, complete with threats, wars in the press, and strikes that closed the house down. In the summer of 1961, in fact, the negotiators for the musicians' union demanded ludicrously impossible terms and refused to compromise.

Bing then announced that he was canceling the 1961–1962 season completely, because all the major singers were being forced to make other plans, and if it did open the Met would be putting on the equivalent of community opera.

With the weight of her reputation, Leontyne Price appealed to President Kennedy, and the president asked Secretary Of Labor Arthur Goldberg to negotiate with the union.

The season was saved, and Goldberg told Bing that Kennedy was looking forward to one of the Met's greatest seasons ever.

And Bing replied, "Perhaps the President would like to run the Met and let me handle Berlin."

Highway Robbery

Can you believe it? Rudolf Bing was mugged in Central Park while dog walking on a Sunday evening.

"Give me your money and your watch," said the thief, showing Bing a large knife.

Well, Bing had plenty of money, but his watch was a keepsake of his days as a fire warden in England during World War II. Its sentimental value was priceless, though in actual monetary terms it was worth no more than $25, as he freely told the press.

Later, back at the ranch, Zinka Milanov lectured the chief on bon ton. "The general manager the Metropolitan Opera," she told him, "does not carry a watch wort' twanny-five dohllars."

Yes Is the Answer

A journalist once asked Régine Crespin for a few words on Rudolf Bing. What, for instance, is his best quality?

"He has the memory of an elephant," said Crespin. "Especially when someone says no to him."

You Can Do Anything, Leontyne

The 1959 *Macbeth* with Leonie Rysanek was such a success that Bing tried another piece of early Verdi, *Nabucco*, again with Rysanek. After all, he reasoned, both Lady Macbeth in the one and Abigaille in the other are sort of similar—very dramatic roles with a bit of coloratura now and again.

In fact, you can ham and egg your way through Lady's few florid lines. Abigaille, however, is much more challenging. It's heavier, too, and something of a voice-killer. In any case, *Nabucco* did not score a hit—but the Met had a sensational Verdi soprano on hand in Leontyne Price, and Bing had a thought: What if Price took over Abigaille from Rysanek?

Bing asked Price about this, and, as she didn't know the work, he suggested she attend one of the *Nabucco*s and judge for herself.

The next day, Price met Bing in his office. Trying to be his most charming, Bing made it official: would Price consent to add Abigaille to her repertory?

And Price answered, "Man, are you *crazy*?"

Parte Donna Elvira

Bing waited a long time before inviting Elisabeth Schwarzkopf to join the Met roster, either because he already had several house regulars for Schwarzkopf's three great roles (Donna Elvira, the

Marschallin, and Mistress Ford), or because he was suspicious of her politics. She had, after all, been a Nazi Party member, but so had many others working in the arts in Nazi Germany. In some cases, it was more a formality than a commitment—and as Bing said of one artist he never invited, the Met banned "a mediocre conductor who was an outstanding Nazi," preferring "an outstanding conductor who was a mediocre Nazi."

Was it Bing's revenge that Schwarzkopf's voice was giving out by the time she finally graced the Met stage? Her Marschallins in the 1964–1965 season were incomparable, but Donna Elvira, in the following season, found Schwarzkopf struggling. After the prima, a broadcast matinee on January 29, Schwarzkopf canceled the rest of her Elviras "because of illness," so the *New York Times* reported, and "returned to her home in Switzerland that night."

But there might be something else to it. In *A Knight At the Opera*, Geraint Evans recalls rehearsing Leporello in this production. It was the old Herbert Graf staging in the very picturesque designs of Eugene Berman, one of Bing's better productions of the 1950s. Cesare Siepi was, as so often, Giovanni, Teresa Stich-Randall the Anna, and Jan Peerce the Ottavio. While Evans and Schwarzkopf were working with the director on the scene of the Catalogue Aria, Schwarzkopf's husband, Walter Legge, took exception to something or other and strode up onto the stage to dispute the direction, a major break of protocol.

"I kept out of it," says Evans—a wise move, as the moment Bing heard Legge's voice contending with the director on Bing's magic intergalactic intercom, the manager was up and moving, and when he got into the theatre he went straight into the war zone and ordered Legge to leave the stage.

So Schwarzkopf sang the prima and then went home, either because, one, she was not singing well (as surviving tapes attest); two, she was ill; or, three, out of loyalty to her husband.

The remaining Elviras were sung by Lucine Amara and Pilar Lorengar.

The Trip To Paris

In 1966, the Met took two of its productions to Paris for a short season at the Théâtre de l'Odéon, *The Barber Of Seville* and *The Marriage Of Figaro*. Presumably, the pair were chosen because both were drawn from classic plays by Beaumarchais—and the Odéon, a smallish house, couldn't handle the Met's big showpieces such as *Turandot* or *Aida*.

However, when you guest, you want to be seen in full dress. Further, though the *Barber*, staged by Cyril Ritchard in something like musical-comedy style, was thought delightful, Ritchard's *Figaro* was ordinary. And the casts assembled for Paris didn't show off Bing's company with the truly gala names typical of an evening on Thirty-Ninth Street—Corelli, Tebaldi, Nilsson, Bergonzi, Crespin, Rysanek. If these singers didn't suit the two selected operas, then the whole trip was a bad notion in the first place. The operas were wrong, the Odéon was wrong, and the Met was wrong.

True, it was not as if Paris was used to great opera from its own two venues, the Opéra and the Opéra-Comique. They were arguably the least prominent of all the famous houses in the West, insular and even provincial. Still, the Met scored an own goal with its two paltry offerings. There were boos from the audience and more or less blistering notices from the press, especially for Roberta Peters' poorly sung Rosina.

All the same, Bing replied in his customary witty style.

"Miss Peters has had a bad night," he said. "The Paris Opéra has had a bad century."

L'enigmi Sono Tre

Franco Corelli was playing Calaf opposite the Turandot of the Finnish soprano Anita Välkki in 1966, when he decided to indulge in some vaudeville hanky-panky during "In questa reggia" (In this palace). This was Corelli's second *Turandot* with Välkki that season, and he knew what a formidable voice she fielded, so, as the aria started, he mimed holding a hand to his ear as if Välkki's sound were too thin to hear.

Big mistake.

Välkki spent the aria expanding the brilliant fire of her instrument till, at the repeated line at the very end, where both singers rise up to a high C, she all but blew him off the stage.

Fancy Our Meeting

One of Bing's most loyal employees was Francis Robinson, head of the Met's press office, who had an amazing ability to remember names and faces—but *really* remember them, seemingly forever.

One day, Met bass Louis Sgarro decided to challenge this incredible memory: Sgarro happened to have met a woman who knew Robinson when they were in school together.

Thirty-five years before.

It was a great test, because Sgarro and the woman and Robinson were all in Bloomington, Indiana, a long way from Henderson, Kentucky, where Robinson and the woman had gone to school. So Robinson could be caught off-guard, not expecting to see someone from his youth.

Sgarro was fairly brimming with glee when he brought the two together. But before he could say, "Francis, I'd like you to meet someone," Robinson smiled and said, "Hello, Helen."

Take My Life . . . Please

Francis Robinson was often told he should write his memoirs. Just think of all the great singers he had known, what wonderful stories he could tell of backstage life at the Met. And of course there was steely, condescending Rudolf Bing, with a heart as full as a pawnbroker's and a sense of compassion that would be the envy of a great white shark.

And that was why Frances Robinson could never write his memoirs. "I'd have to call it," he once said, "*My Life in the Fourth Reich.*"

Competition Rusticana

Plácido Domingo made his New York City Opera debut in 1965, and one year later he earned stardom in Ginastera's *Don Rodrigo* with the same company. Two years after that, he reached the Met—but not, at first, on the bills, only as a cover. As it happens, he was covering for Franco Corelli in *Adriana Lecouvreur* when the phone rang at Domingo's New Jersey home. It was Rudolf Bing.

"Come to the house at once," Bing told him. "You're making your Met debut tonight."

Domingo scored a success, and Corelli, one of the most competitive tenors of the day, grew wary of this upstart who thought nothing of making a last-minute debut at the Metropolitan Opera in a role he had never sung before.

Now it's two years later. Leonard Bernstein is conducting *Cavalleria Rusticana* at the Met when Corelli, the evening's Turiddu, creeps mournfully into Bernstein's dressing room, pleading exhaustion, illness, rickets, dropsy, and everything else he can think of.

"You do look terrible," Bernstein allows, toying with Corelli's vanity. "Not to worry, though. I can have Domingo here in fifteen minutes. I can't wait to hear his Siciliana—he has such robust A Flats. *Genere fantastico!*"

"*Domingo!*" Corelli cries, straightening up and all but dancing with renewed energy. "Never mind your Domingo! Franco Corelli is going on!"

And Corelli bounded out to his dressing room to warm up for *Cavalleria*.

Putin On the Ritz

Bing had married a ballerina many years before all this, when he was still in his twenties, and though she moved with him from the continent to England and then the United States, she never mastered either German or English (his languages) and he knew no Russian (her language).

So, when in 1971 Martin Mayer and his wife began to have lunches and dinners with the Bings while Mayer was ghosting Bing's memoirs, Nina Bing had nothing to say.

Well, almost nothing. She did know enough English to utter one remark, and she trotted it out after every single meal. It was addressed to Mrs. Mayer, and it ran, in its entirety, "Habb some gorgonzola. Iss gut here, not yellow like in Chermany."

A Ghostly Presence

Marilyn Horne's Met debut came unreasonably late in her career, at first because she was offered the mother parts—not the Azucena mother parts: the Teresa in *La Sonnambula* mother parts. Strictly minor roles.

Then, in the mid-1960s, the Met proposed a new *Norma* to Joan Sutherland, and Sutherland demanded Horne as her Adalgisa, offending Rudolf Bing's sense of autocracy. No one was allowed to influence casting in his Metropolitan, and that put Horne on his blacklist.

Still, sooner or later the Met had to put on a Sutherland *Norma*, and by 1970 Horne was so big a name that in fact what the Met had to put on was a Sutherland-Horne *Norma* after all.

At the dress rehearsal, because Adalgisa does not appear in the last act, Horne decided to slip into the auditorium to enjoy the Sutherland *Norma* for herself, and stood in a side aisle enraptured. As Horne recalls in her second book of memoirs, *The Song Continues*, at one point Horne couldn't help but murmur, "My God, sometimes I forget how fantastic she is!"

Suddenly she heard someone behind her—Bing himself, materializing as if by magical incantation in his usual manner. Said he, "You are not so bad yourself, Miss Horne."

Pop Goes the Weasel

As the Met's Director Of Productions in the 1970s, John Dexter introduced Met audiences to the unit set. Certain bits of furniture or whatnots could be flown in, but the overall view never changed. Dexter's *Le Prophète*, with Marilyn Horne (now in the greatest of all mother parts, Fidès), James McCracken, and Renata Scotto, was very much in that line, and his next staging, Poulenc's *Dialogues des Carmelites*, took place entirely on a vast white cross.

At a cocktail party just before *Carmelites'* premiere, Dexter encountered an operagoing grande dame who said to him in a questioning tone, "I trust you will not make *Carmelites* as austere as *Le Prophète*?"

To which Dexter replied, "Madame, the production of *Carmelites* will make Bert Brecht look like a Renaissance voluptuary."

Advantage To Volpe

Long before he ran the Met, Joseph Volpe sported a beard, which Bing asked him to remove.

Volpe chose not to shave. Later, he asked Bing for an advance on his salary to buy a cottage for summer getaways, and Bing agreed—on one condition. The beard must come off.

This time, Volpe gave up his beard, got the advance, and made the down payment on his cottage. Then he started growing the beard back again, and Rudolf Bing was not pleased.

"Mr. Volpe," he said, "you promised me you were going to shave off that beard, did you not?"

"I did shave it off," Volpe answered. "But I didn't promise to *keep* it off."

Pause.

His features tight and his tone crisp and even, Bing said, "Mr. Volpe, this will be the last time that you get the better of me."

The Firing Of Joan Sutherland

It wasn't exactly a firing, true—and Sutherland did return to the Met (after four years). Still, the Bonynges and the Met more or less broke off relations in the late 1970s, when that impossible Board (as opposed to a Gatti or Bing) was in charge, which made negotiations over repertory very tricky. Because a Gatti or Bing knows repertory. The Board does not.

The specific problem with the Bonynges was *The Merry Widow*, for Bonynge and his team had concocted an edition of Lehár's operetta that Sutherland was comfortable with. This version changed a few minor things here and there but also added a lengthy ballet to the start of the third act and interpolated a number from Lehár's *Paganini* for Sutherland as a grand finale.

The reason Sutherland was so set on her particular *Merry Widow* was its (for her) playability: here was a role she felt dramatically comfortable with, dialogue and all. Somehow, the flirty and secretly loving widow brought out Sutherland's latent Lynn Fontanne, and she wanted to show this livelier side to the Met public.

To sweeten the deal, the Bonynges were to agree to new productions of *Semiramide* and *Die Entführung Aus Dem Serail*. But as time went on, Sutherland's daily vocal exercises convinced her that these two roles were moving out of her reach, and she retreated conclusively from both titles.

Had she been discussing this with a knowledgeable general manager, they might have resolved the problem with new productions of other operas—*Manon*, for instance, which would have been at least a Sutherland novelty. True, no one longed to see the party-size Sutherland as Massenet's convent girl. Still, a great singer in great music is the business of an opera house, and the role actually wouldn't have been all that musically different from Lakmé, an established Sutherland part.

But there was no knowledgeable general manager at this point in the Met's history. There was the Board and Anthony Bliss. They didn't think it mattered whether Sutherland sang at the Met or not. So, instead of negotiating, they told the Bonynges, "If no *Semiramide* or *Entführung*, then no *Merry Widow*."

So it really was a sort of firing. For four years, Sutherland did not appear at the Met. And, as far as that goes, the Met has since then put on two different productions of *The Merry Widow*: so why didn't it put on one for Sutherland?

When Sutherland finally returned, in *Lucia Di Lamermoor*, there was an ovation after her first aria, and when someone in the house shouted, "Welcome back!," the applause got even warmer. Not long after, the Met gave Sutherland a new staging of Donizetti's *La Fille Du Régiment*, another sweetly comic role that brought out the dickens in the diva, and at last the Bonynges and the house put their differences behind them.

The Firing Of Kathleen Battle

It is well known that Battle's opera debut was in 1976, with Michigan Opera Theatre, followed by an engagement with the New York City Opera. However, Battle really stepped into opera the year before— on Broadway, no less—as the matinee alternate in the title role of Scott Joplin's *Treemonisha*.

It was a very suitable role, that of a lighthearted young leader personality who rallies her people against superstition. And that, from the start, was the character Battle projected: tender yet strong-willed.

Unfortunately, as her career progressed, Battle began to emphasize the strong will, and in bizarre ways. Like an Italian prima donna of the eighteenth century, Battle took to isolating herself and treating her colleagues with contempt. Arriving at the Met for a *Marriage Of Figaro* in 1985, Battle found that the Countess, Carol Vaness, had occupied Dressing Room 1 and promptly threw Vaness' costumes and kit into the hallway, though by rights of role prestige Dressing Room 1 belonged to Vaness. The latter said nothing at the time, but, two years later, when the Met took *Figaro* to Japan, Vaness walked up to Battle after the last performance and told her that Vaness would never sing with her again. "You," she concluded, "are the worst colleague I've encountered in my entire career."

Well, so far, so good. But Battle's stunts became ever more provocative, as if, each season, she must top herself. She appeared to be sending a message of some kind, but nobody could read it. When she stormed out of a Met rehearsal for Handel's *Julius Caesar* over a disagreement with Christian Thielemann's tempos and demanded an immediate audience with general manager Volpe, she seemed to beg for trouble. One can't *demand* an audience with the head of the house. Volpe didn't respond, so Battle quit the production on the spot.

The last straw was Battle's interaction with Rosalind Elias in 1994 during a rehearsal for *La Fille Du Régiment*. This is a joyful production, but Battle damaged company morale by coming and going as she pleased and warning the other singers not to look at her. Worse, Battle criticized Elias' piano playing, in a music-lesson scene, as incompetent.

Elias was by then a very well-liked Met veteran, having sung with the company from 1954 on, in a wide variety of roles. Though not an international star, Elias was a performer of interest, whether as Cherubino, Carmen, Charlotte, or, especially, the "niece" (presumably the title character's illegitimate daughter), Erika, in the world premiere of Samuel Barber's *Vanessa*. It was one thing to provoke newcomer Carol Vaness, but quite another to pick a fight with a piece of Met history.

As with Bing's firing of Maria Callas, Volpe's of Battle was not euphemized. Volpe had had it with Battle's "unprofessional actions" that were "profoundly detrimental to the artistic collaboration among all the cast members."

Callas eventually sang at the Met again, but so far Battle has not done so.

He Broke Her Jaw

In 1986, Eva Marton and Plácido Domingo sang the sweethearts in a revival of the Franco Zeffirelli *Tosca* production, facing off against the Scarpia of Juan Pons. The conductor was the flamboyant Luis García Navarro, and while Domingo had been heard often enough as Cavaradossi and Pons was, dramatically speaking, a lump, this was a big night.

There was added excitement when, during the Tosca-Scarpia scuffle just before "Vissi d'arte," Pons accidentally hit Marton's jaw so hard she heard a crack and now had to devise a new way of shaping the words and music in order to get the sound out. Somehow or other, Marton—often difficult with colleagues but in the end a noble trouper—got through the act.

Backstage during the intermission, her dressing room was filled with staff concerned about what would happen next—suspend the performance or ask Marton to finish out the evening, even though the big Act Three duet would call for much heroic singing?

But heroic singing is what Wagnerian sopranos like Marton are made of, and she bravely determined to go on for the last act. It went well, as it happens, and while the story made the papers, it became a curiosity rather than a scandal. And no bones were broken, after all, so who knows what actually happened? Indeed, Marton and Pons recorded the opera together just two years later, without incident.

Nevertheless, Marton felt entitled to a bit of tea and sympathy over this. The Met's bureaucracy assigns "liaisons" to each of the principal artists, particularly to help foreigners unused to the house and New York culture in general. Marton's liaison, Sissy Strauss, famed for her annual New Year's party, asked Marton to dinner at her place. Just a quiet meal for two and soft food for Marton's delicate jaw. Something light and soupy.

"Yes, yes," said Marton. "Something light is good. But you know what's really soft and so right for a broken jaw?"

"What?" Sissy asked.

"Filet mignon."

The Firing Of Bing's Second Wife

Nina Bing died in 1983, and, helpless in the onset of Alzheimer's disease, the eighty-five-year-old Bing somehow came under the influence of a woman half his age. A restaurateur overheard her asking Bing to marry her, and he supposedly answered, "Yes. But who are you, again?"

They did marry. She then took him out of the country for nearly a year, traveling widely and running through much of Bing's fortune. They ended up in a homeless shelter in England—a citizen of which Bing had become many years before, never changing his national status thereafter—and there Bing's lawyers managed to separate the couple, bring Bing home, and have his marriage annulled.

That same year, 1989, Bing was admitted to a senior's hospice, where he lived for eight more years, dying from complications from Alzheimer's.

Met Gallantry

While singing at the Met, Renée Fleming managed to total her BMW in the middle of Manhattan, and Joseph Volpe hired a car to take Fleming to and from the house.

When Fleming thanked him, he replied, "It's not for you, it's for me. We need you in one piece."

Well, they did: Fleming was one of the few singers of the day whose appearance drew sell-out houses no matter what the opera was.

At another time, Fleming got a menacing letter from an anonymous crazy, and she began to notice strange men following her around. Uh-oh.

But they were a security team. Volpe had hired them to keep an eye on his prize diva.

No Wiggle Room

Angela Gheorghiu did not like the blond wig they gave her to wear as Micaëla in the Met's *Carmen*, and during the dress rehearsal of the 1997 Japan tour she made her entrance in Act One showing her own dark hair.

Joseph Volpe came backstage during the first interval and cut to the chase. "Angela," he said, "where's the wig?"

Gheorghiu tried a number of stalls—the wig isn't Spanish, it doesn't suit me, I'd rather die.

"The wig," Volpe countered, "goes onstage. With you or without you."

"I'm not wearing the wig," she told him.

Leaving her, Volpe sought out the person in charge of the production—Sarah Billinghurst—and told her to warm up the understudy, who happened to be the delightful Ainhoa Arteta. *She* played the prima, and, chastened but still combative, Gheorghiu wore the hated wig at the second performance, but askew, showing plenty of her own hair and thus obeying the letter of the command, not its spirit.

Again, Volpe dropped in on Micaëla in her dressing room at the first interval. "Wear the wig right," he warned her, "or Arteta gets the run."

Micaëla wore the wig right.

Met stage director Peter McClintock, who witnessed the incident, shares this tale with us:

You Can't Get a Man With a Gun

Robert Carsen's production of *Eugene Onyegin* starring Dmitri Hvorostofsky and Renée Fleming offered unique visuals for every scene. Designer Michael Levine arranged great empty spaces covered or bordered by banks of leaves—but conversely, for Tatiana's bedroom, he created a tiny enclave just big enough for bed, night table, and writing desk, entered by a trap door in the floor.

In the Met's typical extravagance, the small role of Tatiana's nurse went to Irina Archipova, in her prime the key mezzo of the Bolshoi Theatre. Archipova had been a teenager during what Russians call "the great patriotic war," in the early 1940s, and while Levine's version of Tatiana's bedchamber may have been meant to suggest her claustrophobically unworldly life, it suggested to Archipova the tiny attic nests from which Russian snipers would shoot at Nazi invaders.

With her hands on her hips, a skeptical Archipova surveyed the set and cried, "Tatiana, shto ona li partizanka?"

Which means, roughly, "So Tatiana is with the Resistance now?"

Peter Stein's Visa

The German director had worked for a year on a new *Boris Godunof* for 2010 when he abruptly quit. The Met told the press that it was for "personal reasons," but they were unusual ones: first, someone at the American consul's office in Berlin had been rude to Stein when he applied for a work visa and sent him away without one. Then a Met official flew to Berlin to help Stein get his visa—but when Stein wrote to the Met's chief, Peter Gelb, in a cri du coeur, Stein felt Gelb's answer was thin on sympathy and possibly even vaguely threatening, as Gelb asked for Stein's assurance that he would fulfill his contract. Or, Gelb explained, "I will be forced to look into alternative plans."

Gelb no doubt felt that Stein, a mature man and an experienced traveler who must have encountered impedient bureaucrats before, was behaving like a crybaby. And Stein did quit.

"I'm not used," he said, "to working in a factory."

About the House

Leontyne Price always felt territorial about the Lincoln Center Met, as she had opened it, in 1966, in Samuel Barber's *Antony and Cleopatra*, in a role especially tailored to her gifts. At this writing, the building is fifty-three years old, and, on the television documentary *The Opera House*, Price says, "It will endure for another fifty years, my dear. Trust me."

Composers

HECTOR BERLIOZ

"With his eagle's countenance and his hedge of hair he looked like a French-speaking bird of prey and was every bit as daunting as he looked," writes Eleanor Perényi in *Liszt*. "He combined intellect with bad judgment, wit with irrationality...and was unusually disaster-prone. Let everything hang on the fate of a certain concert and the heavens opened."

Mendelssohn called him "genius without talent," because by the standards of the time—he lived from 1803 to 1869—Berlioz's wild nonconformism seemed a violation of craft. His ideas were seen as unique and thrilling, his composition itself bad housekeeping. Nevertheless, he was the greatest composer between Beethoven and Wagner, like them an absolute original who left music different than it had been when he first met it.

Oddly—and unlike Beethoven and Wagner—Berlioz had a zany side. For unknown reasons, all the wags in Paris started shouting about someone named Lambert. "Ohé, Lambert!" they would cry—on the boulevards, from rooftops, out of windows. "Where's Lambert? Who has seen Lambert?" And Berlioz joined in; he found the bizarre charming, and one hears it from time to time in his music.

And he was clever, Berlioz. A wag. Expert in the art of the bon mot, he said that Meyerbeer "had the luck to be talented and the talent to be lucky." Berlioz's considerable journalistic output—he basically supported himself and his family with his periodical writing—could be scathing about other composers. Yet he was always brilliant, and, contrary to what Mendelssohn said, Berlioz was no inflamed primitive. He knew music from top to toe, and whatever his opinions were (he didn't care for Wagner, for instance), he grounded them in knowledge and discernment.

True, he was impulsive; this, too, comes through in his music, which often swerves from one idea or one tempo to another without warning. Four times he tried to win the Prix de Rome (an arts scholarship whose recipients could live in the historic capital of Europe at the expense of the French government), and in 1830, aged twenty-seven, he finally won. Then, still in Italy, Berlioz learned that his intended bride had been promised to another, apparently through her mother's intervention. So Berlioz resolved to disguise himself as a lady's maid, travel home, and kill mother, daughter, and rival. But somehow he lost his costume on the way and, stopping at Nice, he decided to give up the whole plan and write an overture to *King Lear* instead.

Wait, there's more: when the winning composition of the Prix de Rome, a cantata called *Sardanapale*, was premiered, a horn player fudged his entry, so the tympani (who were supposed to take their cue from the horn) didn't come in. And the cymbals (waiting for *their* cue from the tympanist) didn't come in, either. And *that* threw the big bass drum off, so the gigantic explosion toward which the entire piece was heading didn't happen.

Nothing is heard!" Berlioz recalls in his *Mémoires*. "Nothing!" And, as he was the one conducting, he threw his score at the players with a cry of rage, and Maria Malibran—an opera star well known to the audience—jumped from her seat as if she had been shot. So of course a riot broke out. That was life with Berlioz.

He had to do battle with most of the world around him, from instrumentalists and singers to critics and public; few composers were as wronged as he. His gigantic opera of Romanticized Classicism, *Les Troyens* (The Trojans), was never staged complete in his lifetime, and it took a century before everyone realized how magnificent it is. Most important, Berlioz emphasized the union of music and great literature, in major works based on Virgil, Shakespeare, and Goethe, even adding a sequel to his *Symphonie Fantastique* in the form of a dramatic recitation with musical interludes, *Lélio*. Not simply a composer (and, in opera, sometimes his own librettist), Berlioz was a very mentor of music, making his epoch a revolutionary one. Of the Romantics, Beethoven was the first. But Berlioz was the most.

Many of the Berlioz stories come from his *Mémoires*, so let us sample a few…

The Director Of the Conservatoire

Sooner or later, a budding French composer would have to enroll in the Paris Conservatoire, and an interview with the formidable head of the place, Luigi Cherubini, was essential—but most students put it off till later.

As did Berlioz, who blithely walked into the Conservatoire ignorant of one of Cherubini's latest rules, that all male students had to use the front entrance of the building and all the female students the back. Headed for the library, Berlioz was stopped by an underling who ordered him to go out and re-enter the establishment by the men's entrance.

Berlioz ignored him, and was engaged in studying his beloved Gluck in the stacks when Cherubini himself stalked in, "his face like a skull," Berlioz recalled, "his hair on end, his eyes evil, and his tread menacing."

"And there he is!" the underling cried. Cherubini, so angry that his French stuttered and his native Italian accent made it hard to understand him, shouted, "And you're...the...the...one? You who...who...dares enter by...by...the forbidden portal?"

Berlioz promised to use the right door the next time.

"Next time? Next...You are too bold, sir! What is your name?"

"You'll hear it one day!" Berlioz proudly replied.

"*Seize the miscreant!*" Cherubini cried, as he and the underling pursued Berlioz around the room, crashing into desks and throwing over books and papers. Berlioz escaped, swearing to return whenever he wished to.

And that was Berlioz's interview with Cherubini.

The Perfectionist

In the 1820s, all Paris was enjoying Castil-Blaze's desecration of Weber's masterpiece *Der Freischütz* as *Robin Des Bois* (Robin Hood). Castil-Blaze had changed everything, cutting numbers, adding other music, and monkeying with the storyline. There was much to object to, and during one performance, a spectator rose to his feet crying, "No, not two flutes, you villains! Two *piccolos*! Oh, what ruffians they are!"

The young playwright and novelist Ernest Legouvé was there, startled to see how agitated this man was. Wasn't it odd to object to a trifle of orchestration when the entire production was a debauch? Yet this figure, with his fists clenched and eyes a-fire, acted as though all civilization must crumble because of a few bars of flute.

Of course, it was Berlioz. And Legouvé, who made his acquaintance shortly thereafter, became one of his closest friends, as we shall see.

Why Don't You Sing What Rossini Wrote?

In the *Mémoires*, Berlioz recalls riding in a carriage with Gilbert Duprez, the tenor who flabbergasted the music world by singing high C in chest voice (a piercing sound to those unused to it) instead of the tender falsetto typical of tenors in that age. Active roughly from 1830 to 1850, Duprez became a sensation, the Opéra's marquee name. But he could be stubborn in refusing to sing a role as written.

And he wasn't the only one by any means. Many singers threw tantrums over this phrase, that lyric. Why don't they simply honor the score? "A quarter of it is because they can't," Berlioz explained, "a quarter because they're ignorant, and half is sheer caprice."

In the following story, Duprez will give Berlioz a terrible time on the premiere production of *Benvenuto Cellini*, but on this carriage ride they seem to be friends. Berlioz, in one of his moods, hummed a phrase from Rossini's *Guillaume Tell* that Duprez always sang incorrectly. It occurs in the last act, in "Asile héréditaire," on the line "Je viens vous voir pour la dernière fois!" (I come to see you for the last time!) Rossini directs the singer to hit a G Flat over the chord of F^7, a harmonic kink that is immediately smoothed out when the vocal line moves up to a G.

But Duprez invariably sang a harmonious F instead of the G Flat, because he feared the public might think he had made a mistake if he sang the line as Rossini, needing that dramatic stabbing sensation, had composed it.

Hearing Berlioz hum the passage—correctly, of course—Duprez cried, "You're criticizing me!"

"Of course I am," Berlioz replied. "Why don't you sing the phrase as it's written?"

They argued a bit, till Duprez promised to sing the G Flat, "for your sake."

But he never did—"neither," Berlioz goes on, "for my sake nor for his nor for Rossini's. Nor for common sense or for music itself." Sheer caprice.

"Singers!" Berlioz concludes. "What a race!"

Now we expand our base from the *Mémoires* to pull back for the long view...

Berlioz In the Snake Pit

Like everything else Berlioz did, his first opera, *Benvenuto Cellini* (1838), was innovative. "I have always drawn inspiration," he often said, "from great works of literature," and here the source was Cellini's autobiography. But such an unruly hero, both artist and outlaw, would not likely suit the Paris Opéra and its high-toned characters, so Berlioz planned *Cellini* as an opéra comique. This vastly misunderstood form is not "comic opera," but something more like "theatrical opera."[1] With its conspiratorial plot and at times colloquial libretto, *Benvenuto Cellini* would disconcert and thus infuriate the Opéra public. The piece *had* to be an opéra comique.

However, the Opéra-Comique itself turned *Cellini* down, and, amazingly, the director of the Opéra, Charles-Edmond Duponchel, took the work for the big house, though he thought Berlioz was (this in the composer's sarcastic wording) "a lunatic whose music was an amalgamation of absurdities beyond any possibility of

---

1. The French word *comédie* means both "drama" and "comedy," as with the national theatre, the Comédie Française, which stages plays of all kinds, not only comedies. Although opéra comique varied in format over its long history, not till the 1900s did it offer strictly comic pieces. It was sentimental and lively rather than humorous, though it eventually allowed more serious and even tragic narratives, such as *Carmen*.

redemption." Naturally, Berlioz knew how risky this would be, but there were advantages—the Opéra's glorious voices, for one: now Cellini would actually sound like a world-beater, in Gilbert Duprez's trumpet tones. And the huge Opéra orchestra would make an exhibition of Berlioz's bold scoring.

Unfortunately, Opéra protocol forbade composers' conducting their own music, and *Cellini* is rich in hazardous fast movements. Worse, *Cellini*'s conductor was to be François-Antoine Habaneck, whom Berlioz cordially hated and who seems to have played Berlioz in performances varying from capable to desultory.

Still, the Opéra was the Mt. Olympus of European music, and Berlioz had scaled it, even if, as he wrote in the *Mémoires*, "One must be free of all subsidiary labor when creating an opera," though he had a wife and child to support. So now comes an anecdote-within-an-anecdote, as our old friend Ernest Legouvé comes by to ask how *Cellini* is going.

"I don't have the time to work on it," Berlioz replies, "what with these damned articles I have to write."

"What if you *had* time?" Legouvé asks.

"Ah, well then I would compose from dawn to twilight!"

"So. And what would you need for financial independence?"

"Two thousand francs," Berlioz tells him, gloomily. Why not ask for the moon? And the sun, to light my candles?

"And if someone were to…if he wanted…" Legouvé pauses. "Devil take it, help me finish, Hector!"

Berlioz was much confused.

"All right," Legouvé continues, "what if one of your friends *lent you the two thousand francs*?"

"What friend could I ask that of?" Berlioz cries, still not getting it.

"You don't have to ask," says Legouvé, with a hand on Berlioz's shoulder. "I offer it to you."

And, says Berlioz, who recorded the scene (in different wording) in the *Mémoires*, "I leave it to the reader to guess how I felt."

Actually, all of this was the good part. Because once Berlioz had finished composing *Cellini* and Duponchel had accepted it—he called the music "preposterous" but the libretto, by Léon de Wailly and Auguste Barbier, "captivating"—the piece had to get into line as the lumbering, rehearsal-heavy Opéra processed the previously accepted titles.

When *Cellini* finally went into production, it seemed as though everyone at the Opéra was Berlioz's enemy, though the two women leads loved their parts and sang beautifully for him. Duprez was at his considerable worst, scarcely even trying to bring Cellini to life, and Habaneck kept trying to turn the orchestra against their music. Indeed, Berlioz once caught two of them amusing themselves by playing a popular song, "J'ai Du Bon Tabac" (I've some good tobacco) instead of their parts. Even so, others in the pit began to realize the extraordinary quality of the music, its fresh solution to the old problem of how to narrate a story in musical terms.

When the first night arrived, the public loved the opera's overture but then went dangerously quiet. The unconventional libretto, the mixture of sacred and profane in the tricky Roman Carnival scene (which revives the ancient fairground playlets, too rude for the Opéra; and includes an onstage murder), and the irreverent title character, less a poet than a bloodthirsty prankster, shocked the audience into an intense rejection of the work.

After three performances, Duprez threw off his part; there was but one last repetition (in the following season), with a different tenor. That was all the *Cellini* Paris would see for well over a century. Franz Liszt put it on with success (in a revision) at Weimar, in 1852, but *Cellini* managed only a single performance the following year in

London, at Covent Garden, where, Berlioz reported, "a gang of Italians virtually hunted [it] from the stage by hissing, booing, and shouting from start to finish."

Hypocrites, idiots, and reactionaries: this was the world of Berlioz. But then, the transformative genius composers of the nineteenth century tended to develop their revolutions gradually. It was Berlioz alone who wanted to break out all at once: an impossible arrogance for which the gods—or at any rate the public—punished him.

Will the Real Der Freischutz Please Stand Up?

Not long after *Benvenuto Cellini*'s fiasco, the Opéra got a new intendant, Léon Pillet, who proposed mounting *Der Freischütz* in its authentic form, to erase the bad memory of Castil-Blaze's adulterated version. Of course, by Opéra rules, the spoken dialogue would have to be set to music, and the piece sung in French translation.

To prepare the edition, Pillet called upon Berlioz. The latter hated the notion of adding music to the work, but he feared that someone else would make a mess of it, whereas he, Berlioz, could inhabit the spirit of Weber, musician to musician, and create recitatives consonant with Weber's style.

"But everything else must be absolutely true to the original," Berlioz told Pillet. "No Castil-Blazade of any kind!"

"Yes, yes, of course," Pillet rejoined. "How you do go on. Do you think I want another storm of abuse from the critics? A visitation from Weber's angry ghost?"

So Berlioz accepted the job. Ah, but whom did he have in mind for the singers?

"Well," Pillet began, "Madame Stoltz, of course."

Of course, of course, Berlioz was thinking, as all Paris knew that Pillet and Rosine Stoltz[2] were as close as two shipwreck survivors floating on a piece of driftwood. A mezzo, Stoltz had created the role of the apprentice Ascanio in *Benvenuto Cellini,* so she was known to Berlioz as a fine singer—but not one who could get through *Der Freischütz*'s Agathe without tranposing the music down, which would diminish its brilliance. So we're off to a great start. Oh, and wait—I'll bet he'll want my treacherous Cellini, Duprez, as Max, though he'll hem and haw and yes and no and finally throw the role over at the last minute.

"As for Max," Pillet went on, "the public will surely want to hear Duprez."

"He won't sing it."

"Why not?"

"You'll find out. And whom do you see as the Hermit?"

"Oh...yes. Well. It's sort of a draggy role, don't you think? Just when we're ready for a joyous finale, this eerie old man comes pontificating in about matters that no one else cares about. Let's just drop him from the action and speed along to the—"

"I quit," said Berlioz.

"Oh, all right, all right! Have your Hermit, then. Goodness, how stubborn you musicians are!"

The Show-Off

Berlioz toured Germany several times over the years; he was more popular there than in Paris, with its cultural politics and personal

2. This singer is not to be confused with Teresa Stolz, identified with Giuseppe Verdi both personally and professionally.

cabals. In the early 1840s, he was in Berlin, where he caught a performance of *Die Hugenotten*, with Meyerbeer himself conducting. And Berlioz rather enjoyed it, admitting one blatant exception—the Valentine of one of the most famous singers of the nineteenth century, Wilhelmine Schröder-Devrient.

She is famous yet today, mainly because of Wagner, who was so inspired by her *Fidelio* Leonore that he seemed, at least in part, to model his heroines on her portrayal. She even created three of them, in *Rienzi*, *The Flying Dutchman*, and *Tannhäuser* (as Venus).

Berlioz, too, had admired Devrient's Leonore, some time before. But now, some twenty years later, she was vocally weakened. "She never *sings* such words as 'Heaven!,' 'Impossible!,' or even 'Yes' and 'No,'" Berlioz wrote, "but always shouts them as loudly as she can."

Then, too, she would overwhelm the stage action with extra business for herself. This became especially irritating during *The Huguenots'* "conspirators" scene in Act Four, when Valentine's father, St. Bris, lays out the plan to massacre Paris' Protestants. A great moment: Valentine's betrothed, the Count de Nevers, refuses to participate, defying the others all by himself and suffering arrest lest he give the plot away.

However, to Berlioz's annoyance, "instead of hiding her anxiety and staying almost passive as Valentines normally do, Madame Devrient goes right up to Nevers and makes him walk toward the back with her as she seems to coach him in the defiance he is to make."

Berlioz thought it robbed the scene of its power, as the count was demoted from a hero to a hen-pecked husband.

Worse yet, at St. Bris's German equivalent of "À cette cause sainte" (To this holy cause), Devrient threw herself hysterically into his arms, "carrying on so intensely that the bass singing St. Bris, startled by these hysterics, seemed to say, 'For heaven's sake, Madame, this is my big moment in the whole five acts. Now, kindly get off me so I can sing my music unmolested!'"

Crime Of Fashion

One of the things Berlioz noticed in German orchestras was the use of the antique piano we of today call the "clavichord" as a *continuo*, clonking along throughout the orchestral writing even in a performance Berlioz heard of Bach's *St. Matthew Passion*.

And what a piano—"the worst that could be found!" Berlioz reports. "It spread a totally unnecessary cover of monotony over everything." Then he realizes that is exactly why they were using it: "The worse a tradition is," he observes, "the more sacred it becomes!"

You Were At My Wedding, Denise

One potential achievement above all haunted Berlioz: *Les Troyens*, his recounting of the Trojan War and Aeneas' visit to Carthage on his way to found Rome and jump-start civilization in Western Europe. It was an epic of history and romance, duty and appetite, so it could come to life only at the Opéra. And that made it mission impossible. But Berlioz's confidante the Princess Carolyne Sayne-Wittgenstein berated him with encouragement (so to say): "If you prove too feeble to set Cassandra and Dido on the stage as only your artistry can," said she, "then never dare to call on me again. I will not receive you."

Well. That forced Berlioz forward. Playing the diplomat if it killed him, he forged on with the composition while finessing the stalling games of the Opéra management. And powerful people were on his side. But when the Empress Eugénie asked when *Les Troyens* would be ready, Berlioz told her, "Your Highness, one could live for a century before the curtain rose on one's work at the Opéra."

Then Léon Carvalho, intendant of the Théâtre-Lyrique, sought *Les Troyens* for his house—but the Lyrique couldn't do justice to so grand a work, and, worse, Carvalho proposed whopping cuts. Berlioz was pulverized: this was the worst good news imaginable. Oh yes, slash away the work's first half, in Troy, to save money. Leave out scenes from the Carthage half, yes, yes, yes, only for heaven's sake *let me hear my music in the theatre before I die*!

The Théâtre-Lyrique did produce the opera's second half only, on November 4, 1883, and with brazen cuts. And the twenty-two performances were not very well attended. But now *Les Troyens* was on the cultural map. In poor health for most of his life, Berlioz died six years later, somewhere between hoping and believing that, one day, all of his *Trojans* music would be heard.

Encore!

Three years after *Les Troyens'* run at the Théâtre-Lyrique, at a charity benefit, the second-act septet, "Tout n'est que paix et charme" (Everything is pure peace and charm), was performed, with the original Dido, Anne-Arsène Charton-Demeur. Incredibly, everyone thought "someone else" had the job of inviting Berlioz, so nobody asked him. He had to secure a seat on his own, ending high up in a balcony, all but incognito.

The music of the septet, a gently rippling Andantino haunted by a softly repeated C unison in the strings and woodwinds, thrilled the audience, which demanded an encore (as had occurred also at the opera's premiere). Then someone noticed Berlioz—no one in musical Paris could mistake that singular visage—and gave him away. The people then rose up in grateful demonstration, demanding that Berlioz, too, stand to receive their homage. Then the whole world, it seemed, wanted to shake his hand, and outside on the street it took him forever to work his way through the crowd and return home.

Berlioz's Last Words

The composer died in 1869, aged sixty-five. At the end, like his Dido at the very end of *Les Troyens*, Berlioz had a vision of the future. "At last," he breathed out, "they are going to play my music."

> Our experience of "modern" opera begins with the Romantic Era, after Gluck and Mozart. Beethoven was the father of Romanticism, but he wrote only one opera, so the movement of Romantic music theatre really starts with Berlioz and now continues through the four most prominent of the line—Richard Wagner, Giuseppe Verdi, Giacomo Puccini, and Richard Strauss...

RICHARD WAGNER, BAYREUTH, AND THE WAGNER DYNASTY

Wagner's life was an opera. No other theatre composer had an existence so replete with drama, from Staircase Entrances to Repudiation Scenes, and so filled with episodes well known to opera buffs. There is Wagner's participation in the Dresden uprising of 1848, which sent him into exile. There are the three performances of *Tannhäuser* at the Paris Opéra, perhaps the most celebrated calamity in opera history. There is Wagner's own theatre in Bayreuth, still in the possession of the Wagner family despite its past Nazi associations. There are the historical figures that entered Wagner's orbit—besotted King Ludwig II of Bavaria, the fascinated then disillusioned Friedrich Nietzsche, the very helpful Franz Liszt, who nonetheless found Wagner personally unbearable.

And that he was: a megalomaniac who shamelessly dunned his friends for financial support while betraying them in word and deed.

"You regard people only in the way they can be of use to you," his brother Albert wrote in a letter, and "after that they cease to exist for you." Wagner demanded worship from everyone around him, yet he himself was insensitive and overbearing. At a dinner to honor a playwright after the première of his play about Schiller, Wagner suddenly asked him how he could write about a great German poet without being a great German poet himself. The party was ruined, but Wagner was content.

His lack of gratitude could be spectacular. He owed much to Liszt, especially, as this piano virtuoso, abbé, and musical revolutionary pioneered the self-transforming Leitmotiv that became a Wagnerian staple. Liszt and Wagner were even personally close: Wagner's second wife, Cosima, was Liszt's daughter. She once asked Wagner, "Didn't you recently say that Father inaugurated a new era in art?"

"Yes," said Wagner. "In fingering."

Met stage director John Dexter wrote in his autobiography, "If I have to choose between the great and the good, I will choose the good. The great are usually shits." Still, they're wonderful sources of anecdotes, because they're never off stage. "You *dare* to bark at the great Wagner?" he once asked his dog Peps.

A very thorough inhabitant of the Romantic Era, living right through the center of it from 1813 to 1888, Wagner termed his art "the music of the future," more Romantic than anyone else's—grander, deeper, more haunted and guilty and glorious. He eventually regretted having coined that phrase, but it was correct: following precepts set down by Gluck, Wagner reinvented opera from a series of musical numbers about courtship protocols to musically free-flowing enactments of myth centered on not vocal display but character interaction. And he did this while eroticizing melody itself, as in the grotto of Venus in *Tannhäuser*, offering (in critic Joseph Horowitz's words) "phallic lunges no previous composer had dared describe."

Wagner not only dared: he scarcely did anything but dare all his life. This same *Tannhäuser* failed badly at the Opéra (in 1861) because the reckless aristos of the Jockey Club, protégeurs of the Opéra's ballet girls, resented the inclusion of the dance at the start of the show (before they arrived) and raised a hullabaloo through all three performances. But was it also xenophobia—as it was well known that Princess Pauline von Metternich of Austria had induced Napoléon III into ordering up the production? And was it *also* because Wagner had ranged the spiritual with the sexual so sincerely that even *Tannhäuser's* redemptive finale couldn't placate puritanical fury?

"Que Dieu me donne une pareille chute!" (God give me a failure like that one!) was Charles Gounod's summation, and all Paris enjoyed a new verb: *tannhauser* (pronounced "tann-o-*zay*), combining "tanning hide" with the opera's title to mean "beating Wagner up." Thus: *nous tannhausons, vouz tannhausez, tout le monde tannhause.* Nevertheless, to restate Princess Pauline's famous grandfather Klemens von Metternich, when the Paris Opéra sneezes, European music catches cold, and by 1876, when Wagner presented the first complete *Ring* cycles, at Bayreuth, he was one of the most famous men in Europe.

He was especially famous for his anti-Semitism, prevalent in his Germany (Nietzsche once said he himself was the sole German he knew of who didn't hate Jews) but acute in Wagner. Part of this grew out of his loathing of Meyerbeerian grand opera, the epitome of the presentational "number opera" he was replacing. But these feelings ran more deeply than the matter of aesthetics. Wagner's hatred wasn't policy but rather a visceral revulsion that he actually turned into an opera in which Jews attempt to destroy Western Civilization: *Der Ring des Nibelungen* (The Nibelung's Ring).

Naturally, it is all done with nineteenth-century dog whistles, fronted by the gods, dwarfs, giants, and men of the old Norse sagas.

The aggressor—this four-part opera's title role, no less—is first seen lusting after Aryan maidens, a favorite stereotype right into the Nazi era. Then he switches missions and steals the gold of the Rhine to forge the ring, powerful enough to enslave the world. Moreover, his brother, devious and complaining—another stereotype—is characterized by music that whines and nags.

Everyone in nineteenth-century Europe would have easily read this subtext, but most today would miss it, concentrating on the Apocalypse Now! of the work's more generalized symbols. Thus, the gold is nature, the ring is industrialization, and the politics are anti-authoritarian, doting on the revolutionaries Siegfried and Brünnhilde. This layering of meaning begs for Regie opera, in which the stage directors conceive of a space-age *Ring*, a storybook *Ring*, a Chernobyl *Ring*, an updated *Ring*, a wackadoodle *Ring*. So Wagner really did set forth the artwork of the future: it isn't finished yet.

And Bayreuth, too, is ever under new regimes, as the Wagner descendants, now in their fifth generation, fight with one another for control of the theatre. First there was Wagner's widow, Cosima. George Bernard Shaw, an early Wagner enthusiast, claimed she had "no function . . . except the illegitimate one of chief remembrancer," brooking no deviation from The Master's stagings.

Wagner and Cosima's son took over next. Named Siegfried, he was nothing like the fearless godling of the last two *Ring* operas, being physically modest, passive, and pleasant. Wagner's opera Siegfried is an arrogant muscleboy; the American tenor Claude Heater enjoyed a one-man franchise in the role in Germany because he was tall, handsome, and heavily gymmed up, striking the public as, for once, the real thing.

Further, Siegfried Wagner was gay, which posed problems for the continuity of the dynasty. Nevertheless, he was married off to Winifred Wagner, an English girl living in Germany who led the festival through the 1930s and the war years, nestled in the loving friendship of her "Wolf"—Adolf Hitler himself. A fervent Nazi who even so tried to assist threatened Jewish artists (officials dreaded her letters because they invariably demanded favors bound to ire Nazi bigwigs), Winifred Wagner was one of the few German public figures after the war who not only admitted being a Nazi but did so proudly. Death camps? "All lies and propaganda!" When the Festival was restarted, in 1951, she made a point of inviting as her special guests various Nazi remnants. The boldface names—Goebbels, Göring, Himmler, and of course Hitler—were dead, so she unearthed sons and daughters, nieces and nephews.

But she was no longer in charge: her sons, Wieland and Wolfgang, ran Bayreuth now, the former offering sparsely decorated, stylized productions emphasizing lighting effects and psychological stage direction that served as all Europe's laboratory of postwar experimental stagecraft. Wieland coached singers as if they were actors— Birgit Nilsson's Isolde grew from a strictly vocal achievement into the embodiment of a tortured, then passionate, and at last evanescent heroine entirely through Wieland's direction at Bayreuth.

He could be churlish, too, banning singers from his demesne over the lightest of slights. Frederic Spotts tells us that Dietrich Fischer-Dieskau learned that he would never appear at Bayreuth again because he had chafed at having to wear a hunting hat as *Tannhäuser*'s Wolfram because it impeded his hearing.

After Wieland, Wolfgang inherited the family playhouse, with the feuds and snubbings expected of this family, all of which are minutely dissected in the German press. Yet through all its transformations, from a temple of Wagner worship to a museum of antiquated stagings to a Nazi tabernacle to a living instruction manual in how to create "new" (as Wagner himself put it), Bayreuth has remained the world's capital of the Romantic ideal of opera-as-myth.

The Turning Point

Wagner's third opera, and his first interesting one, *Rienzi* (1842), came to light in Dresden. Set in ancient Rome and boasting in its title character the founder of a line of Wagnerian tenors who hope to change the world for the better, *Rienzi* is also another of those looooong Wagnerian works, and on the night of the premiere—during the performance itself—Wagner worried that it was too long after all. But the audience was clearly enjoying itself, though the curtain had gone up at six and it was now nearly ten, with another act to go.

At the end, around midnight, the public gave *Rienzi* a fifteen-minute ovation, and, back at home, Wagner reflected on his future. Had he reached a turning point, with his dreams of love and death commingled as one? Beauty is agony; night enlightens; the gods dwindle into rumor. All this was whirling in his brain as subjects for future operas: an entire world set upon the stage!

But did Wagner wonder also if his wife, Minna, was the correct partner for a revolutionary artist? Herself an actress, she was all the same a bourgeoise at heart, scornful of Wagner's grandiose schemes. Perhaps he needed a more intellectual partner—and Minna could pair off with a shopkeeper or solicitor.

For Wagner, like his heroes, was going to change the world. He would not only create Siegfried: in the musical world, he was Siegfried.

Ending It All

Wagner met the woman who could embrace his revelational vision in Cosima—the daughter of Franz Liszt, as I've said, but also the wife of conductor Hans von Bülow. True, a technicality like adultery never stopped Wagner. It didn't stop Cosima, either, though she at least felt guilty. At first.

One day in 1858, she and Karl Ritter, one of the many disciples Wagner collected over the years, went boating on Lake Geneva. Karl was uneasy in his marriage, too, as he had a tendency to develop neurotic hero-worship fixations on formidable men. (That's what they called it in the nineteenth century; today, we call it "gay.")

As the two glided over the water, they sympathized with each other, for she really wanted to be with Wagner, and he really wanted to be with…Wagner…till finally Cosima offered to make a Great Romantic Gesture and drown herself in the lake. Give me Wagner or give me death!

Karl was presumably thinking exactly the same thing. In any case, he said he would drown himself, too.

Thus brought up short in her theatrical ecstasy, Cosima changed her mind. So did Karl. Because, really, the act of suicide should always be a single. And so, they rowed gloomily back to shore.

It's Lonely At the Top

Wagner loved dogs. We've already met Peps, and now we take in a Newfoundland named Russ, faithful to the end—or so Wagner thought.

One day, Wagner found himself Standing On the Edge Of the Abyss (as he always liked to put it) and went out with Russ to think things over. He was gone for hours, night fell, and then Russ returned on his own. Worried, Wagner's housekeeper got the houseman to accompany her with a lantern as they went off on the road to find their master.

Eventually, they spotted a figure trudging toward them in the dark: Wagner, still forlorn. As they gathered him up to take him home, he told them, "I thought no one cared about me anymore. Even Russ got tired of being around a worthless soul like me and went home for his dinner."

As the three of them headed back, Wagner sadly added, "Even Russ."

A Little Night Music

Years later, during the composition of *Parsifal*, his final opera, Wagner was in Italy, and one evening three young Wagnerians (one of them Engelbert Humperdinck) came to call. As they left under a silvery moon in the gentle night, they heard Wagner singing on a balcony the words of the Three Ladies at the end of the first scene of *The Magic Flute*:

To guide and keep you safe from harming,
Three handsome boys, and wise as well as charming...

To which Humperdinck and his companions answered with the music that caps the scene:

And so, we leave! Godspeed! Amen!
For now, farewell! We'll meet again!

It was a singular moment, a kind of ritual ceremony of the musicians' tribe, inspired and enchanted by art.

Little Cuties

It's difficult for us today to realize how vast an event was the first Bayreuth season of *Parsifal*, in 1882. A new opera by Wagner: it was as if someone had discovered Beethoven's Tenth Symphony. No current composer has a hold on operagoers comparable to Wagner's in his last years, and there was the special glamour of being the first people in the Western World to hear the piece—not at the piano or in concert excerpts but on stage in Wagner's own bespoke theatre.

Among those making the pilgrimage to the Green Hill on the northern edge of Bayreuth, where Wagner's playhouse stood, was a party of French Wagnerians, musical bons vivants, and the usual curiosity seekers. In the group was Léo Delibes, who was to immortalize himself the following year with *Lakmé*, silent now as the others buzzed in excitement. Finally, someone asked Delibes what he thought.

"The second act pleased me the most," he replied.

"Not the grail scenes?" someone asked.

"Or the Easter music?" said another.

"Oh, yes. Very nice, certainement. But that second act! [This sounds right only in the original French:] "Il y avait des petites femmes, et que les petites femmes, c'est toujours amusant."

Or, roughly, and referring to the seductive flower chorus, "The second act had little cuties, and little cuties are always fun."

Shop Talk

Hermann Levi was Bayreuth's first *Parsifal* conductor, and Julius Kniese was his chorus master. In those first years of the Festival, from 1876 well into the 1900s, everyone had to outdo everyone else in Devotion To the Music, and Levi's reverence may have come up short when he questioned Kniese about his tempo in a certain passage.

"Not my tempo," Kniese replied. "And not your tempo. *The* tempo!"

Levi was Jewish, by the way, but Wagner never let his bigotry get in the way of a good performance of his music.

Klingsor Casts His Spell

Although Mozart mingled strains of the sacred and profane in *The Magic Flute*, it was Richard Wagner who liberated opera of its "Victorian" view of sex in both the stories and the music, and *Parsifal* especially sets the sensual and spiritual side by side, as the magic garden of erotic delight is but a walk away from the temple of the knights of the holy grail.

The music leans toward either religion or sex, though heroine Kundry, like a combination of the Gospel's two famous Marys, embodies both. Interestingly, Wagner, obsessed and driven as he was, could joke about his art. There is a lilting waltz in the magic garden, where the women's chorus, divided into two vocal groups of three parts each with six separate lines of soloists, raises exotically erotic melody—the scene that so delighted Delibes. And Wagner said, "With the knights of the grail I had to be sparing of the sensual harmony. But once I get to the magic garden, I take out my old paint pot."

Wagner Conducts

During the last performance of *Parsifal*'s premiere season, on August 29, 1882, Wagner entered the already famous covered Bayreuth orchestra pit after the first scene of the third act, to take the baton from Levi and lead the last half-hour of the work himself. The singers later said that he drove the music with such intensity that they almost went hoarse, and the audience, helpless before this impassioned spiritual pageant, cheered for ten minutes, though it had been informally established that *Parsifal* was too sacred for applause.

Finally, Wagner rose at the conductor's stand to address the house even as the curtains parted with the entire company—including the creatives—onstage. It was a tearful occasion, as all were amazed at what the sixty-nine-year-old Wagner had made of his life and wondered what work could possibly follow *Parsifal*. Some dared say that Wagner's course must be at an end—that this opera was terminal, a way of reconciling shameful deeds with the concept of eternal peace.

Half a year later, Wagner was dead.

Wagner's Last Words

In Venice, Wagner was suffering little seizures. Seated at his desk, he suddenly felt a large one overtake him. It would be the last. "My wife!" he cried, "…and the doctor!"

The housemaid called Cosima, who raced in to find Wagner with his eyes closed and his features distorted in pain. He did not move again.

After the doctor pronounced him dead, Cosima stood guard over the body for twenty-four hours, and even then they had to drag her away.

And all of musical Europe went into mourning.

Mistress Of the House

Cosima ran Bayreuth as a tyrant, refusing to countenance suggestions from anybody. In her memoirs, Lilli Lehmann, a stalwart of the first festival back when Wagner himself was in charge, observed that Cosima could bat away any challenge with either of two responses.

If Lehmann wanted to try something new, Cosima would say, "No, The Master wanted it *this* way."

And if Lehmann wanted to do something as it used to be done, Cosima would say, "Yes, The Master wanted it that way—but then he changed his mind and wanted it *this* way."

You can't beat the woman who was sleeping with the boss.

Horse Opera

Both Lehmann and Cosima were very spirited personalities, quick to snap at observations they disapproved of. Once, when Lehmann praised the horsemanship of Therese Vogl in *Götterdämmerung*'s Immolation Scene, leaping onto Grane's back and riding momentously into the fire, Cosima spat out, "*Circus tricks!*"

The Thrust Direct

Richard and Cosima's son, Siegfried, was as sweet-natured as his mother was sour, but there were people even he didn't like, and one of them was Richard Strauss. In his twenties, Strauss worked as a musical assistant at Bayreuth, but was never allowed to conduct there at that time, which may have contributed to the pair's frenemy relations.

One time, Strauss let slip that, during a stay in Berlin, he put up at the Hotel Adlon, the most prestigious and expensive in the city.

"Ja, wahr?" Siegfried replied, in a sarcastic tone. "So your music is making you good money, is that the point?"

"Yes," Strauss answered, "and it's my own music. Not my father's."

Goebbels Vs. Goering

Among the top echelon of Nazi chieftains, Josef Goebbels had an official stranglehold on the arts, but Hermann Göring was always nibbling away at the edges of Goebbels' fiefdom. The two hated each other, and if Göring staked out a position, Goebbels always sought to outmaneuver him.

Hitler encouraged these wars among his leaders, thinking it toughened everyone up. Thus supported, Göring did battle with Goebbels over Max Lorenz, the glory of Bayreuth *Ring* cycles—so much so that when Hitler himself decided to ban Lorenz from its stage, Winifred Wagner threatened to close the festival down. She meant it, too. She loved Hitler, but no one was going to order her around in Bayreuth.

The "Lorenz Question" stemmed from his marriage. Lotte Lorenz was Jewish, and, defying Nazi edicts, Lorenz refused to divorce her. Her mother lived with them as well.

Göring made a point of favoring the Lorenz family, so Goebbels placed a phone call or two and, in 1941, the S.S. came to arrest the two women at a time when—as the S.S. must have known—Lorenz was not at home. When he returned, it would be fait accompli.

However, Göring's sister had given Lotte Lorenz an emergency phone number, and, while supposedly packing her things, she called the number and put the S.S. officer on. He was told to halt the action and await further instructions.

A few minutes later, the phone rang again. "Leave the flat at once," came the order, "and do not return under any circumstances."

And Göring immediately issued a proclamation that Lorenz and his family were under "my personal protection"—based, no less, on "a decree by the Führer."

Goebbels, known even among his fellow hard-line Nazis as "the poison dwarf," was beside himself for weeks.

Where Is This Opera Taking Place?

When Bayreuth reopened after the war, in 1951, Wieland Wagner's *Parsifal* production, which seemed to be made of little more than lighting, divided the audience. Some thought it transcendent and others hated its lack of...well, where was the swan that the young hero kills? The grail temple walls, the garden? Even the conductor, Hans Knappertsbusch, demanded to see the little dove that Wagner directed should appear overhead at the very end. Very well, anything to keep the peace in the family: Wieland arranged for a little puppet dove to appear—but so high up in the flies that only Knappertsbusch could see it.

After one performance, a furious member of the public accosted the conductor, asking how he had the gall to take part in such a travesty. Why didn't he say something at the dress rehearsal?

Thinking fast, Knappertsbusch replied, "I thought the scenery was held up at customs."

I Remember It Well

Wieland had hopes of hiring Otto Klemperer to conduct, even after Klemperer—who was Jewish—opened up their interview with "So what was it like sitting on the Führer's knee?"

Klemperer never did end up conducting at Bayreuth.

Venus Envy

Wieland's new staging of *The Flying Dutchman* in the 1959 festival was a huge success. With George London, Leonie Rysanek, Fritz Uhl, and Josef Greindl to work with, Wieland was emboldened to announce, very publicly, "For the first time since the reopening, I have, once again, *Weltklasse* (world-class singers in the leads).

Some in the audience were skeptical about the appearance of the spinning maidens in the second act—twenty-eight very buxom girls tightly encased in the kind of pastel sweaters that Lana Turner had made notorious.

"They're supposed to look so," Wieland explained during the rehearsals. "Those are peasant girls. They're sweet but they're rough, and they all smell of cod liver oil."

During the first night's curtain calls, Wieland was gleeful. I gave them a scare, he thought, and now it's their turn to come roaring back at me. I've earned their hisses, and I can't wait.

London, Rysanek, and the others went out to cheers from the house, but when Wieland took his turn...he got cheers, too. As he came backstage, Rysanek was amused to hear him say, in genuine wonder, "What can I have done wrong?"

Winifred Wagner's Legacy

Filmmaker Hans-Jürgen Syberberg taped an interview with the former mistress of Bayreuth in 1975, and while Winifred insisted that certain comments remain unfilmed, Syberberg let the tape recorder run throughout, so Frau Wagner left her mark on history with the following much-quoted comment: "If Hitler were to walk in through that door now, for instance, I'd be as happy and glad to see and have him here as ever, and that whole dark side of him…doesn't exist for me."

Where's Waldo?

This is one of those crazy fables, such as How the Fox Got His Tail, and it starts in 1930, when the French recording company Pathé decided to make an extensive survey of all four *Ring* operas spanning forty twelve-inch 78 sides. (The discs actually ran at 80 RPM.) A total playing time of about 170 minutes limited the set to just highlights, but a local Wagner festival had attracted to France many of the best *Ring* singers of the day, including Frida Leider, Lauritz Melchior, and Friedrich Schorr, with Franz von Hoesslin conducting.

As it happened, most of the marquee names were under contract or at least an "understanding" with other recording labels, and Pathé was left with a rather mixed bag of principals. Still, Pathé went ahead, and while the results couldn't compete with HMV's much more complete *Ring* albums with gala casts, still Pathé's discs offered a less cumbersome and less pricey alternative.

However, Pathé's casting of the Jewish Henriette Gottlieb as Brünnhilde enraged German nationalist sentiments, so when the Nazis came to power, in 1933, they made it a sacred mission to confiscate and destroy every copy of the Pathé *Ring* that they could find, just as they did with other "offensive" recordings, such as the *Threepenny Opera* 78s of the 1928 Berlin cast. These had been sold in America and thus escaped destruction. But the *Ring* records seemed to have been utterly annihilated. Collectors had the odd sides, but no one owned the entire release, and when in 1999 the Gebhardt label sought to effect a CD transfer and scoured the aficionado circuits of Europe, nothing turned up.

Then somebody thought of something. What was the one place in Nazi Germany that might have acquired the Pathé *Ring* while being invulnerable to interference by the Party's culture police?

That place was Wahnfried, the Wagner family home in Bayreuth. Why, yes, they had the Pathé *Ring*. Yes, it was complete to the last side. Yes, Gebhardt could make a copy.

And that's how the fox got his tail.

There He Was In His Prize Song

Christian Thielemann tells how he was coming out of the shower in his dressing room after conducting a Festspielhaus *Meistersinger* when in walked his boss, Wolfgang Wagner.

Thielemann is naked, wet, and holding just a small towel, but Wolfgang blithely starts giving the conductor notes on the performance. Tempi, a choral entry, this or that singer in such and such scene, a passage that might not have gone quite the way The Master would have liked.

Finally, Thielemann gets a bit of silence in which to explain that he isn't dressed to receive visitors. Indeed, he isn't dressed at all.

Well, so what? "It would not be first time I've seen a naked man," Wolfgang assures him. Now a few more notes, perhaps a tiny bit of praise. Then it's Gute Nacht and away Herr Grandson Wagner goes.

Just another day in the family theatre.

GIUSEPPE VERDI

It's tempting to compare Verdi with Wagner, as the two most popular composers of opera in the nineteenth century. Both men were born in 1813 and worked through early defeats to build on great success to the end of their lives. They epitomized the eclipse of the "number" opera of recitative alternating with arias and ensembles as it ceded to a flowing stream of music, and both cultivated strong democratic politics.

There the resemblance ends. Verdi was a born villager and remained one all his life, suspicious of or simply exasperated with the mores of the city flatterers, whereas Wagner hobnobbed with dandies and sycophants and even got into the court politics of the King of Bavaria, Ludwig II. The theatre was Wagner's life; Verdi hated it. "My long career," he was glad to say on the night of the premiere of *Otello* (1887) at La Scala, "is now over." In fact, it wasn't: *Falstaff* (1893) was yet to come. Still, Verdi couldn't wait to get out of Milan, out of the public eye, out of opera altogether. For centuries, it had been protocol for the composer to hang around for a new work's first three performances, more or less superintending, and Verdi honored the etiquette, but at the reception after *Otello*'s third rendition, when they cried, "Speech! Speech!," Verdi told them, "Till midnight I remain Maestro Verdi." Cheers, blessings, evvivas. But wait: "Then I return to being the peasant of Sant'Agata."

Sant'Agata was Verdi's country estate near his hometown of Busseto, a complete working farm. Had Wagner owned something of the kind, it would have been for the purpose of presiding over it from a distance. But Verdi actually ran his place, fascinated by (or simply duty-bound to) the day-to-day of husbandry, crop rotation, expenses, profits. As early as in mid-career, he constantly threatened to abandon music for farming. In his letters, we find such sentiments as "Farewell, my public, my work among you is ended, and now I take my leave of you to go and plant cabbages."

Verdi's longtime partner, soprano Giuseppina Strepponi, had been born in Lodi, to the northwest of Busseto, but she no more than tolerated the rustic life. She and Verdi lived together for eleven years, then married, so Strepponi was technically a farmer's wife: thus she became perforce the mistress of Sant'Agata. But Strepponi was no peasant, and neither was Verdi. Middle-class in background, he was a cultured man, grounded in the classic authors (especially Shakespeare). Furthermore, he had a superb command of the theatre, shaping the dramatic arc of his collaborators' librettos and hectoring the singers into executing his vision.

His influence—his sheer historical and cultural importance—cannot be overstated. As not only composer but producer of opera, Verdi became the superintendent of the art after the era of Rossini, Mercadante, Donizetti, and Bellini and before that of Puccini and the so-called verismo generation. Opera itself was so basic to Italian self-esteem in that time that Verdi was in effect the central Italian. From 1859 on, a graffito appeared everywhere, reading "Viva Verdi"—but this was understood to mean "Viva Vittorio Emanuele, Re d'Italia": defiance from the Risorgimento, the "resurgence" of the spirit that would free Italy of foreign occupation and unite her city-states into the first genuine Italia since the fall of the Roman Empire. (The idea of a conjoined nation was so innovative that the uneducated thought "Italia" was the name of Vittorio Emanuele's wife.)

At last, in 1871, after the evacuation of Rome by French forces and the collapse of the resistance of the fanatically anti-republican Pope Pius IX, the unification was complete. And through all of this intense history, Verdi's music was ubiquitous: *Rigoletto, Il Trovatore,*

La Traviata, Un Ballo In Maschera, La Forza Del Destino, Don Carlos.
It was a time of battles and politics and the emergence of an encom-
passing countrywide ethnicity: and Verdi wrote its anthems.

This makes him an ideal subject for biography, though his gruff
"all business and no playtime" exterior rejected any participation in
the world of backstage intrigue. Yet Verdi could be as stubborn and
irritable as anyone; his scornful criticisms of his most constant and,
really, subservient librettist, Francesco Maria Piave, are a study in
abuse. Those closest to Verdi worshiped him—for his genius but
also for what he represented to Italy. Still, he had a misanthropic
side, and cut offenders out of his life. Even La Scala was not immune.
Irate at the inaugurating production of *Giovanna d'Arco* (1845),
Verdi vowed never to enter the theatre again, and though he eventually changed his mind, he did not allow the house a Verdi premiere
for some thirty-five years.

Given an industrious life's work of over twenty-five operas (the
precise total depends on how one counts certain revised works),
and given as well that Verdi not only staged their premieres but
some succeeding mountings as well, this composer offers surprisingly few anecdotes. We know him, rather, from his countless letters,
in which he delivers himself of blunt opinions of everyone and
everything ("Words don't influence me—actions do!" he writes,
when yet another friendship collapses).

We have as well the voluminous correspondence of Verdi's longtime pupil and amanuensis, Emmanuele Muzio, who is even more
outspoken (as in "The English declare that on Sundays, in the
London streets one sees only dogs and Frenchmen"). Between the
two men, we learn how much composers of the early and middle
nineteenth century had to defer to singers and impresarios. Yet
Verdi fought—in the long run successfully—to install the composer
as the absolute authority in opera production, because all the other

participants were his artistic inferiors. Impresarios were liars, cheaters, skinflints. Publishers? Greedy do-nothings. The censors were the stooges of tyrannical regimes and the public was ungrateful. And what of the critics, you ask? Stupid little parasites, terrified of innovation. Worst of all were singers—vain, impossible, stubborn, arrogant. In short: no one is professional and everyone's an idiot.

He Almost Died

Verdi's real hometown was actually the village of Le Roncole, little more than a small parish near Busseto: a church, a tavern-*cum*-grocery (run by Verdi's father, Carlo), houses. When Verdi was a babe in arms, Russian soldiers chasing the French passed through the village, raping and killing. Verdi's mother hid with little Giuseppe in the church belfry, where they were safe.

Just a few years later, Verdi was a rent-paying guest in Busseto, attending school. Yet he had as well a job as Le Roncole's church organist, and had to walk three miles back and forth to execute his duties.

One Christmas day, he mistook the path and fell into a deep watery irrigation ditch, common in rural north Italy and almost invariably unmarked, as the locals all know where they are. And now Verdi was not safe.

If a passing farmer had not heard Verdi's cries for help, his story might have ended here, a tragedy for not only Verdi but the future of opera itself.

Here follows one of opera's most famous stories, told and retold for well over a century. No collection of opera tales would be complete without it…

Musicabilissimo

In 1831, aged eighteen, Verdi moved to Milan to pursue his musical studies, and before long he was married with two children and embarking on a career as a promising composer linked to La Scala. But now there really was a tragedy: Verdi's entire family died, one by one. He had presented the world with two operas, the serious *Oberto* (1839) and the comic *Un Giorno di Regno* (King For a Day, 1840), but had really gotten nowhere, and was so miserable that he spent his time reading cheap novels. Given Verdi's gifts, it was a form of slow suicide.

However, La Scala's intendant, Bartolomeo Merelli, knew that Verdi needed no more than a first-rate libretto. Donizetti could make music about anything—honor, love, courtiers, then the mad scene. Verdi, however, needed a *story*, something with a severe father and a wayward daughter, or a hero compromised by his own ideals, an uprising, a macabre regicide. Something flavorsome.

And Merelli thought he had just the story: *Nabucodonosor* (Nebuchadnezzar), by Temistocle Solera. Merelli had offered it to Otto Nicolai, but, he told Verdi, you know these Germans. They think they're all Beethovens, so nothing pleases them unless it's a second *Leonora*! But what a splendid drama from Solera, this. Magnificent! Such great effects, such entrances! The grandest of attitudes, beautiful lines! That Nicolai is so obstinate—and a Berliner, so what else can you expect? Now, if *you* take Solera's libretto—

"Why should I?" Verdi barks at Merelli. "What do I care if it's Nicolai sì o no?"

"Just look at it, Verdi, will you? Are you a second Nicolai? And where will *he* end up, turning everything down? But this Solera, now—what poetry and catastrophe! What surprises! You never know what he'll do next!"

Verdi knew exactly what Solera would do next, as Solera was the credited librettist on *Oberto*: he would write a little this and a little that and then immediately do a disappearing act. At various times, Solera made his living as a circus performer, a composer, an antique dealer, a plagiarist, and a spy. And he legendarily lost his virginity before he was a teenager.

"Solera again!" Verdi cries, leaving Merelli's office—but Merelli shoves the libretto into Verdi's coat pocket before he can get away. When Verdi gets home, he throws the pages onto a table, where they fall open. Merelli and Solera, Verdi is thinking, they deserve each other. But his eyes happen to light on the libretto, at the first lines of a chorus of Hebrew prisoners: "Va, pensiero, sull'ali dorate" (Fly, thought, on golden wings).

Other lines arouse him. Interesting. Promising...*Bah*! Who cares? I'm finished with all of it!

The next day, Verdi brings the libretto back to Merelli.

"Well?" the impresario asks, with a victorious smile. "Beautiful, no?"

Verdi agrees.

"So set it to music!"

Verdi shrugs.

"Beh, mio caro Verdi. Consider. Is this not a fine libretto for an opera?"

"Musicabilissimo," Verdi admits. Utterly made for music.

"Then start setting those verses and we'll say no more about it."

"I won't have anything to do with it, I tell you!"

Again Merelli stuffs the manuscript into Verdi's overcoat pocket, shoves him out, and locks his office.

"*Go home and write the opera!*" Merelli shouts through the door.

Much later, recalling the incident, Verdi said, "What could I do? One day a strophe. The next day another. A melody, then the recitativo before it, the cabaletta. The monstrous Abigaille, with a monstrous range, the pathetic king, the stern Jewish patriarch." It was as if they had seized him, had leaped out of myth to take over his thinking. "And page by page," he concludes, "the opera was composed."

Nabucco. A smash hit that was soon singing all over Italy—La Scala alone gave it seventy-five times within the first ten months, an all but phenomenal run—and over Europe as well. Verdi expert Julian Budden called it "the expression of a new personality in Italian music."

We have Merelli to thank for giving Verdi the opportunity, even if the impresario had to impose it on him. Unfortunately, as time went on, Merelli's slapdash productions outraged the composer, especially Merelli's habit of raiding the conservatories to give leads to inexperienced (but cheap) singers. Yet here, at least, Merelli proved a godsend. For with *Nabucco,* Verdi's career really begins.

No Changes! Not a Note, Not a Word!

Verdi's very next opera, *I Lombardi alla Prima Crociata* (The Lombards On the First Crusade, 1843), again with a libretto by Temistocle Solera, was threatened by censorship. Verdi, Solera, and Merelli were ordered to appear before the Chief Of Police.

Verdi refused to go, and he told the other two that he would agree to no changes whatsoever. Censorship of the theatre was routine in Italy at the time, for reasons both political and religious, and *I Lombardi* (as it is more commonly called) was filled with depictions of spiritual commitment, including a baptism. To mix the sacred with the profane world of the stage was edgy, and the Archbishop of Milan was, we might say, very unhappily "interested" in all this. Was Verdi thinking of him many years later when composing the big scene of the tyrannical Grand Inquisitor in *Don Carlos*?

Luckily, the police chief was sympathetic to Verdi, perhaps an enthusiast of *Nabucco*. He gave Solera and Merelli an irresistible offer of compromise: if Verdi but change the first two words of the heroine's establishing solo from "Ave Maria to "Salve Maria" (which at least would free it of textual blasphemy), he will trouble to reassure the Archbishop of the opera's piety.

Adamantly opposed to negotiating with tyrants—it only encourages them—Verdi nonetheless thought it over. Two words? And nothing else? Very well. He gave in, and on opening night he had another smash hit.

I Hate Paris In the Springtime

All his life, Verdi felt comfortable only in the countryside. Cities enervated him, and of course they all centered on the opera houses where he constantly battled with the enemies of his life. And Paris had that dreadful Opéra, "la grande boutique," as Verdi called it: the great notions shop.

"Everywhere I go," he noted of Paris, "I deal with things in twos—two impresarios, two librettists, two music publishers. Nothing is done alone—they all go hunting in pairs."

The Premiere Of Attila

Attila (1846) was one of Verdi's most martial operas, with an irresistible crash-bang athleticism in the way the orchestra goads the singers on to glory, as the title character, a bass, plans to destroy Rome and the tenor and soprano, of the ruling class of doomed Aquileia, defy him.

The baritone, Ezio, a Roman leader, tries to make a deal with the Hun, reaching a superb line from that crazy librettist Temistocle Solera:

EZIO: Avrai tu l'universo, resti l'Italia a me.

"You will have all the world," Ezio promises Attila, "just give me Italy." Attila is disgusted by Ezio's treachery of his own people, but Italians of Verdi's day saw in these words a meme on their own wish to drive out all foreign occupation and take ownership of their own country. Immediately popular, *Attila* was done all over Italy till Verdi's later more sophisticated titles overshadowed it.

The premiere was given at Venice—a smart move, as one scene shows the very founding of the city by Aquileians, fleeing Attila as they row through the lagoon to land on a few lone islands. There was one accident, when candles burning at a banquet in Attila's camp gave off an unpleasant smell. But the line that Ezio sang in his duet with Attila sent a thrill of patriotism through the audience. Verdi set it to an arching melody striving upward to the baritone's high F— always a "money note" in Verdi—and the rest of the phrase has the ring of victory. "Sì!" came the answering cry from the audience on the opening night in Venice. "Italia a noi!"

Let Italy be ours!

Do Your Job!

Writing *Macbeth* (1847), Verdi was especially careful to get the drama as authentic as possible. He wrote a prose version of the libretto, then sent it to the faithful Francesco Maria Piave to versify. He demanded that Lady Macbeth be not "a fine-looking woman... [but] ugly and evil." He inquired of English theatre experts exactly how the dead Banquo's apparition in the Banquet Scene should be managed, proudly explaining to the intendant of Florence's Teatro della Pergola, where the premiere was to take place, that the advice he was given reflected stage practice in London, "where they have been playing *Macbeth* continuously for the last two hundred years."

Banquo, Verdi had learned, was to rise through a trap door in the deck to occupy Macbeth's seat at the banquet table, his face obscured by a ghostly veil and wounds clearly visible on his neck.

But the Banquo, Nicola Benedetti, balked at this. Why should he appear at all if he has nothing to sing? Is he supposed just to sit there looking eerie?

That's exactly what he was supposed to do, Verdi told him.

"But I have no music in that scene!" Benedetti insisted.

And Verdi answered back, "You weren't hired only to sing. You were hired to sing *and to act*!"

No Singing!

Verdi thought of *Macbeth* as being less sung than acted, chanted, whispered, breathed out with "a thread of voice." The chorus and the supporting roles were vocal creations, yes—but not the two leads. This wasn't the usual romantic tale but a thriller, to be above all realistic.

Everything, Verdi felt, rested on the Macbeths' duet "Fatal mia donna" (My murderous wife) and Lady Macbeth's Sleepwalking Scene. Verdi was so determined to keep his singers from getting "operatic" during them that, on the eve of the premiere, just before an invited dress, he dragged the Macbeth and Lady, Felice Varesi and Marianna Barbieri-Nini, into the theatre's foyer for one last of the countless rehearsals of the duet.

"But, Maestro," said Barbieri, "we are in our costumes already." An invited audience was in the house, and the conductor and orchestra were ready to play. "How can we appear like this in the—"

"Put on a cloak, then," Verdi told her, "and come with me."

"We've gone over this scene one hundred fifty times!" Varesi cried.

"And in a few more minutes," Verdi answered, "it will be one hundred fifty-one. Ecco."

The maestro was adamant, and, more to the point, the two singers must have been aware of how innovative and special *Macbeth* was. Varesi, Barbieri thought, seemed threatening as he grabbed the hilt of his sword, but he went along with the composer for, yes, the one hundred fifty-first rehearsal of the duet, arguably one of the three or four most brilliant inventions Verdi had created to that point: a breathless, anxiety-filled waltz of sheer evil.

And, as it happened, that duet made a sensation at every performance.

"Once," Barbieri later recalled, "we had to encore it five times!"

The Wife Of the Gentleman Farmer

Writing to Léon Escudier, Verdi's French publisher, Giuseppina Strepponi described the couple's life at Sant'Agata. "His love for the country has become a mania, a craze, a wildness—use any extreme word you can think of. He gets up with the sun to inspect the corn, the wheat, the little vineyard.... But we do both like to see the sun rise. He sees it out in the fields, and I see it from my bed."

It's Not Nice To Fool Mother Nature

In 1849, Verdi was in Naples for the premiere of *Luisa Miller*, where his friends formed a kind of cordon sanitaire around him to protect him from a local musician named Capecelatro, who was said to have the *malocchio*, the evil eye.

Verdi thought the very notion absurdly primitive; besides, he and Capecelatro were friends. Still, many Italians did believe that anyone cursed with the evil eye cannot help but cause catastrophe, and Verdi's allies were determined to keep Capecelatro away from the maestro, at least in the vicinity of the Teatro di San Carlo.

On *Luisa Miller*'s opening night, all went well for both the opera and the anti-Capecelatro brigade. But then there was a glitch in security, and Capecelatro was able to reach Verdi, embracing his beloved maestro and lauding *Luisa Miller* as an opera among operas. When Capecelatro went away, one of the security team apologized for the slip-up, and Verdi no doubt told him the whole *malocchio* thing was village superstition.

But wait. "Did not Capecelatro similarly embrace you at the prima of your *Alzira* here?" the Verdian would have countered. "And did not *Alzira* fail?"

"*Alzira* failed," Verdi said, on more than just this occasion, "because it is an ugly piece of work. I, Verdi, say this. There is no such thing as an evil eye."

And just then a piece of scenery broke loose and came crashing down. Had it fallen inches closer to Verdi, he would have been killed.

A preposterous tale, perhaps, but it's in all the biographies in one form or another.

Who Asked You?

The unmarried partnership of Verdi and Giuseppina eventually resulted in marriage, but for a bit over a decade they lived together as man and wife, shocking the townspeople of Busseto, for the 1850s was not a golden age of live and let live.

Indeed, Verdi's former father-in-law (that is, the parent of Verdi's deceased first wife, Margherita), Antonio Barezzi, wrote him a scolding letter over the matter. And we have Verdi's reply, which underlines how resolutely the composer stuck to his beliefs, because he knew he didn't see the world the way others saw it and had no wish to adapt to their views. They saw him as contrary; he saw himself as liberated. He was agnostic on the subject of religious ceremony, and he hated it when others (even Barezzi, Verdi's benefactor when he was a teenager) tried to make him a tool of their will. So, in his reply to Barezzi, Verdi wrote, among other things:

> In my house there dwells a free and independent woman…and neither she nor I need to account to anyone for the way we live.

Note how Verdi sees his relationship with Strepponi as one of equals:

> What rights have I over her, or she over me?

and even:

> Who knows, indeed, whether or not she is my wife? And if she be my wife, who knows why we do not make it public?

And just in case Verdi hasn't yet made it clear that Strepponi is not a mere au pair, a house guest, or a contrivance of a spouse:

> In my house she receives as much respect as I do. More, even. And no one on the premises is allowed to forget this for any reason whatsoever.

Verdi Filosofo

Il Trovatore (1853) was a tremendous success. Together with the immediately preceding *Rigoletto* and the immediately ensuing *La Traviata*, Verdi created a kind of self-contained trio of operas that swept the Western World. This was not only because of their immensely lovable music but because the realistic character development of *Rigoletto* and *La Traviata* vividly affirmed Verdi's break with the bel canto titles that were more about singing than about drama.

True, *Il Trovatore* is less innovative than its two siblings, and many writers thought it horribly dark. The most common objection was that it was filled with death—a mother and a baby burned alive, the soprano a suicide, the tenor beheaded. Like Berlioz and Puccini, Verdi had a cultivated woman as a confidante, the countess Maffei, and he wrote to her about this in an almost Shakespearean tone.

"Really," he said, "what is there in life but death?"

Verdi's King Lear Opera

Intensely stimulated by Shakespeare's plays, Verdi planned, all his adult life, to adapt *King Lear*. In approach-avoidance fashion, he was drawn to yet fearful of it—so terminal a piece, too big, perhaps, for the opera stage as Verdi knew it.

Macbeth. Otello. Falstaff…but *Il Re Lear*? Historians agree that, at one point, Verdi was actually going ahead with the project. It was when he was in Paris preparing *Les Vêpres Siciliennes* (1855) at the Opéra. The opportunity occurred by fluke, when Sophie Cruvelli, rehearsing Hélène in Verdi's new piece while singing Valentine in Meyerbeer's *Les Huguenots* in the evenings, suddenly disappeared.

It would be a treat to report that Cruvelli's aides gave it out that she was hiking the Appalachian Trail (in the Mark Sanford manner), but no statement was forthcoming in public or private. Cruvelli had simply vanished.

Thus, with his schedule suddenly cleared, Verdi decided to attack the *Lear* project in earnest. Antonio Somma had written the libretto, and now Verdi was composing the music.

Meanwhile, no one was particularly worried about Cruvelli, as she was known to be impulsive and unpredictable. And she blithely reappeared in due course, having simply sped off somewhere with a lover in the nobility, a certain Baron Vigier, to enjoy a short passion break (also in the Mark Sanford manner).

So Verdi dropped his work on *King Lear* to recommence the *Vêpres* rehearsals, and he never did complete a *King Lear*.

Alas. *Macbeth* is one of Verdi's greatest works in his early years, and *Otello* and *Falstaff* are generally thought his masterpieces. Shakespeare really brought out the best in him—but perhaps *Lear* was simply out of reach, given the resources of Italian opera in Verdi's time.

Charles Osborne, who read Somma's *Lear* libretto, remarked intriguing correspondences between lines written for Cordelia and the little aria Leonora sings at the start of *La Forza Del*

Destino, and he felt as well that the father-daughter relationship in *Simon Boccanegra* may have been first musicalized in Verdi's *King Lear* sketches.

More About Cruvelli

The Paris Opéra was so central to European music that Sophie Cruvelli's disappearance from the *Huguenots* performances became the talk of the continent. Verdian Francis Toye tells us that a spoof entitled *Where's Cruvelli?*, opened at the Strand Theatre in London. Best of all, when Cruvelli returned to Paris and made plans to marry her baron, she leaped back into *Les Huguenots* and perforce had to make her second-act entrance only to hear the soprano playing Queen Marguerite de Valois ask her in recitative, just as Meyerbeer had set it:

Ma fille, allons, courage,
Dis-moi le résultat de ton hardi voyage!

This translates as "My dear, come now and tell me what happened on your audacious trip!," at which the theatre—and all the rest of musical Europe—rocked with laughter.

Oops, Wrong Toast

Few opera composers were so intensely industrious as Verdi was in youth yet so reluctant to write in their seniority. *Aida* (1871) was meant to be his last work for the stage.

Ah, but then his publisher, Giulio Ricordi, suggested Shakespeare's *Othello* as a subject for opera, and Verdi couldn't resist. Besides, he now had the best librettist of his career, Arrigo Boito. Considering how much trouble his earlier collaborators had caused him, it would be all but monstrous to waste someone with Boito's gifts, which included among other qualities an unprecedentedly rich vocabulary. This was something Verdi in particular would appreciate.

Yet Verdi continued to demean the entire operation, as was his habit. Some acquire cynicism; Verdi was born with it. "Should I finish this *Otello*?" he would say. "But why? For whom? It is a matter of no importance to me at all, nor to the public."

Still, he persevered. At one point, Ricordi paid a visit to Sant'Agata, to hear Verdi play scenes from his new score. Silence afterward, in the glow of being the first outsider to hear the wonderful new music, and Strepponi says, in the local dialect, "L'è ancamò, el me Verdi!" (My Verdi still has it, eh?)

We might say that Verdi continued to be unalterably opposed to pursuing his career except when he wasn't. But *Otello* (1887) reaffirmed Verdi's place as the leader of Italian music. And now, Verdi was *really* going to retire.

Oh, but except. Verdi hated the theatre yet was made of the theatre, part of it, owned by it. And now—secretly!—he was at work on *Falstaff*. News of the project began to trickle out, and, finally, everyone went out to celebrate in anticipation of another triumph.

Verdi, Strepponi, Ricordi, and some friends were dining in state at Milan's Grand Hotel when Strepponi proposed a toast honoring the new piece. "I drink," she said, "to the big belly."

Silence. Nobody moves. Then Strepponi realizes that the table is embarrassed for Ricordi's daughter, who is very noticeably pregnant.

Quickly but suavely, Strepponi adds, "...*of Falstaff*." And the company exhales in relief and merrily clinks glasses. Yes, the big belly of Falstaff, what else?

And this opera, too, is a smash hit. In a way, it is the *Nabucco* of Verdi's old age: his opera of operas.

Iago Had a Credo and Verdi Has One, Too

Eleven years after the premiere of *Otello*, La Scala was closed for an entire season, after which a new regime took control of the opera house, led by impresario Giulio Gatti-Casazza and music director Arturo Toscanini. At the start of Gatti's reign, Verdi treated the young intendant to some advice. "The critics don't matter," Verdi told him. "What matters is the box-office receipts. Not because of the money, but because only the public can tell you if a piece is worthy. They're the real critics."

Ah! Here's Verdi's cab, and, as he gets in, Verdi concludes with "The theatre is meant to be full. Not half-empty with aficionados and sycophants."

Verdi bangs his cane on the roof of the cab, to signal the driver to proceed.

"Full, mio caro Gatti," Verdi tells him, leaning out of the cab as the horse starts off. "Full of those who love a good story with good music. Not empty, Gatti."

Full.

Get Me To the Bar On Time

Verdi once observed that the Italian operagoing public could sit still for at most forty minutes.

Did Verdi ever go over the limit?

Maybe: "The first act of *Otello*," he supposedly said, "is forty-two minutes—two minutes more than necessary."

We have the tale from the not entirely reliable Gino Monaldi,
who brought out his *Verdi 1839–1898* in 1899. The composer may
have said something of the kind about something or other, but
none of *Otello*'s four acts is even forty minutes long. The third act
spans over forty minutes if the ballet is included, but the dancing
is usually cut.

Verdi's Tosca

Here's another story from Monaldi. Though he tended to speculate
and mythologize as much as compile data, he gives us a tantalizing
view of Verdi praising the subject of *Tosca*, even saying that he would
have liked to set it to music himself. Yet he felt it was essentially a
young man's opera, not suitable for the Grand Old Father of the
Italian musical stage.

There was this as well: like many others at the time, Verdi felt the
plot of *Tosca* was simply too brutal. People die in Verdi's operas, but
in *Tosca* all three of the principals are killed, and the tenor is tortured. Yes, it's offstage, but we hear his cries.

Yet Verdi says he would have gone ahead anyway if only Sardou,
author of the play *La Tosca*, would consent to changes. It was apparently not the second act, containing the torture scene, that Verdi
had in mind, but the third, when the tenor is shot by a firing squad
while he and the soprano think it's going to be fake—more torture,
in effect!—and the soprano then leaps to her death. Verdi even told
Gino Monaldi exactly how he would alter the action, and Monaldi
called Verdi's new ending "very beautiful."

Oddly, Monaldi, so generous with anecdote and quotations
elsewhere in his Verdi biography, didn't specify what changes Verdi
had in mind. And now we'll never know.

RICHARD AND PAULINE STRAUSS

Strauss illustrates the difficulty of being "apolitical" in a political age. However, to paraphrase Trotsky, you may not be interested in politics, but politics is interested in you.

Further, it was impossible for anyone living in Nazi Germany to be apolitical, because the state was the Party and the Party was the state. You were a Nazi fanatic or at least a collaborator—or a very hostile government viewed you as an enemy. Was Strauss a Nazi or just a German in a Nazi epoch?

Well, he wasn't a Nazi—and he had a family to protect: his only offspring, Franz, had married a Jewish woman, and the couple had children. As long as Strauss placated the rage of the regime, he and his kin were safe.

However, the Nazis were not easy to placate, even if you were the nation's outstanding international figure in music and thus crucial to nationalist prestige. In 1935, when Strauss insisted on crediting the librettist of *Die Schweigsame Frau*, Stefan Zweig (whose name had been omitted from the program because Zweig was Jewish), Strauss precipitated a Party upheaval. The helpless intendant of the opera was fired, the work was banned after four performances, and Strauss, ever after, was held under suspicion as "unreliable": i.e., neither a fanatic nor a collaborator. An enemy.

Strauss had made music under the Kaiser and under Weimar democracy; he thought he could easily make music under the Nazis. Things around his life might change, but—he thought—his life wouldn't. He was wrong. During the nationwide Kristallnacht pogrom, in 1938, Strauss' daughter-in-law had to be hidden from arrest by a family doctor, and Strauss' two grandsons were physically attacked and forced to spit on Jewish prisoners. As Goebbels wrote in his diary, "It is too bad that we still need [Strauss], but there will come a time when we will have our own music, and then we will have no use for this decadent loon."

And yes, Strauss was indeed Germany's musical star, along with Puccini the last grand masters of Romantic Era classics. Yet Strauss and Puccini were not mutual admirers. Browsing through the score of Strauss' *Die Frau Ohne Schatten*, Puccini exclaimed, "It's all logarithms!" For his part, Strauss found Puccini's operas relentlessly melody-based, where the Straussian model is more symphonic. *Salome* (1905), *Elektra* (1909), *Der Rosenkavalier* (1911), *Ariadne Auf Naxos* (1912; revised 1916), the *Frau* (1919), and *Arabella* (1933), mostly with librettist Hugo von Hofmannsthal, let the accompaniment tell the story as much as the singers do. "Louder, louder the orchestra," Strauss joked at an *Elektra* rehearsal during a passage for the Klytemnestra, Ernestine Schumann-Heink, "I can still hear the Heink!"

Though an extraordinary musician, Strauss was thought personally on the boorish side, not least by north Germans who found the composer's Bavarian ways too informal. Still, the objectionable Strauss was not Richard but his wife, Pauline de Ahna. The daughter of a Major General in the Bavarian Army (and an opera soprano herself), Pauline was a notorious termagant. She never tired of telling Strauss what a lout he was, in contrast with her highly cultured background, and if one of his operas failed to equal the smash success of his early titles—the ones cited above—Pauline would openly scold him for it.

Strauss biographer Matthew Boyden writes, "Even her own family thought her a handful," and, throughout the Strausses' married life, everyone was flabbergasted at her behavior. When visiting, Pauline would run her hand over the furniture to check for dust and then remark to her hostess on how well (or ill) she kept house.

Oddly, Strauss seemed never to mind Pauline's excesses. He even turned her into characters in his music, in the tone poems

Symphonia Domestica and *Ein Heldenleben* and two operas, *Die Frau Ohne Schatten* again (as the Dyer's Wife, her spite hiding a regretful tenderness) and, in a gentler version, as Frau Storch in *Intermezzo*. She maintains a fascinating presence in opera history, for even the aficionado knows little or nothing of most composers' wives. Who was Frau Mozart, Frau von Weber, Signora Mascagni, Lady Walton?

Of course, there's the startling exception of Cosima Wagner, Bayreuth's She Who Must Be Obeyed. Yet even Cosima wouldn't have dared take on various state officials, as Pauline did. "Nazi trash," she called them—and she didn't care who heard her.

The Reluctant Wagnerian

We start with Strauss' father, Franz, the first horn of the Munich Court orchestra and a very conservative musician who revered Mozart and hated Wagner. Actually, there were plenty of people Franz disliked, chief among them Pauline, who loved reminding him of the gulf between her exalted family profile in the Bavarian military and his humble situation. Social status mattered greatly in Wilhelmine Germany, so even the pepper-tongued Franz Strauss had no effective comeback for this abuse.

In truth, there was nothing humble about the senior Strauss. He refused to play at Bayreuth, and Wagner himself once asked him why he'd play the *Ring* in Munich but not in the theatre it was composed for.

And Franz replied, right in Wagner's face, "Hier bin ich Staatsbeamter, hier muß ich ja blasen!"

Which means, roughly, "Here I'm an employee of the state, so I have to play what they give me!"

Blasen, literally "to blow," means also "to play a wind instrument." Munich was the first center of the Wagner cult because of King Ludwig II of Bavaria and his infatuation with the music. But Munich was as well the first center of Wagner hatred (because of the composer's arrogance and his meddling in state affairs), so Franz fit right in. At Wagner's death, the orchestra stood in memorial silence, except for one man.

Franz Strauss.

Engaged

It's in all the biographies: Pauline was singing in Strauss' first opera, *Guntram* (1894), when, at a rehearsal, she got annoyed at Strauss and threw her score at him—and that is one heavy score. In the popular version, she is upset because he has corrected her once too often. But in fact it appears that she knows her music and he has been busy correcting everyone else in the cast. Eager for attention, Pauline complains that he is ignoring her.

"Of course I am," Strauss replies. "You don't need my help."

Completely missing the point, Pauline cries, "But I want your help!" And this is where she heaves the music at him.

"She was aiming at my head," he later recalled, "but to everyone's amusement it crashed down on the music stand of one of the second violins."

Pauline then stormed off, but Strauss followed (along with everyone else), and through the door of Pauline's resting room came her shouts of fury and the silences when Strauss would be replying. Then the door opened, and Strauss appeared alone. The concertmaster expressed the entire orchestra's sympathy at the appalling behavior of Fräulein de Ahna and offered to refuse to play for her in the future.

"That would make me very sad indeed," Strauss responded. "For I have just proposed to the Fräulein, and she has consented to become my wife."

Ever the Hostess

The Strausses had but one child, a boy they named Franz, after Strauss' father. It was a difficult birth, and Pauline had to be sedated. When she came to, she immediately said, "Doctor, would you like a cognac?"

Happiness Is Just a Thing Called Salome

In 1905, bursting upon a scene that was not ready for it, *Salome* was a shocker—a young woman makes love to the head of a man she has had decapitated, and this in a Biblical setting! The Kaiser famously said, "I admire this fellow Strauss, but that *Salome* will cause him no end of trouble."

When Strauss heard the remark, he answered with "That trouble made it possible for me to build my villa in Garmisch."

The house (which became the Strausses' permanent home), was a handsome three-story building in white with a sloping red roof and a turret at the right front corner. It was set amid lush green-ery and a view of Germany's highest peak, the Zugspitze, outside the village of Garmisch, some fifty miles southwest of Munich, scarcely inches from the border with Austria. When the district was occupied by the U. S. Army in 1945, Strauss came outside to make peace with the conquerors, and when he identified himself as the composer of *Salome*, the soldiers knew who he was. In the end, then, *Salome* not only didn't cause Strauss trouble: it might have saved his life.

With a Song In My Heart

Strauss often accompanied Leo Slezak in song recitals, but the tenor felt the composer was rushing the tempi.

"My dear Strauss," said Slezak, "must you play so fast? You're sabotaging your own beautiful melody."

"God in heaven," Strauss replied, "it isn't that beautiful."

Winging It

In 1921, Strauss undertook an American tour with Elisabeth Schumann, and though the concerts were a huge success, her diary records many a mishap.

For one thing, Strauss' son, assigned with superintending the practicalities, failed to secure their luggage at one point, and they arrived in Detroit with their trunk missing—including all of the music. Some of the pieces were found locally, for every music shop in America would have had a Schubert album at least. But Strauss had to play all of his own songs by heart, and as soon as he started "All Mein Gedanken" (All My Thoughts), Schumann could tell that he had forgotten the accompaniment and was making up a new one on the spot.

"I leaped along with him," Schumann says, and "the words fitted perfectly." So no one but Schumann and Strauss knew what had happened. (Those in the audience who were aware of the song would have supposed that Strauss had used an unpublished alternate accompaniment.) After the set, backstage, Schumann asked Strauss to write down the wonderful new piano part. This was history! But Strauss had already forgotten the whole thing.

Famous though Strauss was, some of the media really didn't place him. When the tour reached St. Louis, one local paper crowed, "THE WALTZ KING IS HERE" and ran a photo of the Johann Strauss statue in Vienna.

The Strange Tale Of Mieze Mücke

If ever there was a one-woman man, it was Richard Strauss. Still, Pauline could be insanely wary of the possibility of a liaison, especially as her husband was always off on a job. One time, she opened a letter addressed to him and read a message from a certain Mieze Mücke:

Dear Herr Strauss:

I looked for you yesterday in the Union Bar, but you didn't show up. So I am asking by post: could you let me have those opera tickets for one night this week?

With my sincerest gratitude,

Mieze Mücke

Pauline was outraged. The Union Bar—a modern Sodom, to be sure! And this...no, she couldn't even think of the name...would be one of those cabaret hussies one hears of! The way is clear: divorce! *Now* and *forever*!

In truth, this was a misunderstanding based on a confusion of Strausses. *Our* Strauss had never met this woman or even heard

of the Union Bar. When he wrote Pauline an only mildly exasperated letter of explanation, she accepted it. At that, a total separation
from her Richard would have destroyed Pauline, and they both
knew it.

But Strauss got an opera out of it, the aforementioned *Intermezzo*.
Strauss thought the story would show how endearing Pauline was
after all, but von Hofmannsthal was so revolted by the very idea that
Strauss had to write the libretto himself. He spared nobody, even
including their little boy in a speaking part, reproaching his mother
for her abuse of his father.

Now for the cherry atop the sundae: after the performance on
the first night, Pauline exclaimed, to everybody's horror, "And that's
exactly how it happened!"

Advantage To Kessler

In 1926, the Strausses attended an *Elektra* in Berlin and found themselves seated near man about town Count Harry Kessler and the
painter Max Liebermann. Pauline invited the two for a late supper.

The conversation was cultured, and when it turned to Georg
Büchner's play *Woyzeck* and Alban Berg's brand new opera adaptation (renamed *Wozzeck*), Pauline expressed disdain.

"What do I care about the horrid doings of a mere non-
commissioned officer?" she said, knowing that all at the table were
aware of her father, the General.

"Yes, but the wonderful opera *Carmen*," Kessler reminded her,
"is also about a non-commissioned officer."

"Ah, but *Carmen*...romance, Spain, Mérimée," Pauline pointed out.

"What's the difference between a German non-commssioned
officer and a Spanish one, really?" Kessler went on. "As far as that

goes, I find humble Gretchen much more interesting than, for example, the lordly Mary, Queen Of Scots."

Pauline leaned in to Liebermann for a whispered touché: "They do say that Count Kessler has become quite the Red nowadays."

"No, meine Frau," Kessler replied. "Just a good old-fashioned democrat."

Prosper Mérimée of course wrote the short novel that *Carmen* is drawn from, and Gretchen is the heroine of Goethe's *Faust, Part One*, so famous in German culture that she is known simply by her nickname, short for Margarethe (Marguerite in Gounod's opera). She has even given her name to a "thing": the laden question whose answer may cause trouble. It's known as the "Gretchenfrage" (the Gretchen question), after the moment in *Faust* when she asks the protagonist if he believes in God.

Strauss the Anti-Nazi

Little did Strauss know that the Gestapo was opening his mail, so unlike many others he did not trouble to keep his messages free of risky statements. Thus, in a letter to his mid-1930s librettist, Stefan Zweig, Strauss defied the first tenet of Nazism, that all humankind could be typed by race or ethnicity:

Do you think that Mozart wrote Aryan music? I know only two kinds of people: the ones with talent and the ones without.

Strauss went on to pursue his peculiar notion that everyone in the world was useful only in making him wealthy, giving Zweig a radical new interpretation of the Nazi buzzterm Das Volk. Literally, it means "the people," but in Nazi parlance it meant "the Aryan people of the Reich," superior to all other peoples:

> The people concern me only at the moment that they become [my] public. Whether they are Chinese, Bavarians, New Zealanders, or Berliners is of no importance. What matters is that they pay for tickets to hear my music.

We know that Goebbels had been eager to cast Strauss out of the regime altogether, and once he and Hitler received copies of this letter, Strauss became a Party untouchable, forced to resign his position as head of the Reichskammer[3] and no longer able to count on help in protecting his family from Nazi terror.

Strauss continued to compose and conduct. His music was performed. His operas received big premieres, well publicized and with the best people available. Yet he had to be extremely self-censoring in everything he said, every agreement he made, every plan he discussed—and there was always the hazard of Pauline's interaction with Nazi bigwigs on formal occasions.

Even so, Strauss really seemed to be living in an imaginary world. He may not have felt truly affected by Hitler's war till the premiere of his final opera, *Die Liebe Der Danaë* (Danaë's Love), at the Salzburg Festival, was canceled after the dress rehearsal, in observance of the closing of the theatres for "total war." For all the eighty-year-old Strauss knew, the opera might never be heard again. My, that hurt.

---

3. Reichskammer is untranslatable. The word denotes "National Music Chamber," but the organization was simply a propaganda bureaucracy ruling on musical matters in Germany.

GIACOMO PUCCINI

To repeat, the five composers especially highlighted in this section are unique as opera's great masters of post-Beethoven Romanticism. Berlioz stands out for the headlong nonconformism that had to wait till long after his death for vindication, Wagner for his mythopoeia and colossal themes, Verdi for the intensely individualized "voices" of his characters, Strauss for the wonderful literary quality of the librettos he set.

But Puccini is unique because even today, well over a century after his first major works appeared, he has little if any support among the intelligentsia. *La Bohème, Tosca,* and *Madama Butterfly* are regarded virtually as guilty pleasures. Even other opera composers, who know how hard it is to gain the ear of intellectuals, have been quick to condemn Puccini. Catalani—from Puccini's own hometown, Lucca—called him "insincere." Strauss said he couldn't tell one Puccini score from another. Benjamin Britten told Shostakovich that Puccini's operas were "dreadful," to which Shostakovich replied that the music was dreadful but the operas themselves were marvelous.

Another difference between Puccini and his colleagues is his musical style, which didn't change all that much from his first opera, the one-act *Le Villi* (The Spirits, 1884), to his last, *Turandot*, unfinished at his death, in 1924. True, the timbre of his orchestration, so to say, changed over time, and *Turandot* balances intimacy with epic flash and comedy with tragedy in a way no other Puccini title had ever done before. It is his only bizarre piece, his one-of-a-kind. It is notable that, in the rare case of academia exploring Puccini with zest and curiosity, it is usually *Turandot* the professors turn to.

Puccini stands out as well for his lifelong inability to settle on a subject and then execute it with art's traditional "careful haste." On the contrary, Puccini waffled endlessly—this story; no, that one;

but what about…?—and badgered his poets for revisions so end-lessly that they dreaded working with him more than once.

Yes, Verdi was meticulous about his librettos, demanding improvements before he would set them: but not endlessly. And Verdi always knew exactly what he wanted from a story, while Puccini was never certain about what was needed and sometimes let his collaborators figure it out and surprise him. He went through so many librettists on *Manon Lescaut* (1893) that the published text and score bore no credit for the words.

So it fell to Puccini's publisher, Giulio Ricordi, to play referee and healer in Puccini's dealings with his collaborators. Ricordi was the publisher also of Verdi, as we've seen, and between the two com-posers the House of Ricordi, founded by Giulio's grandfather and eventually run by four generations of Ricordis, became central to Italian music. This is because the publisher was far more than the source of the printed material: Ricordi maintained relationships with the theatres to put his composers ahead of others, assisted in getting the best out of the resulting productions, and kept the peace of Italian music despite accusations of monopolistic tyranny and the menace of the other major Italian music publisher, Edoardo Sonzogno.[4]

Puccini did have something in common with Richard Strauss: Each man dearly loved his spouse, to the bewilderment of their friends. Elvira Puccini—most unusually for the era—left her first husband for the composer, lived with him, and even gave him off-spring, all for some twenty years, till her husband died and she and Puccini could be legally wed.

4. Ricordi published such other promising composers as Riccardo Zandonai, Franco Alfano (who finished *Turandot*), Ottorino Respighi, Italo Montemezzi, and Ildebrando Pizzetti. Sonzogno had the other big names of the day—Pietro Mascagni, Ruggero Leoncavallo, Umberto Giordano, and Francesco Cilea.

Like Pauline Strauss, Elvira was what we now term a control freak. However, Puccini was not as submissive as Strauss, so the Puccini household was a fraught one. Ever wary of her husband's interest in other women, and certain that his many male comrades might cover up an assignation for him, Elvira would burst in on some masculine party in high suspicion or simply shout angrily down from upstairs, "What are you two talking about?"

The worst of it was Elvira's stalking of poor little Doria Manfredi, a village girl who was a servant in the Puccini household till Elvira threw her out, accusing her of adulterous contact with Puccini on no evidence whatever. Trying to turn her neighbors against Doria, Elvira made herself the village harpy, terrorizing her victim till Doria finally poisoned herself.

Then it was revealed that she had died a virgin: an innocent victimized by outside forces, like Butterfly, Angelica, Liù. That the Puccinis' marriage survived this enormity can be credited to the typical Italian need to "far' bella figura": for Puccini to be able to present himself nobly to the world. To cast Elvira out of his life would have seemed more shameful than staying with her.

So it was not surprising that Puccini contracted a lifelong out-of-wedlock relationship with a *petite amie*, more understanding and indulgent than Elvira. This was the Englishwoman Sybil Seligman. Arts history is filled with these special liaisons, sensitive rather than erotic—or was it?

Puccini's biographers cannot tell us the precise extent of this entente. Mosco Carner, Puccini's most exhaustive analyst, had Sybil's sister's word that Sybil and Giacomo were physically intense at first and then "settled down" in a platonic sympathy of great depth. But one of Sybil's sons told Julian Budden that "his mother's aversion to sex" made him wonder "how he had been conceived in the first place."

Puccini's crucial relationships with two such different women as the domineering Elvira and the immensely supportive Sybil have led many writers to psychologize the composer, seeing in his operas an encoded fear of engulfment by the one and a wish to rhapsodize about the other, as if Elvira were Turandot and Sybil Mimì. Such commentary sees sadism in Puccini's theatre, a need to play Elvira himself in torturing his so to say "Sybil" heroines.

However, Puccini didn't see all his Sybils as helpless. Gilda dalla Rizza—one of the composer's favorite sopranos, his "cara dolce Gildina"—told Lanfranco Rasponi that Puccini would coach her to be "girlish but firm," establishing a strong point of view even as the traditionally timid Lauretta in *Gianni Schicchi*. This girl must be neither "coy [n]or modest...but a determined young woman." Right from her first line, she must let the audience feel that she knows what she wants and intends to get it.

In the end, though, all this obscures Puccini's central importance as the man who emerged from the plethora of active post-Verdi Italian opera composers as The One. The Mascagnis and Zandonais were the sensations of the art; Mascagni once enjoyed virtually simultaneous six premieres of a single work, *Le Maschere* (The Masks, 1901). Yet after the first decades had passed, only Puccini succeeded in replenishing the core repertory with multiple masterpieces. In the end, here—in his very own way—was Verdi's heir.

Safety In Numbers

Puccini's first opera, the short *Le Villi*, is sweet but unimportant, and his second, *Edgar*, underwent revision after revision till the composer simply gave up on it. But his third opera, *Manon Lescaut* (1893), proved a triumph.

Some had questioned the wisdom of tackling a subject that had recently proved so successful in Massenet's version, *Manon*. Multiple settings of the same story or even the same libretto were once extremely common; the texts of Pietro Metastasio, the most prominent librettist of the eighteenth century, were routinely set by as many as fifty or more composers over the years.

But it was happening much, much less by the late nineteenth century. True, Verdi challenged Rossini in *Otello* and Otto Nicolai in *Falstaff* ("replacing" *Die Lustigen Weiber Von Windsor*). At that, Massenet's *Manon* itself challenged Auber's *Manon Lescaut*, famous as the first opéra comique with a sad ending. Nevertheless, as Puccini saw it, all's fair in love and opera. "A woman as fascinating as Manon," he supposedly said, "can take more than one lover."

Ho Mutato D'avviso

Somehow or other, Puccini never really fell in love with *La Bohème*'s Mimì as he usually did with his heroines. Work on the opera seemed utter drudgery, and of course he was driving his librettists, Giuseppe Giacosa and Luigi Illica, barking mad with his vacillations.

Then, suddenly, Puccini decided to drop everything and write an opera based on a short story by Giovanni Verga, *La Lupa* (The She-Wolf), about a mother and daughter in love with the same man. Verga, who had written the tale that became Mascagni's *Cavalleria Rusticana*, lived in Catania, in his native Sicily, and as Verga's fiction is steeped in Sicilian folkways, Puccini decided to visit the writer and explore his habitat.

To the exasperation of Giacosa and Illica, not to mention Ricordi, Puccini simply took off with two friends. It was sheer reckless fun and thoroughly unnecessary, for no sooner had Verga prepared a treatment for an operatic *La Lupa* than Puccini got bored with the whole business.

In a letter, Ricordi scolded "The Doge" (his nickname for the composer) for wasting time that had been better spent on the matter at hand, closing with "I wish you a ticket on the Rapido heading for station *La Bohème*."

An Audition

La Bohème's first night, in Turin in 1896, did not go all that well, and the reviews were hostile. But the Torinesi kept it running and the piece quickly became a huge international success, with the best singers eager to take part.

One young tenor simply showed up where Puccini was staying and asked to sing for him, in hopes of playing Rodolfo in a production in Livorno. The tenor tried out with the first-act aria, "Che gelida manina" (What a cold little hand), and sang it with such gorgeous, soaring ease that Puccini said, "Who sent you to me? God?"

The singer was Enrico Caruso.

Historical Accuracy

Tosca's third act gave Puccini particular trouble, and everyone wanted to advise him on how best to lay it out. Giulio Ricordi was especially hard on the big duet that anchors the act, seeing it as too broken up into disconnected bits. Of course it was: to emphasize the anxious state Tosca and her lover are in, facing as they are his supposedly fake execution, to be followed by a mad dash to the sea and exile in foreign lands.

Victorien Sardou, author of the play *La Tosca*, was on the other hand wildly enthusiastic about everything. What an ending, he cried, as Tosca hurls herself from the angel of life—St. Michael, the statue atop Castel Sant'Angelo—into the River Tiber, water of death!

True, it's a terribly violent way to bring down the curtain. Opera deaths are usually gentle expirations—Abigaille in *Nabucco*. Mimì. Manon. Thaïs. Some are stabbed or shot, yes, but they just sag to the floor. Tosca plummets.

"Enfin," Sardou concludes. "Absolutely colossal!"

"Ma," Puccini begins. "In effeto … Tosca can't throw herself into the river, direttamente. It isn't close enough."

"No? It's right on the Tiber on my map."

"Sì, ma … because the fortress is so expansively built, it gets wider lower down, and she would simply land on the battlements."

"Yes, but who cares about that?" Sardou replied. "It's art that matters, not facts!"

Actually, Tosca isn't opera's first jumper. We keep reading that Fenella, the mute heroine of Auber's *La Muette de Portici* (1828), throws herself into Mt. Vesuvius. In fact, the opera's final act is set not on the slopes of the volcano—an unheard-of notion for a nineteenth-century opera, anyway—but on a street in Naples. Fenella is on a balcony at the opera's end and, so say the stage directions, "hurls herself into the abyss," meaning the open space below the balcony.

The First Night Of Madama Butterfly

On February 17, 1904, a first-rate company introduced Puccini's sixth opera, at La Scala. Cleofonte Campanini, soon to be one of New

York's major musicians, at Oscar Hammerstein's Manhattan Opera, was the conductor, and the cast was headed by Rosina Storchio, Giovanni Zenatello, and Giuseppe de Luca, all wonderful singers.

They were keyed up with good feelings, because rehearsals revealed that they had something very special to offer. Yet once the curtain was up, the audience sat through the music in a stony silence, even during the very melodic duet between Pinkerton and Sharpless. Waiting backstage for her entrance, Storchio sensed some dark energy thrumming under the silence. Yes, she felt this even from the wings. Something was terribly wrong.

Then it started. During Storchio's entrance vocal, someone shouted, "*Bohème!* That is *Bohème!*" One started to hear things— especially those cries from the back of the house whose wording is unclear but whose intention is to disrupt. The lengthy wedding scene, filled with the atmospheric touches with which Puccini would season his operas (as with the antique dancing lesson in *Manon Lescaut*'s second act or the shepherd boy's song in *Tosca*'s third) only made the public restless. Even the drastic interference of the Bonze and Butterfly's ostracizing failed to rouse them, and at the end of the act—after a passionate love duet, always a sure thing in opera—there was only desultory applause.

Then came Act Two: and now the storm really broke loose. There was constant heckling of the singers, as if there had been a conference during the intermission, handing out assignments. This one will shout. That one will whistle. Everybody laugh.

So, when Storchio made a sudden turn, momentarily inflating her kimono, someone called out, "Butterfly è incinta!" (Butterfly is pregnant!), and another know-it-all, referencing Storchio's liaison with La Scala's chief conductor, added, "Sì, del bimbo di Toscanini!" (Yes, with Toscanini's child!) Later, during the orchestral inter-mezzo that covers the passage from evening to the following dawn, as Butterfly awaits the return of her American naval lieutenant, the effect of bird calls provoked a riot of animal sounds from the audience. Dogs, donkeys, and roosters were in the house; Storchio compared it to Noah's Ark.

Forced, snide laughter at all the wrong places vexed the rest of the act, and at the end the cast was too demoralized to take even a single curtain call. It was just as well, for there was virtually no clapping.

How could this have happened to a work that quickly became one of the fixtures of the core repertory? It is true that there were some problems with the piece, such as the picturesque but irrelevant details of the wedding party, which included a Drinking Song for Butterfly's Uncle Yakusidé, "All'ombra d'un Kekì." Too, the very long second act violated Verdi's forty-minute rule about the amount of time an Italian audience would sit still. And, contrary to the usage of the time, the music was kept secret even during rehearsals, leading some Milanese opinion-makers to accuse Puccini and Ricordi of arrogance.

Nevertheless, the public's hostility started when the opera did, so this was clearly sabotage, almost certainly by operatives of Sonzogno—again, the only major Italian music publisher in rivalry with Ricordi. La Scala was in 1904 a Ricordi house, seldom staging anything by Sonzogno's composers, so the Butterfly fiasco was probably The Night Of Sonzogno's Revenge.

"A genuine lynching," Puccini later called it, and it wasn't serendipitous. Masterly in the use of the claque, the organizers of the demonstration guided the entire audience—some two thousand people—in just when to harass the performance and when to remain angrily silent, in effect drawing even those who were neutral into taking part while intimidating would-be Puccini partisans. As one critic observed, "The spectacle in the auditorium appears to have been orchestrated quite as well as the one on the Scala stage."

The opera was taken off immediately and the next scheduled production, in Rome, was canceled. But everyone connected with the work knew of its quality, and just three months later the same conductor and principals (except for Storchio, who was fulfilling a contract elsewhere) triumphed with *Butterfly* in Brescia, just forty-five miles east northeast of Milan.

During those three months, Puccini revised the opera: changing that fatal "*Bohème* phrase" in Butterfly's entrance (because it did sound a bit like the melody of "Ma quando vien lo sgelo" in "Mi chiamano Mimì"); cutting all the family incidentals of the wedding sequence; breaking the overlong second act into two parts separated by an intermission; and adding an arietta of regret for Pinkerton near the very end, to make his character seem less callow while giving the public one last pleasing new tune before Butterfly's death scene.

Further small alterations were to come, as Puccini was a relentless adjuster. But now *Butterfly* was ready to take the stages of the world. And as for the work's self-validating, gloriously successful return to La Scala: it never happened in Puccini's lifetime. One La Scala *Butterfly* was enough for him.

"You Shut Up!"/"No, You Shut Up!"

Puccini put his librettists through hell on every opera, and even writers slow to anger could get quite, quite peeved. With the touchy Luigi Illica it was "Non tirar la coda al gatto!" (Don't pull the cat's tail, the idiom for Don't you dare go too far!) from start to finish.

At one point, working on a Marie Antoinette opera that ultimately went nowhere, Puccini told Illica that he, Illica, wasn't up to the task by himself and needed a second librettist to write with (as, indeed, Illica had done with Giuseppe Giacosa, on *La Bohème*, *Tosca*, and *Madama Butterfly*).

By letter, Illica replied, more or less in these words, "And maybe you should get a second composer to write your operas for you!"

Old Dog Tray

In New York in 1908, Puccini went shopping for his next opera subject as he always did, by going to the theatre, and he happened to catch David Belasco's *The Girl Of the Golden West*. Originally staged in 1905, this oldtime melodrama ran for half a season on Broadway but toured for two years, returning to New York at the end of 1907, in time for Puccini to catch up with it.

Belasco had already given the composer *Madame Butterfly* as an inspiration, but Puccini wasn't very interested in the western till one of Belasco's cowboys sang the nostalgic tune "Old Dog Tray." Suddenly, it appears, Puccini saw his next opera, *La Fanciulla Del West* (1910), in one tidy vision.

"At last," he murmured, "I've found my theme."

This tale is in all the biographies, but it makes no sense. Presumably, Puccini used the word *tema*, which does mean "theme," and also "topic" and "subject," as in English. But the song's equivalent moment in *Fanciulla*, though one of the opera's best tunes and reprised in the finale, is hardly the "theme" of the work as a whole. Even worse, some writers seem to think that Puccini (who did at times use pre-existing melodies for ethnic authentication) borrowed the music of "Old Dog Tray." He didn't. While *his* nostalgic number, "Che faranno i vecchi miei" (What are my parents doing), does mention "Il mio cane" (My dog), Puccini's tune sounds nothing like the insipid "Old Dog Tray."

Paris Original

In the Met's first tour to Paris—not the disastrous one under Rudolf Bing but the earlier one, in 1910—Puccini tagged along. But he didn't care for the dress Lucrezia Bori was going to wear for the fourth act of *Manon Lescaut*, when she dies in the wasteland of outer Louisiana, dirty and exhausted.

This was a time before organic production design, when star singers performed in their own costumes, and Bori had assembled a trousseau worthy of the most exalted couturiers.

Puccini happened to be holding a cup of coffee when he saw Bori's outfit, and, thinking it much too spruce for a woman who has been more or less crawling through a desert, he tossed the coffee onto Bori's gown.

She was startled, but—she later admitted—he was right to do it.

Puccini's Greatest Opening Night

It occurred on December 10, 1910: *La Fanciulla Del West* at the Met, with Emmy Destinn, Enrico Caruso, and Pasquale Amato under Toscanini. Never before or after was a public so revved up and in so festive a mood for a Puccini premiere. (*Turandot*, as we'll see, was a special case because of Puccini's death, and anything but festive.) *Fanciulla*'s PR bandwagon ran with every possible angle, not least that David Belasco, one of the biggest names on Broadway, was an unbilled creative on the production, teaching an almost entirely foreign cast how to behave like the inhabitants of Gold Rush California.

Then, too, *Madama Butterfly* had been, for the previous three years, one of the Met's marquee attractions, another of the Geraldine Farrar–Enrico Caruso pairings that made these two the rock stars of opera. And here was Caruso again, in yet more Puccini, this time as a really juicy character who didn't disappear for an hour after the love duet, as Lieutenant Pinkerton does. No, *Fanciulla* offered Caruso as a bandit, and, after *his* love duet, he was shot and left crumpled up at a table while Destinn and Amato played poker to see who got him, love or justice.

There was one drawback for Puccini: the social commotion, with receptions and speeches. He liked being around familiar people in casual attire, joking and drinking and getting into silly mischief. Having to play the visiting grandee was so public, so dressy. A Ricordi was in New York with him—Giulio's son Tito—and at one of the countless ruling-class soirées of appreciation that Puccini was forced to attend, Tito suddenly grabbed the composer's arm and hustled him away on some vague pretext.

"Evviva per noi" (Hooray for us), Tito breathed out when they were free.

"Ma perché questo?" (But why did you do it?) Puccini asked, with a conspiratorial grin.

"I just couldn't resist the chance," Tito replied, "to slap a million dollars in the face."

Nevertheless, even Tito, very keen on lively stage production, had to agree that the Met was making a solid show of *Fanciulla*. And, came the day, when the audience sat quietly throughout the first act, it wasn't a La Scala *Butterfly* quiet. They were listening, concentrating. At the act's end, they went wild, and did so again after Act Two and Act Three.

After all, this was Event Opera. That afternoon, despite a sold-out house, a huge crowd of wannagos gathered, forcing the police to arrive to keep order. Legend has it that desperate me-toos somehow got into the Met without tickets, scoffing at the fire laws—and were there really fifty-five curtain calls? *Fifty-five*?

As the public stamped and clapped and shouted, management came out with a laurel wreath of silver—solid silver, not plated, they say—and Destinn placed it on Puccini's head as the audience went utterly berserk with thanks for his music.

What a night! Yet, ironically, after making the rounds of the major houses, *La Fanciulla Del West* settled into quiet supplementary status even in Italy, and never stirred the public so intensely again.

Scissors and Paste

Most of Puccini's operas were drawn from plays, and Puccini habitually admonished his librettists to reduce the original texts to their essence to leave room for lyrical expansion. Lengthy conversations were for the spoken theatre, not the musical one.

"Tagliare," Puccini would tell his collaborators. "Sempre tagliare, sempre, sempre."

Which means, roughly, "Cut, cut, and cut some more."

Will He Like Me?

In Vienna for the German-language premiere of his three one-act operas known as *The Triptych*, or *Il Trittico* (1918), Puccini attended also a performance of *La Bohème*. Backstage, the cast wondered what message he might send to them during the intervals. You know these composers—"unpredictable" would be putting it mildly. He might give them anything from praise to damnation.

But no message came. At the end, the Mimì, Lotte Lehmann, dared find her way to Puccini to ask, "Caro maestro, were you not pleased with us?"

"Look into my eyes," he replied softly, "for there you will see tears of gratitude."

Now for a series of linked stories leading up to Puccini's death and his last, posthumous premiere...

The Feud With Toscanini

Puccini's relationship with the fiery conductor, who was essentially the music director of Italy just as Puccini was emerging as something like Verdi's heir, was uneasy. On one hand, Puccini knew that a Toscanini preparation of a Puccini premiere—coaching the singers, helping to stage the production, and forcing the orchestra to give of its very best—was almost a guarantee of success.

On the other hand, Toscanini had mixed feelings about Puccini's talent.

Puccini took this personally, especially given that Toscanini's favorite post-Verdi composer was Alfredo Catalani, who trafficked in the most basic harmony and was so starved for melody that only a single Catalani aria is commonly heard today, "Ebben? ne andrò lontana" (Very well, I'll go far away), from *La Wally*. Toscanini even named his children after characters in that opera. But there was no Mimì Toscanini.

So Puccini needed yet resented Toscanini, and Toscanini forced himself to admire Puccini because his operas were becoming part of Italian history. But he drew the line at *Il Trittico*, hating its Parisian riverboat violence and sugary sadism in the nunnery. There was no unity in these one-acts. Only the third piece, an hommage to the old commedia style, was worthy. When La Scala mounted *Il Trittico*, Toscanini handed it over to another conductor.

And that meant war. Puccini struck the name of Toscanini from his Christmas list of friends receiving the traditional pannetone (a sweet bread with fruity bits inside), and when the gift went off anyway, Puccini wired Toscanini:

PANNETONE SENT BY MISTAKE PUCCINI

and Toscanini wired back:

PANNETONE EATEN BY MISTAKE TOSCANINI

and that was that.

But then Toscanini lovingly prepared a thirtieth anniversary production of *Manon Lescaut*, with Juanita Caracciolo and Aureliano Pertile, for La Scala's 1922–1923 season. A tremendous hit, it gave Puccini's brand a much needed boost, for Prévost's novel, the opera's source, tells of two young people whose beauty inspires in them the densest hunger. Such passion might throw the very world off its pins. It's a blasphemy, really (the novel was banned at first), and Puccini put that idea into the work. Under Toscanini, the audience heard it in the music.

At the second interval, Puccini was so overcome that he threw himself into the conductor's arms during the curtain call and had the *Corriere Della Sera* publish his letter euologizing the uniqueness of Toscanini.

But then Toscanini produced *Nerone* (Nero), Arrigo Boito's colossal life's work on ancient Rome. He died without having orchestrated it or having set the fifth act, but in a labor of love, Toscanini dedicated himself to bringing this strange and unwieldy epic to life, for Boito and for his brilliant libretti for Verdi, which alone made Boito sacred to Italian art. *Nerone* must be staged.

Working with first one and then another composer on the orchestration, Toscanini heard that Puccini had spoken unkindly of the project, that Toscanini and his assistants were "organizing" Boito for the 1924 premiere, one of the biggest in La Scala's history. It was crammed with musicians, journalists, and even statesmen from all over Europe, and the dress rehearsal was so private that Puccini himself was turned away at the door. Puccini *barred* from *La Scala*!

So now the feud was on again—just when Puccini needed Toscanini to give to him what he was giving Boito, the utmost of La Scala's consecrating power on Puccini's own *Nerone—Turandot*, epic, brutal, wondrous.

But how was Puccini to effect reconciliation with (as he sarcastically called Toscanini) God? In the end, it was the conductor who made the overture, visiting Puccini and Elvira in their new quarters in Viareggio, a seaside town near his beloved Torre del Lago, due west of Lucca.

Puccini was overjoyed. But did he sense that the pain in his throat was a sign of the cancer that would fell him that same year, leaving *Turandot* to come forth, like *Nerone*, unfinished after his death?

Tempus Fugit

If Puccini's librettists over the years moved too slowly for Puccini, *Turandot*'s writers, Renato Simoni and Giuseppe Adami, were the slowest of all. Puccini found himself spending his days wringing his hands and pacing the floor, crazed to set down the music that was bubbling up inside him before... well, before it was too late.

As he wrote to Sybil Seligman, "If those two don't hurry up and finish, they'll have to put my music paper, pen, and inkpot into my coffin with me!"

È Morto Giacomo Puccini

The diagnosis was cancer, an inoperable tumor in the throat. However, a clinic in Brussels offered a radium treatment that held out the possibility of recovery, by the insertion of radioactive crystal needles. The operation seemed to promise success, but then Puccini suffered a heart attack, and soon after he was gone, saying only, "Mia povera Elvira, mia povera moglie" (My poor wife Elvira).

Few outside the Puccini family and the Italian state were aware of Puccini's medical troubles, and the news that he had died swept musical Europe in a tide of despair. In Milan, Toscanini castigated himself for having played petty games with the last genius in the line of Rossini, Donizetti, Bellini, and Verdi. Why, he wondered, must we have these bitter little wars over nothing? Insults traded over a fruitcake!

At least he could promise the composer's memory that *Turandot* would get a mounting as brilliant as the one he had just given to Boito's *Nerone*—which, ironically, was to have received its fifth hearing at La Scala on the day Puccini died. Management pasted a bill over the *Nerone* posters reading, "In segno di lutto per la morte del Maestro PUCCINI la rappresentazione di questa sera È SOSPESA." (As a sign of mourning for the death of Maestro Puccini, this evening's performance is suspended.)

A Tenor's Sense Of Commitment

Puccini had wanted Maria Jeritza to sing Turandot; her personal magnetism and powerful soprano had been in his mind when he created the part, because of her more or less swashbuckling way with Tosca and Minnie of the Golden West. As for Calaf, Puccini wanted Giacomo Lauri-Volpi, whose voice had the power and heady top notes the role demands, including the high C that for many tenors is at best a definite maybe.

However, both Jeritza and Lauri-Volpi were under contract to the Met (where they would indeed sing Turandot and Calaf), and Toscanini cast from the La Scala roster: Rosa Raisa and Miguel Fleta, with Maria Zamboni as Liù and a noted Falstaff, Giacomo Rimini, as Ping.

This was a very good if not tremendous cast—Jeritza and Lauri-Volpi would have generated a lot more spark—but preparations for the prima, scheduled for April 26, 1926, were exhaustive, with, as usual at La Scala, numerous chieftains all at work amid a great deal of simultaneous shouting.

Puccini had died but seventeen months before, making this a bittersweet memorial, and everyone was working feverishly to perfect the rendition. There was Giovacchino Forzano, La Scala's stage director and a Puccini librettist, running from the stage to the auditorium and back, intense and perspiring, exhorting his players in the big throne-room scene in Act II. There was Raisa as the princess of doom and delight, Fleta as the prince who must tame her. "Yes!" Forzano cries. "You fear! You love! You hate!" And the choristers, in their bizarre outfits. "Move forward now," Forzano cries. "Dio mio, not like that. You're the people of China, not railway workers on your lunch break. Suave! Haughty! Back! Again!

And there's Vittorio Veneziani, the chorus master, his arms as rigid as if working semaphore flags, beating out the rhythm. Next to him is Toscanini, who directs along with Forzano, concentrating on the principals and their use of grand gestures. On the huge staircase at the center of the set, Toscanini draws from Raisa a pantomime of rage and challenge. He demonstrates; she imitates.

"Now Fleta," he commands. "You crouch, because she is invincible! She is Turandot! It is fear and wonder. Remember, Puccini is watching us! Crouch, like this!"

Toscanini crouches. Fleta crouches. Raisa triumphs. Veneziani semaphores. Forzano runs back into the front rows to see the effect.

"Chorus, turn to see!" he tells them. "Yes! No!"

"Puccini," Toscanini warns. "Art. Truth."

"Like that, yes!" Forzano thunders. "But now the prince defies the headstrong princess! It is the essential moment of the drama—I'll show you!"

He runs up the gangplank over the orchestra pit to Miguel Fleta, who says, "When can I go and eat?"

What Did Toscanini Say When He Stopped the Orchestra at *Turandot*'s Premiere?

Puccini left the score of *Turandot* at the death of Liù and the ensuing choral requiem. The all-important duet of the two leads, some scene-change music, and a very short finale ensemble preceded by two lines from the heroine were not completed.

Puccini had thought Riccardo Zandonai should round off the opera if it was perforce left unfinished, but Toscanini instead chose Franco Alfano, presumably because Alfano's *Risurezzione* (Resurrection, from Tolstoy's novel) seemed very much in the Puccini line and his *La Leggenda di Sakùntala* used the percussive Eastern orchestration that Puccini adopted for *Turandot*.

Puccini had left some thirty-five pages of sketches that Alfano was ordered to use, and much of the first portion of the duet is almost pure Puccini. However, as the lengthy scene progressed, Alfano couldn't find enough Puccini to justify it, and he had to put in some Alfano. Toscanini, who wanted as much Puccini and as little Alfano as possible, was furious.

But it wasn't possible. The sketches were…sketchy. In the end, Toscanini forced Alfano to cut the music down, though the first scores had already been printed with Alfano's original (longer) ending, which also closes the opera with an odd reprise of the tune we hear when Ping, Pang, and Pong enter in Act Three, rather than just the melody we hear today, the tenor's "Nessun dorma." At the dress rehearsal, Alfano asked Toscanini what he thought of it all, and Toscanini said he had a vision of Puccini "coming from the back of the stage to smack me."

That rehearsal and the first run of performances gave *Turandot* in its completed form except for the premiere, when Toscanini stopped the orchestra where authentic Puccianian composition ended, as the chorus sadly filed offstage in the requiem.

It was a fitting ending, and Toscanini would have no speeches, feeling that the music itself said all there was to say. Yet he did permit himself an explanatory remark on why the work had been halted in suspended animation.

We have various versions of it, including "Here the maestro put down his pen," which is absurdly out of character for Toscanini. He had a sharp and even offbeat wit, and he would never have uttered anything so flossily sentimental. Besides, we have the word of Enrico Minetti, concertmaster of La Scala's orchestra at the time, for what Toscanini actually said. Too moved formally to address the house, he turned slightly to say, "Qui finisce l'opera, rimasta incompiuta per la morte del maestro."

Here the opera ends, incomplete because of the composer's death.

Having sampled the five masters who superintended the Romantic Era, let us catch up with a few more composers, from Handel to Britten…

Billow?

Handel was working on an oratorio with a libretto by the Reverend Thomas Morell, and the latter was awakened quite early one morning—it was still dark—by Handel's pulling up in his carriage outside Dr. Morell's house.

Through his bedroom window, the good father heard Handel call up to him with "Vat de defel means de vord 'billow'?"

Laughing, Dr. Morell said it denoted a wave of the ocean current.

"Ach, de vafe," Handel replied. And he told his coachman to turn around and take him back to London.

A Whopper Of a Cadenza

Handel attended a concert by the violinist Matthew Dubourg, and at the climax of a movement, Dubourg played his solo cadenza so elaborately that he seemed to be exploring every key in Western music, and was traveling very far from the melodic strain he had started with. This wasn't variations on a theme, but a little symphony of the world.

Finally, Dubourg made his way to the trill that signals the close of the cadenza, whereupon Handel shouted, "Valcome home, Mr. Dubourg!"

Do You Know Who I Am?

Luigi Cherubini was an Italian till his mid-twenties. Then, suddenly, he was one of the leading composers of France and even the director, from 1821 to 1841, of the all-important Paris Conservatoire (as we know from his aforementioned run-in with Berlioz in the library). As the chief music pedagogue of France, Cherubini was called, at his insistence, Marie-Louis-Charles-Zénobi-Salvador Cherubini, though all his life he spoke French with a heavy Italian accent.

Cherubini's major contribution to music lay in his operas, such as *Lodoïska* (1791), *Les Deux Journées* (1800), and *Les Abencérages* (1813), all of which pursued Gluck's revolution in naturalizing opera seria. Cherubini's form was opéra comique, the spoken drama with music, yet his emotional intensity anticipated the Big Sing of grand opera. Cherubini's masterpiece, *Médée* (1797), remains a summit of pre-Beethoven music drama even today, and in his lifetime Cherubini was regarded as a French national treasure for his operas especially.

Even so, no matter how big you get, sooner or later you're going to meet someone who just cannot place you. At a reception of some kind, Cherubini met the Secretary Of the Fine Arts, who complimented him on his latest mass.

"But my dear Cherubini," this worthy went on, "why limit yourself to religious music?" Struck by a sudden thought, like Pan inventing the pipes, he cried out, "Why don't you write an opera?"

Now for some opinions from The Great Man himself…

Rossini On Auber

"Auber est un grand musicien qui fait de la petite musique": He is a big musician who writes little music.

Rossini On Wagner

A friend called on Rossini to find him studying the score to *Tannhäuser*.

"I've tried and tried," Rossini announced, "but I couldn't make head or tail of it till I turned it upside down. Then it sort of made sense."

At that moment there came a terrific clatter from another part of the villa: the housemaid had dropped a platter of cutlery.

"Ah!" Rossini cried. "The Venusberg music!"

Now It's Beethoven On Rossini

"He makes music out of the frivolous spirit of our age, but he is especially talented at it, and an outstanding melodist. He writes with such ease that he can compose an opera in a few weeks, while a German will take a few years."

Then these two giants come face to face...

Rossini Meets Beethoven

Rossini was in Vienna, fêted as the king of Italian music, though all he wanted to do was to visit Beethoven.

Consider: Rossini led opera beyond Cherubini into an art of at times marvelous dramatic penetration. Worldly, socially popular, and diplomatic unless offended, Rossini all but created modern Italian opera. A genius.

Beethoven, too, was a great leader, taking the symphony out of the Classical Era into the Romantic. Introverted, socially difficult, and catastrophically blunt, Beethoven created modern music altogether. A genius.

So we anticipate an epochal entente of two philosopher-kings. In fact, this was a sad event, because Rossini, so eager to assist gifted musicians, found Beethoven in shabby quarters, gloomy of mien and refusing help of any kind.

In fact, Beethoven was notorious in Vienna. Even those who worshiped his music couldn't abide him personally. We have Rossini's own narration for the story, as he noticed cracks in the ceiling through which rain would fall and the "ineffable sorrow in [Beethoven's] face."

But "Ah!" Beethoven cries. "Rossini! The author of *The Barber Of Seville*! I present my congratulations! It is a superb opera buffa."

By then, Beethoven was almost totally deaf, but, as he told Rossini, he could read scores and thus "hear" them.

"Never write anything but comedies," Beethoven advised Rossini. "To do anything serious would compromise your talent."

The Italian poet Giueppe Carpani, who had initiated the meeting, immediately told Beethoven that Rossini was a master as well of operas of passion and grandeur, not only comedies. But Beethoven was not familiar with them, and he told Rossini, "Write more *Barbers*!"

Appalled by Beethoven's reduced circumstances, Rossini tried to interest prominent Viennese into giving the great man some financial support, but everyone begged off. "Beethoven is impossible," they all said. Unstable and ungrateful. Yet when his life was over, the entire city went into mourning. They couldn't love him till he was dead.

This famous meeting of geniuses comes from Edmond Michotte, who took it down during the equally famous meeting of Rossini and Wagner in Paris, when the former recounted to the latter his Viennese adventure.

Will He Like Me?

Vincenzo Bellini was not only a wonderful composer but a great charmer of both women and men, and he knew how to use that to his advantage. In Paris for the last opera of his tragically short life, *I Puritani* (1835), Bellini reckoned that he must meet and enchant Rossini. A word from that eminence to journalists would assure *I Puritani's* success.

So Bellini approached Rossini with all flags flying, affectionate to a fault. Would our great Rossini vouch for me? Side with me? Would he condescend to look at the *Puritani* score and advise? Will he be kind? He is kind to others, they say.

And, lo, Bellini said, "Will you help me, brother to brother?"

And Rossini replied, "Yes, as you wish."

"No, not as I wish. Not so suave and polite, but deeply and truly. Do you *love me well*?"

Rossini laughed. Heavens, this delightful boy. "Of course I love you well."

A pause. Then Bellini told him, "Yes, you love me well." He sighed. "But I really need you to love me *best of all*."

An Offbeat Eulogy

Tchaikofsky's death brought vast crowds to the streets of St. Petersburg to see him off to the burial ground. So great was the crush of onlookers that even the doorman of Tchaikofsky's brother's apartment building was impressed.

"And he was not even a general," the doorman murmured.

Pride In His Work

Hans Pfitzner wrote both libretto and music to *Palestrina* (1917), on the relationship of the Renaissance composer Giovanni da Palestrina with the issue of church music at the Council Of Trent. Of all famous operas, it's the dullest, but it has its adherents, and many were the musicians who revered its author, though Pfitzner was a megalomaniac with a tendency to quarrel with everyone about everything.

One morning, he was in a hotel somewhere, quietly composing, when suddenly a burst of noise from road workers outside infuriated him. Rushing to the window, he threw it open and shouted, "Silentium! Hier wohnt Pfitzner!"

The literal translation is "Quiet! Pfitzner dwells here!," but the grandiose wording gives the utterance a ceremonial arrogance. Anyway, it had no effect on the roadwork.

This One Is Scary

Like all great artists, Shostakovich fought to express himself even in the totalitarian hell of Stalinist Russia, when twenty million people were killed to placate the rage of the beast. Stalin himself was especially infuriated by the sensual honesty of Shostakovich's opera *Lady Macbeth of Mtsensk*.

True, Shostakovich did compromise on occasion, when he absolutely had to survive. But he would recover his standing only to defy authoritarian censorship once again. And finally the state decided it was time to eliminate him, as a warning to others, and he was ordered to appear for the "protocol of the interrogation"—Stalinism for torture and death.

Shostakovich duly put his affairs in order, said farewell to his loved ones, and presented himself at the appropriate place and time.

Consulting a list, the gatekeeper blandly told Shostakovich that his interrogator had just been shot.

"It's all over, comrade," he told the composer. "Go home."

Paradise Found

In 1963, for the first recording of Britten's *War Requiem*, his longtime company, Decca, decided to bestow upon its most celebrated living composer for his fiftieth birthday a special disc of the *Requiem's* rehearsals and playback-room discussions, caught on microphones hidden throughout Kingsway Hall.

Decca had to be secretive, for Britten was extremely touchy about his abilities as a performer (even of his own music). The tapes were edited down to a bit under an hour, and the label pressed exactly one copy of the results, complete with the usual printed black Decca label in a specially designed leather sleeve. John Culshaw, Decca's producer, knew that Britten would be at least somewhat resentful about the trickery involved. But if Culshaw had warned Britten what they were up to, he would have stopped him absolutely—robbing posterity of a vital document of a major composer-conductor in his element.

After the Decca team had given the disc to Britten, he told Culshaw, "I shan't forgive you quickly for this!"

But he was smiling as he said it.

Much later, Decca included the edited rehearsal tapes on the remastered CD release.

Don't Quit Your Day Job

A woman asked the young Britten what he wanted to be when he grew up.

"A composer," Britten told her.

Yes. How nice. "And what *else*?" she asked.

OPERAS

Bibbidi-Bobbidi-Boo

Opera librettist Jacopo Ferretti left us a memoir telling how he got the idea for one of Rossini's most popular operas. Ferretti and the impresario of the moment were brainstorming in Rossini's quarters, trying to come up with a worthy subject and getting nowhere, while the composer, "to delve more deeply into the matter," had climbed into bed.

Actually, it sounds as if Rossini was bored with the whole thing—but now something happens. Ferretti, while executing a yawn of fatigue, whispered, "*Cinderella.*"

That's it! Rossini suddenly sat up, Ferretti recalls, "as straight as Dante's Farinata,"[1] and asked, "Would you have the courage to write me a *Cinderella*?"

To which Ferretti replied, "Would you have the courage to set it to music?"

It's an odd exchange—why does courage enter into it?—but that's how Ferretti recounted it. Rossini then asked for the treatment, so he could get started on the music. How long would it take?

---

1. In the Tenth Canto of the *Inferno*, Dante and Virgil come upon the heretics in their burning tombs, and one, Farinata degli Uberti, rises at the sound of Dante's Tuscan dialect, which reminds Farinata of home. Educated Italians reference various episodes of the *Divine Comedy* the way Americans call up bits in popular movies and television shows, and Ferretti is likening Rossini's sitting up in bed to Farinata's sitting up in his flaming coffin.

"If I work all night," said Ferretti, "tomorrow morning."

And that was it. "Buona notte!" Rossini cried, his head hitting the pillow. Two months later, he gave the world *La Cenerentola* (1817).

Advertisment

Bellini's *Zaira* (1829) went over so badly at its first night, in Parma, that not long after the curtain fell handbills were given out reading, "Urgent. Anyone who can locate the musical inspiration of Signor Bellini is requested to take it to the Teatro Ducale at once."

Battle Royal

Donizetti's *Maria Stuarda* got off to a terrible start at its dress rehearsal, in Naples—a city, by the way, that frowned on depictions of monarchical figures in any case.

Maria Stuarda offers Elizabeth I and Mary Stuart, and the opera's big scene is a fictional confrontation between the two. Mary is at first submissive, Elizabeth haughty, and finally the Queen Of Scots rips into her foe, calling her a "vil bastarda." It is one of opera's merry legends that the Mary attacked her lines with such venom that the Elizabeth assaulted her physically. After peace was restored, one of the two, seething, said to someone or other, "Donizetti sides with that whore of a soprano," but Donizetti, standing just behind her, put in, "I don't side with either of you. The two queens were whores and both of you are whores."

Good gracious. In the end, for any of several reasons—one being that it was suddenly announced that the Queen Of

Naples was a descendant of Mary Stuart—Donizetti had to cobble together an ersatz *Maria Stuarda* with different characters and retitled *Buondelmonte*. They used the scenery intended for *Maria Stuarda*, which sometimes suited and sometimes didn't, and the composer lamented, "I don't know what this opera is anymore."

Orpheus In the Underworld

In the last act of Meyerbeer's *Robert the Devil*, Robert and his faithful half-sister, Alice, defy the devil and watch him, defeated, course down to hell through a trap door. However, one night at the Opéra, the Robert (Adolphe Nourrit) was so In the Moment that he doubled down on the defiance and strode manfully up to where the devil (Nicolas Levasseur) had been standing, unaware that the stagehands hadn't yet restored the deck. Nourrit promptly tumbled out of view.

Luckily, the mattress below the trap was still in place, and Nourrit was unharmed. As he pulled himself together and wondered how to get back on stage, Levasseur asked him, "What brings you here? Did they change the ending?"

Not That Chorus Again!

Robin Des Bois, Castil-Blaze's corrupt edition of *Der Freischütz* (discussed elsewhere in this book), thrilled all of Paris. Everywhere one went, people were humming Weber's tunes—especially the Huntsmen's Chorus. Paris didn't just adore that chorus. Paris *was* that chorus, and it was driving a few Parisians crazy.

Finally, a newspaper advertisement for a manservant listed, among the needed prerequisites, "Must not sing that chorus from *Robin Des Bois.*"

The Source Of La Bohème

Henry Murger's *Scènes De la Vie De Bohème* earned in its day a reputation as a remarkable instance of naturalistic fiction. But then, Murger had himself lived the bohemian life in Paris, and in using the people he had known and the things they did, he caught the spark of life.

Scenes From the Artist's World first appeared as separate stories during the late 1840s, but a play version created a demand for a collection of all the tales in one volume, and its success turned Murger into—as he phrased it—"the Emperor Of Morocco who had married the Bank Of France."

Too Many Sharps and Flats

When Thomas Beecham gave Strauss' *Elektra* (1909) at Covent Garden, he loved telling of a famous British composer (who shall be nameless here) who so hated the piece that, upon leaving the theatre, he declared his intention to head home and play C Major chords twenty times on the piano, just to remind himself, after *Elektra*'s cacophony, that there still *was* a C Major.

As Beecham always added, *Elektra* ends with colossal repetitions of a single chord, blasted out by the full orchestra. The chord? C Major.

Here now is one of the legends of Parma, Italy, home of a severely knowledgeable and critical public . . .

Turkey Parmigiano

Many years ago, the intendant of Parma's Teatro Regio had trouble casting Rossini's *William Tell*. Of course he needed a major baritone for the title role, but the only singer available was somewhat past his retirement date, though still active.

The anxious impresario sent a trusted deputy to meet the baritone at the train station and inquire—delicately—about his current vocal condition, as he had never sung in Parma before and might not be ready for the turbulent Parma opera buffs.

The baritone seemed chipper as he stepped off the train, a good sign. The deputy asked him how he was, how was his love life, how was his liver . . . the usual Italian things. Oh, and what was his last engagement? The Puccini Marcello? And how did that go? Ah, bene, bene.

But Marcello is a cinch. Guglielmo Tell is a challenge.

"Tell me," the deputy asked as they headed off to the baritone's lodgings, "are you ready to give us a splendid 'Resta immobile' (Stay still, the aria Tell sings to his son just before shooting the apple on his head)? You know, the Parma public is very keen about the piece, especially that last phrase, with the *acuti*, the Fs and E Flats on those very exposed lines, so wondrous and dramatic."

After a pause, the deputy continued with "How *are* your *acuti*, *incidentalmente*?"

"Ah, bah. They don't come as easily as they once did. All those years in teatro, you see."

The deputy nodded compassionately, and then said, "Get back on the train."

I've Nothing To Wear

The heroic soprano Gina Cigna, a Turandot and Norma on complete 78 sets in the 1930s, was due in Brazil to sing a work new to her, Carlos Gomes' *Lo Schiavo*. Whatever the music was, Cigna knew she could master it; after Norma, anything is possible. But she needed to know what kind of costumes were involved, as she always traveled with her own.

As she explained to interviewer Lanfranco Rasponi, the opera company's representative told her, "Senhora, bracelets and necklaces, and that is all."

Cigna must have been taken aback, but, after all, these Brazilian operas were so often about adventures in the jungle. As she dryly told Rasponi, "I managed somehow to follow these instructions."

That Arabella Is as Long as the Ring

Early in his career, Karl Böhm asked Strauss about cuts Böhm wanted to make in *Arabella*, but Strauss cut him off with "If I wanted cuts in *Arabella*, I would have written cuts in *Arabella*!"

Sudden Fear

Don Giovanni was Ezio Pinza's most famous role, with a wonderful moment in the confrontation with the statue when, after an evening of merriment, his face suddenly revealed something new: knowledge of his own mortality.

Once, a fan complimented Pinza on his terrified look, and Pinza replied, "Fifty-fifty terrified! *Pinza* is not afraid, only Giovanni!"

Real Life In Don Carlo

Playing Posa in Rome in his youth, Tito Gobbi wanted his death scene to fill with increasing pain and weakness and to end with a choking sound. A death rattle. But the conductor, Tullio Serafin, told him, "*Don Carlo* is not a crime film, with detectives and murder. You must retain nobility to the end."

Convinced his way was the more honest, Gobbi offered to sing as Serafin wanted at the prima—provided he could do it *his* way on the second night.

Serafin agreed, knowing Gobbi would have a success singing full out on the prima and that would be the end of this nonsense. But Gobbi held firm: on the next night, he would act as well as sing.

"So, you stubborn young *zuccone* (pumpkinhead), you insist on coughing your way through Verdi's aristocratic *cantabile*?"

He did. Gobbi didn't just sing Posa's death scene: he *died* on that stage. Moved and thrilled, the audience rose to its feet to cheer him, and, after the opera, Serafin said, "You are right, Tito. Go on in your career in your own way."

Carmen Smokes Chesterfields

Wasn't the young Risë Stevens lucky to cop a lead in a Bing Crosby film when she was still on the rise? *Going My Way* (1943) even gave Stevens a vocal spot of her own, for which she chose the Habanera from *Carmen*.

Crosby thought it highfalutin. "Wouldn't you rather sing 'Shortnin' Bread'?" he asked.

No, it was the Habanera, and Stevens sang it so persuasively that Chesterfield Cigarettes tapped her for a print ad showing Stevens in full Carmen kit with a flower in her teeth. You could almost hear the castanets.

Geraldine Farrar was not persuaded. "In my day," she observed, "artists became Carmen by singing Carmen."

Britten Is a Bus Stop

Peter Grimes (1945) was so famous when it was first presented that one bus conductor, working on the line that stopped near where the opera was playing, would cry out, "Rosebery Avenue and Sadler's Wells Theatre! All out for Peter Grimes, the sadistic fisherman! Mind the stair!"

Busy Salome

Inge Borkh was celebrated in Strauss' opera, not least for the little doodads with which she amplified her portrayal—looks, turns, gestures. Once, in Bern, she sang it with Strauss himself in the audience.

"That young woman is very talented," he said. "But she shouldn't be doing so much. It's all in the music."

London's Rose Cavaliers

Decca planned its 1953 recording of *Der Rosenkavalier* to capture the work's Viennese charm with a typical Staatsoper cast and Erich Kleiber leading the Vienna Philharmonic.

So imagine young Decca official Christoper Raeburn's surprise when Kleiber told him, "Don't pass this on to the orchestra, but the Covent Garden players are much more authentic in the music."

Gloriana's Premiere

This was a terrible idea: a Coronation Opera on the accession of Elizabeth II that told of Elizabeth I in both eulogy and defamation.

Surely the audience of international diplomats was expecting a hagiography. But Britten and his librettist, William Plomer, sought to investigate the very notion of a sovereign—at that, one in love with a subversive. Worse, after the smash success of *Peter Grimes*, the envious also-rans of the musical establishment, also on hand for *Gloriana*'s premiere, were gunning for Britten.

And they got him. Between the politely frosty first nighters and the critics, *Gloriana* was destroyed, not to make a comeback for twenty years. Britten never forgot how it felt when the curtain fell on the last act and a Covent Garden full of bloodless European foof-fenpoofs made little plopping noises with their white gloves.

"Clap, damn you," Britten muttered, in his box.

Mind the Drop!

James McCracken made his Viennese debut as Bacchus in *Ariadne auf Naxos* with so little rehearsal that no one warned him that within the set was a huge drop to the basement, something like thirty feet down. Or maybe someone did warn him, but in German, which he didn't understand.

Bacchus arrives very late in the "opera" section of the work and sings a duet with Ariadne that goes on more or less forever. Then the opera ends. At one point, attempting a dramatic effect of some kind, McCracken began to back away from his Ariadne, Teresa Stich-Randall, only to hear her cry, "Vorsicht! Vorsicht!" (Watch out! Watch out!)

McCracken knew that wasn't in the score, but as he couldn't tell what she was saying, he kept backing away, right to the edge of the drop. Finally, Stich-Randall more or less screamed, "*Stop!*" And he did, finally.

Gott sei dank.

Louche Cannon

Nicolai Gedda started out with a lyric tenor that he protected from the more heroic roles, yet, very early on, he couldn't resist trying Huon in Weber's *Oberon*. It's a part usually taken by big voices, but this was the Paris Opéra, and Gedda was collecting bookings in major places, such as Milan and London. Paris seemed irresistible.

Alas, he found the experience almost disturbing, as the Opéra functioned at that time in chaos and the singers were ruthless with one another. Someone else in the *Oberon* cast took an intense dislike to the Rezia, a Brazilian, and enlivened one rehearsal by saying, "If she intends to go on making that dreadful noise I'm not staying here."

"Mais, chère amie," the Brazilian replied. "That is my voice, and my voice is my voice, comme ça, you see? Besides, you French singers are just shit, anyway."

Blue Oyster Cult

Joan Sutherland is not known for modern music, but she did create Jenifer, the heroine of Michael Tippett's *The Midsummer Marriage*, on its Covent Garden premiere, in 1955, and this allegorical tutti-frutti gloss on *The Magic Flute* had the entire cast utterly bewildered. Tippett had rehabilitated myth with a psychological subtext in a contemporary setting, as though an oracle had appeared in the English countryside to make obscure pronouncements inside a huge clam shell while the ballet corps performed ritual dances and everyone behaved as symbolically as possible.

When the singers asked Tippett what the work meant, he said, "I don't know, darlings. It was something inside me that had to come out. Just sing it beautifully and it will be all clear and right."

Alone together, they commiserated with one another. John Lanigan, the tenor of the Second Couple, offered only a tight-lipped "I know my role." Baritone Otakar Kraus hated the ending. "Just once," he said, through a thick German-Czech accent, "I would like to be in an opera where I am still alive at the final curtain. Always they are killing me."

"You think you've got problems?" said contralto Oralia Dominguez through an interpreter, as she spoke no English and had learned her role by rote. She was playing one of Tippett's more fantastical characters, the clairvoyante Sosostris. "I'm sure the music is most interesting and modernesque," she conceded. "But how am I to charm the public when my face is painted blue?"

A little Jung, a little dance, a little seltzer down your pants. But, lo, it was Art.

Pret à Porter

Donizetti's French grand opera *Le Duc D'Albe* (on the same story line as Verdi's later *Les Vêpres Siciliennes*) lay unfinished at his death, in 1848. A completion by others was staged in Rome in 1882, but the work soon vanished from the stage.

Then the Spoleto Festival revived it in 1959, in a new edition by Thomas Schippers. *Il Duca D'Alba*, the Italian version, had been heard on radio, but this would be the first staging in nearly eighty years. Luchino Visconti, the director, decided to recreate ottocento style: singers delivering their solos downstage, choruses just standing around, and old-fashioned picture-book sets.

So, at the Parravicini scenery warehouse, Visconti asked if they had something in the line of The Brussels Grand Place, A Brewery, A Room In the Brussels Town Hall, A Prayer Room, and A Harbor.

"Certo," came the answer—and the Parravicini man offered Visconti exactly what he asked for, all five visuals in splendid old style.

Stunned, Visconti asked where they came from.

Consulting his notes, the man said, "These are the work of Carlo Ferrario, signore. Last used in…let me see…yes, in 1882 in Rome. For Donizetti's *Il Duca D'Alba*."

I Call Myself Phoebe

Renata Scotto was singing Gilda in Venice, and the famously beloved Toti Dal Monte came backstage to say, "Cara, this is not the way to sing Gilda."

As Scotto stifled an "Excuse me?," Dal Monte went on with "You play her like a woman, too dramatic and knowing. And where are your long blond braids? You should sing Gilda as I sang it. Ah, that was the era of the authentic verdiana Gilda. I can see that I shall have to open up my schedule to give you some Gilda lessons."

One Fine Day

The soprano Camilla Williams—the foremost exponent of George Gershwin's Bess between Anne Brown and Leontyne Price—was singing Butterfly at the Long Island Festival (on the C. W. Post College campus) in 1963. It tells us how intensely Williams related to the drama in opera that, when her long-awaited naval officer's boat was sighted in Nagasaki's harbor, she impulsively cried, "He's coming!"

The performance was in Italian, and the audience buzzed a bit in response, but there's only one word for this.

Commitment.

It's Not One Of the Great Overtures, Though

When Gianandrea Gavazzeni conducted *Anna Bolena* at Glyndebourne, he did a lot of cutting, even omitting the entire overture. Three years later, Lamberto Gardelli opened all the cuts. Someone asked him why he had brought the overture back, and Gardelli replied, "Because Donizetti wrote it."

If Looks Could Kill

The world of opera stories tells of Toscas stabbing Scarpia with a banana, a lamp, a fruit bowl, but one night at the Paris Opéra-Comique Régine Crespin stabbed him with . . . nothing. It seems the knife had got caught in a seam of her gown, and as the music screamed of murder and Crespin tugged at the stubborn blade, the Scarpia, René Bianco, frantically whispered, "Stab me, already!"

Finally, Tosca struck—with the evil eye. That was good enough for Bianco, who immediately dropped to the floor. Good, at last I'm dead.

And wouldn't you know that the Cavaradossi, Albert Lance, was making his role debut that night, so the critics were present. One wrote, "It's the first time I ever saw Scarpia die of fright!"

Once Is Never Enough

The old Philadelphia Lyric Opera was a buffs' favorite for its rough and ready production; there was scarcely a major name in the Italian-French repertory that didn't drop in in a warhorse role. But the Lyric was always short in cover singers. On March 3, 1963, Gianna D'Angelo canceled a Lucia with Daniele Barioni, Manuel Ausensi, and Bonaldo Giaotti, and the Lyric brought in the unknown Tina Garfi. When she came to grief on the Mad Scene's high E Flat, she fell upon her knees and begged the conductor, Walter Herbert, to allow her to sing the entire Moderato ("Spargi d'amaro pianto") again.

He allowed it, and as she began, one of the extras, playing a page, collapsed on the floor in a faint.

You Say Regie, I Say Fiddlesticks

A Covent Garden *Idomeneo* had the Elettra, while telling of her love for Idamante in the aria "Idol mio," paint a heart with the letters E and I within it.

Whereupon an exasperated spectator in the balcony cried out, "For heaven's sake, just *sing*!"

La Morte È Una

At the opening of the San Carlo's 1973 season, in Naples, a *Turandot* with Amy Shuard, the booing was intense after the second act.

Backstage, everyone helpfully screamed at everyone else till it was decided that one Franca Como would take over for the third act. As the Calaf and Liù were rather less than ideal, the evening concluded badly, and the conductor, Fernando Previtali, demanded the return of Shuard in the coming performances.

In fact, Shuard, Covent Garden's fine resident dramatic soprano, may have been suffering from the disease that was to fell her just fourteen months after this, at the age of fifty. In any case, Mario Del Monaco, in town for a *Stiffelio* with Angeles Gulin, gave an interview extolling Shuard's instrument as "the perfect Turandot voice."

The Eyes Have It

Way back at the beginning of surtitles, Eva Marton was singing Tosca in Houston. In the first-act duet with Cavaradossi, on her line "Ma falle gli occhi neri!," the audience read, on the title screen, "Give her black eyes!" and broke into laughter.

Marton stormed offstage, vowing not to continue the opera, but peace was soon restored and she completed the performance in fine style.

Still, everyone in the opera world realized that this surtitle business was not as easy as it looks.

The translation malfunction stemmed from an ambiguity in the Italian. *Neri* means both "black" and "dark" (i.e., "brown" eyes).

For "black eye" as an injury, an Italian would more likely say *occhio pesto*.

A Voice In the Crowd

They were booing another Turandot, that of Marion Lippert, this time at the Paris Opéra. Suddenly Régine Crespin rose to her feet, turned, looked upward, and shouted, "Vous êtes des laches!" (You are cowards!)

And that was the end of the booing that night.

The Carlo Bini Gioconda

Yes, it's another booing story. The post-Bing Met suffered many a fiasco, while Bing seethed over not being asked to return and save the house from such didoes as a *Tristan* without Birgit Nilsson. Whose idea *was* that?

One of several notable disasters was the night Plácido Domingo canceled after the first act of *La Gioconda*. Giuseppe Patanè was conducting, the Gioconda was Eva Marton, and Domingo's cover was Carlo Bini.

An amiable tenor—a shock in itself—with a wonderful ability to pick up roles and staging at short notice, Bini was irresistible to an opera house determined never to have to cancel a performance. Bini sang scheduled leads, but he was as well contracted to cover certain roles, and he suddenly found himself being costumed and made up to go on as Enzo and sing his major aria, "Cielo e mar," right off the bat. In the excitement, Bini had not warmed up properly, and "Cielo e mar" did not go well. Unusually for the Met audience, a number of spectators not only booed him hideously but continued to shout at him throughout the rest of the act.

Patanè, notoriously temperamental, called the orchestra to a halt and turned to the auditorium. "At least have respect for the composer!" he cried. "If you don't like the singing, then don't clap!"

It had no effect. The public seemed determined to imitate Italian audiences when they don't like a singer: they scream the music off the stage.

Patanè, who reckoned that every performance was about him, decided to faint after the third act. He, too, had a cover, Eugene Kohn, who was ready to go on—but wait! How will Eva Marton react to this? She can be temperamental, too. Met officers went to Marton's dressing room to sound her out.

"If the orchestra plays," she grandly announced, "*Marton sings!*"

What a trouper! And out she went to finish the show, as the New York press regaled its readers with point-by-point reports and quoting remarks by Bini himself, in his charmingly Italianate English.

"Everything," he said, "is making a big casserole."

Spectacular Voyage

One of the unique qualities of the Met is how willing it is to spend big money on big shows. As Joseph Volpe put it when he was running the house, the Met can afford it, even if "you want the moon to jump over a cow."

So, when Philip Glass was working on his Met commission for *The Voyage* (1992), a complex look at long-distance travel from Columbus' arrival in America to interplanetary missions, he worried that he and his librettist, David Henry Hwang, would be asking too much of the company's resources.

Glass expressed his apprehensions to Volpe. But not to worry. "You write it," Volpe told him. "We'll stage it."

The Guy Who Fell Into the Orchestra Pit During War and Peace

In 2002, the Met mounted its first production of Prokofyef's adaptation of Tolstoy's monumental story, one of the biggest productions in the house's history. On opening night, one of the supers appeared to slip near the edge of the stage during a battle scene and went crashing into the orchestra.

The performance was stopped and the super, one of Napoléon's soldiers, was presented to the audience by Volpe himself, as proof that there was no serious damage (except to the bow of one of the violinists). The story made all the papers, though a pertinent fact was missing: the super hadn't slipped. He had apparently jumped to make a little name for himself.

It made a name for the Met's *War and Peace*, too, for the publicity excited ticket sales, and the remaining nine performances sold out. Volpe was pleased, but the super can't have been: he was fired for showboating.

Conductors

ARTURO TOSCANINI

Even now, writing in 2019, I cannot name an opera conductor with a profile as marked as that of this brilliant, recklessly dedicated, and politically engaged musician—not the dreamy Furtwängler, the grandiose von Karajan, the witty Beecham, the coruscating Solti. They were larger than life; Toscanini *was* life, the conductor who saw music as a mission, moral and liberating as all great art has been in the history of the West. Controversially, one could say that those who don't believe in the Christian God might still believe in the arts that the Christian belief system fostered, from Dante to Shakespeare to Beethoven to Picasso. One might believe in music. And one might believe in Toscanini.

Yes, he was difficult: temperamental, rude—no, brutal—with the lazy, the sloppy, the half-artist who ham-and-eggs his or her way through a score. He was doctrinaire about everything: when his daughter Wally got engaged to a count, he cried, "When has an aristocrat ever been worth anything?"

Or when someone asked him why he always stood when conducting, even in *Die Meistersinger*, the longest opera in the repertory, he replied, "Sitting is when you eat dinner."

Or when people noticed that, after his years in the United States, at the Metropolitan Opera, the New York Philharmonic, and the

NBC Symphony, he still wasn't quite fluent in English, he snapped back with "Speaking foreign languages is for writers and tour guides."

He was a perfectionist, coaching singers individually to bring forth, even on a single line, exactly the shade of musical or dramatic coloring he felt was called for. He threw an hour of his life away before the radio broadcast of the first half of *Otello* trying to get the Iago, Giuseppe Valdengo, to execute Shakespearean nuance on two words, "Non so" (I don't know). Valdengo was a marvelous baritone but he simply didn't understand what Toscanini wanted, and the frustrated maestro gave him a verbal beating.

On the other hand, when Lotte Lehmann dared a *Fidelio* under Toscanini at Salzburg before World War II, she greatly feared how he would react to her. A personable and even ecstatic performer, she could nevertheless be sloppy in her observance of note values. And yet. Lehmann was the Leonore of the age and Toscanini led a very powerful *Fidelio*. Here was a production that simply had to be.

So Lehmann took a chance. And at one point in rehearsal, Toscanini suddenly called the orchestra to a halt, looked hard at Lehmann, and thundered, "*You* are an *artist!*"

Were his standards too high? Even in its golden age, opera has a limited number of Lotte Lehmanns. Is it fair verbally to assault those who are unable to function on opera's high wire at the genius level?

Short answer: Toscanini saw music as holy, a sacrament in the temple of civilization, and he demanded a near-mystical, blind surrender to it from all its adherents. If he could so immerse himself in the perfecting of the art, then so should everyone else. Not only could: *must*. Not to please Toscanini—to affirm the nobility that separates mankind from beasts. Tolerating the inadequate, the maladroit, the apathetic in Verdi or Wagner was in effect to surrender to the forces of barbarism that periodically rise up to attack the ideals of the human race.

A reformer who grew ever more revolutionary as his innovations infuriated narcissistic singers, foolish critics, and the public, Toscanini thought nothing of banning encores. They compromised the integrity of the drama, after all—and, indeed, in her memoirs, Frances Alda recalled preparing a Met *Otello* with Toscanini, who insisted that her Willow Song and Ave Maria will cast a spell and must not be sabotaged by those sheep in the audience, led by a few hysterics into spoiling the mood with their applause and calling for the *bis*. Verdi wrote the scene to capture a woefully beautiful moment, a stillness in this otherwise busy opera, and Toscanini intended to honor that.

"Senti, Aldina," he told her. "You will kneel and sing the Ave Maria. Then you rise—without turning your face to the audience, or they will start barking like seals. You will simply get into your bed like a good pure virgin."

Alda says the house clapped, anyway. But "I felt Toscanini's eye upon me," and "dared not look up." And, she concludes, "the scene went on with its poetry uninterrupted."

We should note as well Toscanini's photographic memory, which could bring an entire opera back into his repertory without his ever having to review the score, even after twenty or thirty years. Rehearsing the first act of *Tristan und Isolde* at Bayreuth, Toscanini asked what happened to the cymbal crash at the end. Had the percussionist lost count of his entrance? No: there is no cymbal crash, the player explained. Indeed, there wasn't one in the parts the orchestra was playing from, but Toscanini had the holy relic of Wagner's original manuscript brought forth from its security crib in Wahnfried, the Wagner family villa, and there, sure enough, was the cymbal crash, omitted by Wagner's imperious widow after his death. "Hier steht" (Here it is), Toscanini told them, virtually the only German he could speak. Here it is, because I was right.

He was always right; that was the problem. It emboldened his worst quality, that tendency to attack in the fiercest terms any musician who failed to live up to his high standards. But then, did he not hold himself to them as well? And his reputation as a tyrant was tempered by his "other" reputation as a foe of fascism, both in his native Italy and Nazi Germany. Toscanini's refusal to conduct again in Bayreuth after Hitler was appointed Chancellor and the Nazis were swept into power in effect sounded the first alarm bell of warning to ring through Western Civilization.

This suggests that Toscanini was the first truly international conductor, emissary as well as musician. From leadership positions at La Scala, the Met, the New York Philharmonic, and at length the NBC Symphony Orchestra and its radio concerts before, all during, and after World War II, Toscanini became not just the most famous but the ultimate conductor. Joseph Horowitz's wonderfully provocative book *Understanding Toscanini* explores the wily marketing techniques behind the corporate "presentation" of the man in all his aspects. Still, however we look at it, he ended as a symbol of Western music, inspiring and unique. It is typical of the power of his opera conducting that his broadcast recording of Verdi's *Otello*, now some seventy years old, is still the most often cited Best Opera Album Ever.

Was his conducting really that good? Long answer: Yes.

The Karma Train Pulls Into Town

Toscanini asked Richard Strauss for the Italian premiere of *Salome*, in 1906. And Strauss agreed.

But then Turin lured the composer into letting their opera company jump the gun on Toscanini.

The conductor read it in the press—Strauss hadn't even given Toscanini the courtesy of a heads up. Astonished, the conductor actually boarded a train to Vienna—where Strauss was at the time—to confront him personally.

Is this true? You have given the Salome premiere to those crafty Torinesi?

The affable, reckless Strauss admitted it was true. But, you know, Turin offered me more money.

So. "Strauss," Toscanini said, "for your music, I take off my hat to you. But for you as a man...I put on ten hats!"

A Letter From Illica

As I've said, in the old days of Italian opera, a music publisher was more than the firm that brought out the scores for commercial sale and supplied the orchestral parts for performances. The publisher could at times actually control the choice of works that a given theatre might put on—especially at La Scala, whose repertory was thought to reflect the who's who of Italian music.

At one point, in 1918, Sonzogno, the house of Mascagni and Leoncavallo, seized control of La Scala, and Toscanini fought back and prevailed. But his heart was heavy, for now La Scala would be a place of money-changers rather than a temple sacred to music.

The prominent librettist Luigi Illica, sensitive to Toscanini's depression, wrote to the conductor's son Walter, trying to get him to explain to his father that opera was as much a business as an art.

"Your father," said Illica, "suffers from the Verdi disease. Great maestro that he is, he wants the theatre trembling with the conscience and aspirations of the Italian nation. Of our very being. But it cannot be, my friend. And to pursue this vain idyll will bring to him only anger and sorrow."

Klaatu Barada Nikto

One of Toscanini's favorite assaults on male singers who displeased him was "You sing like a dog!" For the worst offenders, it was "You sing like a police dog!"

Giovanni Martinelli, a mainstay of Metropolitan tenors and eventually famous as the house's great Otello, fell prey to the maestro's fury during a rehearsal of Giordano's *Madame Sans-Gêne*. The Met had assembled a sharp cast, with Geraldine Farrar, Pasquale Amato, and Andres de Segurola alongside Martinelli, but, at a piano rehearsal, Toscanini went nuclear on Martinelli with his "police dog" attack.

Silence.

Then, surely realizing that he was out of line and needing to atone, Toscanini offered his hat—men always wore hats in those days, sometimes even when they had sex—to de Segurola and said, "Put some pennies into the hat."

Amato, same thing. Farrar. Pennies. Then Toscanini walked up to Martinelli and said, "I don't know how much there is here, maybe twenty cents. Go and get a haircut."

So everyone laughed, and from then on the rehearsal continued splendidly.

Alert the Media

When accompanying Lotte Lehmann's master classes in London, in 1957, Ivor Newton loved spending the downtime just sitting with

Lehmann as she spun out her reminiscences. Toscanini, for instance: was he as terrible as his legend?

Lehmann said no—as long as the singers were dedicated to the work at hand and endowed with some imagination. He hated mediocrities, she said. But with the imposing talents, like Lehmann, he could be quite accommodating, for instance in lowering the key of the difficult cantabile section of the "Abscheulicher!" scene and devising a transitional bit to connect the foregoing recitative to the rest of the music harmonically.

What? A change of key and an edit in Beethoven? But wasn't Toscanini doctrinaire in the extreme about playing everything as written?

Not always, Lehmann told the fascinated Newton, who realized that a piece of opera history would have to be rewritten. Lehmann went on to say that, in the long run, it was the quality of the performance that mattered, and Toscanini's 1935 Salzburg *Fidelios* were thought the greatest rendition of the work anyone could hope to hear.

At some point in that Salzburg summer, Lehmann approached the maestro to tell him—because *somebody* had to—that everyone in the cast worshiped him, and he responded with "You must not use such extravagant language to me. 'Worship' belongs to Mozart, Beethoven, Brahms. I am no more than a conductor. A good one, I hope. But no more than that."

Mr. Memory

Just before a concert, the second bassoonist came to Toscanini, warning him that one of the keys on his instrument was not working— the lowest note, a B Flat. How were they to handle this?

Toscanini stood in thought with bowed head, going over the program in his head. "Aspetta…aspetta" (Wait), he said, as a few moments

THE NEW BOOK OF OPERA ANECDOTES

passed. Then he looked up and said, "Do not worry, caro. That note is
not needed from the bassoon in any of the pieces we play tonight."

Toscanini's Metaphor

Rehearsing the NBC Symphony for his radio broadcast of *La
Bohème*, Toscanini warned the brass instruments that they were
playing a particular figure too loudly.

"This must be heard from the distance," he explained. "But not
too much distance—Brooklyn."

I Can Cook, Too

Fausto Cleva wasn't the most exciting conductor on the Met staff,
but he was a kitchen wizard. He not only cooked pasta but prepared
it from scratch.

In another of those beloved bits of lore kept alive over the years
by Met standees, Toscanini comes to Cleva's for dinner, and finds
it—as the Michelin guides liked to put it—"worth a detour."

"Bravo, Cleva," says Toscanini, enjoying his dish.

"Careful what you say, Maestro," replies Cleva, beaming. "Or
I will tell everyone how you praised me with the 'bravo.'"

Toscanini gives him a look. "Only for the noodles, Cleva."

HERBERT VON KARAJAN

Born in 1908, the future so-called Generalmusikdirektor of all
Europe was scarcely in his twenties when he became one of the two

conductors of the opera house in Ulm. It was a great all-around experience, but after a few years the company chief fired him.

"You are too good for Ulm," the man explained. "This is a backwater, and you are destined for great things. You have learned all you can in this place, and now you must begin your journey toward higher things."

Karajan did so, moving to Aachen and then Berlin. There his former boss from Ulm came to hear von Karajan conduct and popped in backstage to say hello.

"You see?" the man told him. "I was right, wasn't I? Once, you were little Karajan, for a little public. And now..."

He was das Wunder Karajan (roughly, "Karajan the wonder boy"), not just a prodigy but a glamorous one. With his stern good looks and chiseled haircut (he actually became better looking the older he got), von Karajan was by the 1970s the movie-star version of himself, as at home in the celebrity magazines as on the podium. He skied, flew his own plane, and had the lighting technician bathe him in a sacred glow when he conducted. When he recorded Wagner's *Ring* for Deutsche Grammophon, a photographer caught him with his arms outstretched, one hand holding Thor's hammer, as if he was about to slay his enemies and rule the world.

It is impossible to imagine any other conductor daring to pose thus, even Leonard Bernstein. Every orchestra wanted to play for von Karajan; every singer wanted to work with him. In his own way, he really *was* ruling the world. To repeat one of opera's best-known jokes, Karajan gets into his limousine and, responding to his driver's "Where to, mein Herr?," replies, "Just drive. I'm in demand everywhere."

His conducting style, interestingly, is hard to describe, and it has changed from time to time. We know of Toscanini's tense precision and Furtwängler's mysterious grandeur. But von Karajan is hard to pin down so neatly, as he could pound some scores into submission and soothe others, navigate in monumental blocks of sound or seek out lovely details others missed.

Above all, von Karajan seemed to weaponize the organs of the music world, taking charge of the Berlin Philharmonic, the Vienna State Opera, and the Salzburg Festival; reigning as La Scala's most evident guest conductor; and making countless much admired recordings for three of the top classical labels, EMI, Decca/London, and the aforementioned DG. Von Karajan summed it up himself when someone accused him of being an elitist. "I am not an elitist," he replied. "I am a *super*-elitist."

Unlike most conductors, he was a famous stage director as well, avidly hands-on in rehearsals, acting everything out for his singers—the gestures, the movements, eyes and teeth, profile, even dance steps. They say he was one of the greatest Carmens of the day, even if he couldn't sing.

So he was not just an amazing talent. He was a personality—and a tyrant. Everything had to be as he demanded it. When he arrived somewhere, during the winter months, he would take off his coat and simply hand it to whoever was handy, as if everyone must be his flunky. And woe betide the singer who fell into his disfavor. In an interview in the German magazine *Der Spiegel* (The Mirror, equivalent to America's *Time*), Birgit Nilsson said she could tell when von Karajan was angry because he would conduct too fast for a singer to make any sort of effect.

The interviewer asked Nilsson what made von Karajan angry, and she replied, "Resistance."

Dialogue Of a Carmelite

The sensation of the Bayreuth Festival in 1939 was Germaine Lubin's Isolde, more womanly and sensual than was usual in the role from what von Karajan called "those innumerable German cannons."

Van Karajan did not conduct at Bayreuth till its postwar reopening, in 1951, but he had been working at Bayreuth in 1939 all the same and he thought he might take an afternoon off to tour Lubin through the countryside in his car. Richard Osborne's *Conversations With Karajan* tells us how he took her to visit a beautifully ornate church, not realizing that the devout Lubin's strictly ascetic spirituality frowned on the vanities. As von Karajan opened the church door, her anticipatory expression of interest turned at once to scorn.

"This is not a church," she announced. "This is a boudoir!"

Never Forget

Richard Osborne was as well von Karajan's biographer, and he gives a startling account of a confrontation between von Karajan and violinist Peter Gibbs. The latter had been an R.A.F. fighter pilot during the war, and carried bad feelings about his experiences, as anyone might.

In this story, von Karajan is touring North America with the Philharmonia Orchestra in 1955. Now, the Philharmonia was a British outfit, and Gibbs, the concertmaster at Covent Garden, was called in to substitute for an ailing player. At the tour's penultimate concert, something happened that seriously disconcerted von Karajan. It is not clear what irritated him, but after a performance of Beethoven's *Pastoral* Symphony, he rudely walked off the stage as if deliberately to ignore the public's applause—to express his scorn for it, even. Nor did he give the orchestra players their customary bow.

With only the last concert left, before the entire contingent, Gibbs rose and excoriated von Karajan for his conduct, and said that he could not tolerate playing under him once more. Apparently, some of the instrumentalists tapped their music stands in sympathy with Gibbs, and, thus supported, the former R.A.F. hero added—this is Osborne's reconstruction of Gibbs' wording—"I spent the most valuable five years of my life destroying the likes of you."

Von Karajan let this pass at the time, but he subsequently demanded that Gibbs be fired—for that one final concert!—and the Philharmonia sign a letter of apology down to the last member of the consort. Neither condition was met. Gibbs played and the orchestra made no kowtow, though an official did render unto Caesar a hastily typed (Osborne: "brusque") apology.

The final concert then went on as planned.

It would perhaps have been typical of the way von Karajan maintained grudges if he abandoned the Philharmonia on his return to Europe, but he continued to record and concertize with them for some years. Sad to say—indeed, heartbreakingly so—one day Peter Gibbs, who like von Karajan maintained his own airplane, flew out over the North Sea and never returned.

A Presentiment

Another von Karajan biographer, Roger Vaughan, spent time with not only the conductor but also his longtime assistant stage director Peter Busse. One day Vaughan was walking down a hallway while von Karajan and another of his staff were a few paces behind Vaughan. Just as the latter reached the doors at the hallway's end, they suddenly opened up as if magically offering welcome to a deity. But no: they had been pushed open by Busse. Vaughan gave him a "How did you know we were about to come through here?" look.

To which Busse answered, "After twenty years, one knows."

The Master Of the Rhythm

In the late 1970s, von Karajan was fêted with an honorary Doctor Of Music from Oxford University at the same time as Dietrich Fischer-Dieskau. The event was typically preceded by a general march down the high street to the thrill of trumpets and organ, and Fischer-Dieskau got into the spirit of the thing with a martial gait.

Whereupon von Karajan hissed at him, "Stop walking in time with the music, dummkopf!"

An Offer He Couldn't Refuse

For some reason, Riccardo Muti is in the habit of receiving telephone calls from Big Music Celebrities while he's in odd outposts in North America. Elsewhere in this book, it's Maria Callas who calls; in this tale (which Muti himself recounted in a documentary on the Salzbug Festival) it's von Karajan.

Muti is in Raleigh, North Carolina, sleeping—because it's seven o'clock in the morning—and the phone rings.

Who is this idiot, Muti wonders, picking up the receiver to hear someone say, in Italian, "This is von Karajan."

Oh, sure it is, Muti thinks. But he quickly realizes from the somewhat squeaky voice (von Karajan's sole personal handicap; even the gods have something) that it is indeed The Great One. He has called to invite Muti to conduct *Così Fan Tutte* at the Salzburg Festival.

Still drowsy, Muti has trouble concentrating. "Maestro, this is very flattering," he gets out. "But…but it's so early in the morning, and…well, I am confused. There is so much to think about. Mozart, the singers, the producing team. And my schedule, which, right now…I mean, of course I would love to, yes, but…if you would give me a few days to get my thoughts in order on this wonderful opportunity…"

And von Karajan, with his usual sympathy and understanding, says, "*Yes or no?*"

> Muti did in fact conduct *Così* in Salzburg, in 1983, with Margaret Marshall and Ann Murray as the sisters and Francesco Araiza and James Morris as the suitors. Michael Hampe directed, in traditional style.

The Travels Of Sarah Caldwell, Introducing the Strange Saga Of Imelda Marcos' Shoes

Caldwell was a one-person opera company, as impresario, music director, stage director, and even fund-raiser. She did everything but sing, reigning as Boston's Official Opera Character from 1958 to 1990.

But Caldwell, an adventurer in the best sense, liked to travel, for instance producing the first *Pelléas et Mélisande* in Russia. At another time, our State Department asked Caldwell to run a music program in the Philippines of Ferdinand Marcos, a purely apolitical junket. While there, Caldwell crossed paths with Imelda Marcos, wife of the dictator and notorious for what must have been the most extensive collection of shoes in the world. Yet, as Imelda explained it, it was actually patriotic: she had been encouraging her people to manufacture handicrafts, but all they wanted to make were shoes. Naturally, they were always presenting Imelda with samples.

"I can't throw the shoes away," Imelda explained to Caldwell. Somebody would take offense. So she took to wearing several pairs of shoes every day. "To show my loyalty to Philippine craftsmen."

No doubt; no doubt. Still, this was unfortunately not a time for anyone to be allied, even apolitically, with the Marcos government. Though Caldwell worked with Philippine musicians under diplomatic protocol, she was still burned in effigy along with the leader himself.

Nevertheless, Caldwell was willing to go anywhere she could make music. For a few years, she ran the Wolf Trap Festival in Vienna, Virginia, where Caldwell found her plans for opera productions ran into protests from management. Caldwell wanted not just the usual items but authentic originals—*Don Carlos* in French with all the cut music restored, American premieres of distinctive works from Rameau to Schoenberg, *Les Troyens* complete to the last note.

Alas, some of the Wolf Trap people wanted country music and rock. Cousin Emmy and Herman's Hermits.

One of them told Caldwell that Wolf Trap should be "for everybody."

And Caldwell replied, "If we aren't careful, it will be for nobody."

One more Caldwell…

My Way or the Highway

Caldwell was to conduct *La Traviata* at the Met with Beverly Sills, and someone from the Met's music department was showing Caldwell the cuts the Met habitually made in the score.

Caldwell listened politely, then said, "I do *La Traviata* without cuts."

"Uh…yes, that may be, Madame Caldwell. But these are the cuts we always use in the house." Not without pride, he added, "This is the Met's *Traviata*."

"Yes, but I conduct Verdi's *Traviata*," Caldwell replied. "Without cuts."

No anecdotes collection would be complete without a few turns from Sir Thomas Beecham, not only witty but utterly lacking in tact...

Hear Ye, Hear Ye!

About to lead the dress rehearsal of Strauss' *Elektra*, Beecham faced his orchestra of over a hundred and said, "Those singers up on the stage believe they are going to be heard. It's up to you and me to make damned sure that they won't be."

The Universal Language

For the first-ever recording of *The Magic Flute*, in 1937, HMV sent Beecham to Germany to work with the Berlin Philharmonic and a starry local cast. Walter Legge, producing the album, had not only to work out the side-breaks for the many 78 discs and deal with the usual artistic catastrophes but also to translate for Beecham, who spoke no German.

Beecham thought it a waste of time. All that back and forth, that hemming and hawing: "Any damned foreigner will understand an Englishman if he speaks slowly and loudly enough!"

A Heck Of a Way To Run a Business

During World War I, Beecham founded The Beecham Opera Company, offering such unusual titles as Ethel Smyth's *The Wreckers* and Arthur Sullivan's *Ivanhoe* amid the classics and conducting virtually everything himself.

So the young Eugene Goosens was curious to learn why Beecham summoned the neophyte to the Beecham house in Cavendish Square. As Goosens recalled much later, Beecham wore "an exquisite mauve dressing gown" over "pink pajamas"—the very model of the impresario-conductor who has everything, including his own opera troupe. But perhaps Beecham had too much of everything, for he had scheduled an evening of two brand-new titles, Smyth's *The Boatswain's Mate* and Charles Villiers Stanford's *The Critic* even as all this producing and coaching and conducting had left him exhausted. All he wanted now was a holiday in Italy.

"Would you care to take over these two works?" he blithely asked Goosens while retrieving the scores from the piano. "Yes? Dear boy, how kind you are. Dame Ethel will be thrilled. Be at the Shaftesbury Theatre tomorrow at ten for a piano rehearsal, and tell them you're taking my place, there's a good chap."

Goosens spent most of the night familiarizing himself with the music, and a week later, in January of 1916, the double bill was presented.

Apparently, it all went very well, too.

There were three conductors named Eugene Goosens—grandfather, father, and son. This Goossens was the son.

To the Bitter End

Beecham is in the middle of an orchestral rehearsal when, all of a sudden, the music gives out.

"Gentlemen, gentlemen," quoth the maestro. "Why have you stopped playing?"

To which the concertmaster replies, "There's nothing left to play, Sir Thomas. We've finished the piece."

"*Thank God!*" Beecham shouts, triumphantly laying down his baton.

This tale has been passed down from everyone in the music world to everyone else, but it's worse than apocryphal, because it couldn't have happened. Beecham would have seen from the score that he was on the last page of the work. And if he knew the music well enough to conduct without a score, he would have known exactly when the piece was over. Nevertheless, numerous stories attest to Beecham's conducting music he didn't really know. In another part of the forest, the young Geraint Evans, singing the *Meistersinger* Nightwatchman, was momentarily thrown off when he heard Beecham, at the podium, cry out, "Where the hell are we?"

I Love Paris

Beecham preferred French music above all, that delicious, seductive melody that teased the cultivated ear; Massenet's *Manon* was more or less his favorite opera. Except for Mozart, Beecham found the German-Austrian sound heavy, even Bach: "Too much counterpoint," and, what is worse, "Protestant counterpoint."

Worst of all was Bruckner. What, even the lyrical Seventh Symphony? Ha! "In the first movement alone," Beecham said, "I took note of six pregnancies and at least four miscarriages."

Now to German lands...

A Tale Of Two Cities

In Vienna, when the orchestra made a mistake, Karl Böhm would say, "In New York, this never happens."

But at the Met, Böhm would greet a mistake with "They never do that in Vienna."

The Hamburger Party

After the Nazi takeover of Germany, in 1933, Böhm, then at the Hamburg Staatsoper, was told by a Party leader that Hamburg's intendant was departing for racial reasons and Böhm could assume the position in his place.

"But first," Böhm was told, "you must join the Party."

"I already belong to a party," Böhm replied.

"Which one? The Nationalists? The [Catholic] Center? The Social Democrats?"

Böhm didn't answer.

"The *Communists*?"

Finally Böhm spoke up. "None of them. Nor to a fraternity or a policemen's or firemen's group. I belong to the Music Party, and that's how it will stay."

It was a story Böhm loved to tell over the years, and he would always conclude with "So now we know why I never did become the general manager in Hamburg, ja?"

Otto Klemperer struck many as stodgy because of his slow tempi, but personally he was full of the dickens...

Oh, You Old Miscreant!

Even at eighty-four, weak and often confused, Klemperer still had enough ginger in him to conduct *Fidelio* at Covent Garden. And his flirtatious side was as sly as ever. At a rehearsal, Margaret Price warned him that she had a cold.

"A cold?" Klemperer replied. "Then you must go to bed at once. With *me!*"

I Heard a Brooklet Rushing

After establishing himself as the preeminent interpreter of the songs of Franz Schubert, Dietrich Fischer-Dieskau turned to conducting, and, newcomer that he was, he asked Klemperer if he would attend Fischer-Dieskau's upcoming performance of a Beethoven symphony and give the aspiring conductor some tips.

"I'm not free," said Klemperer. "I told Georg Solti I'd come hear him sing *Die Schöne Müllerin.*"

The First Door On Your Right

Paul Hindemith was to give one of his very learned lectures in Zürich, followed by a Q and A period. But the lecture was so learned that few in the audience dared try to top it with a question, and a lull soon penetrated the hall.

But then Hindemith spotted a familiar face—Otto Klemperer! Surely he would have something to offer.

"Dr. Klemperer," said Hindemith, "may I call on you to share a question with us?"

"Ja, so," Klemperer replied, getting to his feet. "Where's the men's room?"

We move now to the Italian wing...

Do It Yourself

Tullio Serafin is never mentioned on the short list of the greatest conductors, but he was greatly admired for his stylish readings of Italian opera, with a sweep and finesse that most others lack. He also led an unusual number of first performances, both world and local premieres, from American and British works to Spanish and Russian—*The Emperor Jones, Merry Mount, La Vida Breve, Wozzeck*.

Serafin's dedication, too, was noteworthy. Though he made his debut in 1900, he was still quite active in the early 1960s, for example working closely with Joan Sutherland for her career-making Covent Garden *Lucia di Lamermoor*, as we know. Once, a recording engineer arrived in the hall early on the first day of an opera session. He didn't expect to see anyone else in the room, but there was Tullio Serafin, marking up the orchestra players' parts on the music stands.

Yes, someone else could have done it. But no one else would have done it the way Serafin wanted it done.

Correctly.

Remedial Reading

Carlo Maria Giulini was working with a very famous mezzo at La Scala and found that she was sloppy about the note values in her part.

"You are evening out the notes, signora," Giulini told her. "But surely you can see that they are dotted."

"I can't read music, Maestro," she told him. "Do you want me to sing them longer or shorter?"

Don't Make Me Get Up From This Desk

In 1973, Riccardo Muti was to conduct *Il Trovatore* at the Paris Opéra during the regime of Rolf Liebermann, but Muti was at loggerheads with the stage director, who wanted to combine Verdi's original score with the revision made for the Opéra in 1857. Of course, Verdi would have had to add a ballet, but there were a number of small changes in the vocal scenes as well, including an expanded finale, as in the original everything happens too quickly.

Muti deeply resented this director's interference in what the conductor saw as musical matters, but when he complained to Liebermann, Muti got no satisfaction. Liebermann even warned him not to *dare* thinking of walking out on the production.

"You are too young, Muti," Liebermann snarled, "to rise up against the Opéra! This house is old. It is tradition, it is history. No one is bigger than the Opéra!"

Muti turned around, went to his lodgings to pack, and took the next train back to Italy. He was not too young to know that, in opera, no one is bigger than the conductor.

As they put it in Venice, *In casa mia, commando mi.*

The Desert Song

Let it be said, though, that Muti is a somewhat controversial figure, not least in accusations of personal vanity about his looks, especially his rich, floppy dark hair. It was a favorite tale in musical circles back when Muti was running La Scala that, somehow or other, he became lost in the Sahara Desert, crawling over the sands murmuring, "Water! Water!"

And then he saw it: a glass of water atop a sand dune, just sitting there, waiting for him.

"*Water!*" he cries, frantically dragging himself up to the top of the rise. Will it prove a mirage? The fantasy of a fevered brain?

No! Muti grasps the glass of water…and immediately dips his fingers into it and spruces up his hair.

Tales Of La Scala

The prominence of the Teatro alla Scala in opera history is only partly artistic. For starters, it is the only company in a major cultural capital particularly associated with one composer, as it is often thought of as The House Of Verdi. Bayreuth also offers a House, that of Wagner—but it is located in a small town and was specifically built by Wagner for Wagner, while La Scala, in the industrial center of Milan, was built in 1778, before Verdi was born.

But is La Scala truly Verdi's habitat, speaking historically? His main association with it lies at the very beginning and very end of his career, with, respectively, *Nabucco* and *I Lombardi* in particular and latterly *Otello* and *Falstaff*. As I've said, for much of his creative life Verdi maintained a bitter feud with La Scala, refusing to excuse its—he thought—sloppy performance tactics, and his premieres occurred elsewhere in Italy, in Paris, in London, and even in St. Petersburg. One might well say that La Scala is even more the house of Arturo Toscanini, who led brilliant seasons there, or of Maria Callas, who dominated the calendar of imposing new productions in the 1950s.

In truth, La Scala's prominence is also political, because of the cold war between Italy's very urban and cultured North and its largely peasant-class South, the place of—derogatively—the *terroni*, roughly meaning "big stupid people of the big stupid earth." There is even a racial bias in this, as the northerners descend from the "first" Italians, the mysterious Etruscans (and Germans, particularly around the Lombardy of La Scala's vicinity), while the southerners are Greeks. Excepting Sicily, there is only one major opera house in the South, in Naples, while the North has (besides La Scala) Venice, Turin, Trieste, Florence, Bologna, and, in central Italy, in this cold war's no man's land, Rome.

La Scala was originally locked into a little side-street, facing a row of houses with no breathing room; later, these were demolished to open up a piazza to give physical authority to The First Theatre in Italy. It boasted the best orchestra in the land and by the late 1800s was as much a conductor's as a singer's house, not least in the reign of Toscanini, which began in 1898. This was an era marked by intensive reformation, building an orchestra pit (until about 1900, orchestras played on the floor, distracting spectators and blocking their view of the stage), banning encores, darkening the auditorium during the performance, reimposing the curtain to part from the center rather than move up and down, and forcing women in the parquet to remove their hats.

The Scala public *hated* being disciplined in this way—encores substantiated their interactive presence—but Toscanini's white-hot performances woke everyone out of routine into the sublime. Toscanini's aforementioned revival of Puccini's *Manon Lescaut*, for instance, startled the house with its power—how could Milan's music lovers not have appreciated this piece before?

Thus, La Scala's prestige grew. Interviewed by Lanfranco Rasponi, Maria Caniglia recalled, "Once La Scala announced you for a new role...there came an avalanche of requests to repeat it in other theatres....If I was treated like a queen at Covent Garden...and many other distinguished opera houses, it was all due to the fame La Scala had conferred on me."

No wonder Maria Callas made conquering this house in particular her personal crusade. Comparably, however famous Joan Sutherland's Lucia di Lammermoor had become in many theatres, it was nonetheless not properly established till she had deposited it in her La Scala account. And it must be said that, though today's opera houses maintain a venturesome repertory, in the postwar years that marked the end of the Golden Age, only La Scala pursued the agenda of spanning epochs and cultures, with Handel here and Dallapiccola there, now featuring the bel canto revival and then unveiling a world premiere.

The stagings, too, outplayed the plodding conservatism of the Met and the often low-budget look at Covent Garden. Photographs of the original production of Tippett's *The Midsummer Marriage* reveal a few slats of cardboard fit to shame a village runthrough of Gilbert and Sullivan. And at the Paris Opéra, while set designs did call on artists such as Fernand Léger and Erté, the casting was provincial.

La Scala, by contrast, was an international opera temple, even as an official Italian national treasure. At an important prima, the auditorium thrums with prideful anticipation—yet, ironically, there is the "other" La Scala high up in the topmost balcony, where one senses instead the gleeful fury of the *loggionisti*. These professional aficionados often bait singers for the slightest of errors, even for extra-musical reasons.

So, at certain times, a night at the opera is like attending a prizefight. In an interview with Andrew Clark in the British *Opera* magazine, Scots soprano Marie McLaughlin recalled her La Scala debut, imperiled when Luciano Pavarotti pulled out of their *L'Elisir d'Amore* after a tiff with the conductor at the dress rehearsal. No Pavarotti? And who is this McLaughlin, anyway?

In fact, the performance proceeded uneventfully until the last few minutes of the opera, when McLaughlin heard shouts of "Va via, Scozese!" (Get lost, Scot!) and "Noi abbiamo Italiane meglio di te!" (We have Italians better than you!).

"Since then," McLaughlin told Clark, "I've spoken to colleagues who have also had bad experiences there, and who just stick it out and get their fees.... But why should I take that abuse?" She was willing to dare a solo call, even though management insisted on group bows, the better to weather the booing. But after that night, McLaughlin packed up and went home.

Asking For a Friend

Playing 'cello in the orchestra for the Scala premiere of Verdi's *Otello*, in 1887, Toscanini was distressed when the composer didn't appear to notice that a passage for the 'celli marked moltissimo pianissimo (very, very, very quietly) was being played merely pianissimo (very quietly).

Approaching Verdi, Toscanini asked why the maestro was not insisting on hearing the suavely subtle effect he had asked for in the score.

"Beh," came the reply. "I only wanted it very quietly. But if I asked for that, I'd get mezzo forte [somewhat loud]. You have to trick them into playing what you want, because they are too lazy to understand extremes. Mark it moltissimo pianissimo and you will get a fine pianissimo, *corretto*."

The Red Shoes Will Not Be Danced Tonight

Toscanini became principal conductor at La Scala for the 1898–1899 season, opening with a *Meistersinger* notable for being played for the first time in Italy, as *I Maestri Cantori di Norimberga*, and with almost no cuts. Antonio Scotti's Sachs headed the cast, and the production was a triumph, though Toscanini knew that everyone, from the critics to the *loggionisti*, was secretly irritated by the work's length.

The second opera in the Toscanini regime was *Norma*, a piece Toscanini both loved and feared because it is too easy to do badly. For his Norma, Toscanini cast Ines De Frate, an excellent singer of the old school, navigating entirely around the music rather than the words. Hers was a beautiful but not dramatic art, and Norma's music is both beautiful and dramatic. At the end of Act One of the dress, Toscanini stood immobile at the podium while the orchestra players got up and stretched and wandered off.

Noting how pensive and troubled Toscanini looked, Duke Uberto Visconti di Modrone (father of the film and stage director Luchino Visconti) rose from his seat in the auditorium and asked the conductor what was wrong. The duke was the president of La Scala, a scion of one of the oldest families in Europe, and in effect the most responsible man in all of Milan, and if something troubled La Scala's music director, Visconti must know.

But the trouble, really, was a cataclysm in the history of Italian opera. Just a few years before this, the premiere of *Cavalleria Rusticana* as well as that of *Pagliacci* (conducted by Toscanini, at that) unveiled the new art of verismo, the "realism" that would influence not only subject matter but vocal style. Veristic opera told of people pushed to the brink in often violent stories, and bel canto would very quickly give way to emphatic, passionate singing. This innovation would govern not only new music but the old music as well.

Of course, Toscanini wouldn't have wanted his artists turning *Norma* into a shouting match. Still, he was aware that opera was going to be—had already become—less about sheer melody and more about intensity. Ines De Frate's Druid priestess was simply too sweet for the new veristic sensibility.

And Toscanini canceled the production then and there. The announcement rocked not only La Scala but all Milan, and the critics then fell on Toscanini like wolves in wolves' clothing. But there was nothing to be done. This was Toscanini's La Scala now, and any *Norma* it presented would be Toscanini's *Norma*.

Verdi Let Me, So Why Can't You?

In 1899, for his second year as La Scala's principal conductor, Toscanini gave *Otello* a new production with its original lead, Francesco Tamagno, only twelve years after the premiere. One of the outstanding tenors of the day—the *Concise Oxford Dictionary Of Opera* calls him "the greatest tenore di forza of all time"— Tamagno was given to taking liberties with his music. He liked transpositions, but where other tenors wanted the music lowered in key, Tamagno wanted it raised, to show off his brilliant top notes.

That he would dare this with the rigorous Toscanini tells us how big Tamagno was. He even wanted the love duet reimposed in a higher key though his exhibitionistic *squillo* would destroy the loving stillness of the end of Act One.

"Just a semitone higher," Tamagno told Toscanini, quite casually. "Verdi let me do it on opening night."

"I was playing 'cello in the orchestra on opening night," Toscanini told him, "and Verdi did no such thing!"

The conductor appealed to the highest authority—Verdi himself—and the great maestro was dumbfounded. "I do my best to set down the music in proper fashion," he said. "Yet Tamagno isn't singing what I wrote?"

"He isn't singing anything," said Toscanini, bitterly. "He's screaming his way through the entire opera. But send for him, maestro, please. Only you can tame this wild horse."

Tamagno was staying in that very hotel, and he was with the two in short order.

"Do I hear this correctly, Tamagno?" Verdi asked him. "You are singing your own Otello? In my opera?"

"Beh," Tamagno replied. "I'm only helping the music along. You composers never know what you want."

Rare Praise

Now we find Toscanini preparing a production of *Mefistofele* with Caruso as Faust and, in his La Scala debut, Fyodor Shalyapin as the devil.

At a piano rehearsal, the Russian bass marked his way through his part, so Toscanini was unable to judge his performance. He asked if Shalyapin intended to tread the holy boards of La Scala singing in half-voice, so Shalyapin dutifully sang out from then on—but he noticed that Toscanini constantly stopped the music to discuss some fine point with the other singers and never said a word to Shalyapin.

The Russian wasn't sure how to take this. The following day, they all rehearsed again, and once more Shalyapin sang out as he would in performance, and this time Toscanini did say something, because suddenly he stopped, sitting there at the keyboard, and quietly uttered, in the hoarse tone one sometimes heard when he was moved by the power of music, "Bravo."

He Plays the Violin

Filippo Sacchi's *Toscanini* recalls the conductor's war against a violinist in the Scala orchestra who would enter into a dainty ballet every time he had to play—adjusting the handkerchief for his chin, limbering up his address of the bow, and assorted other minstrations which were not only exhibitionistic but absurd because the violins seldom stop playing during an opera in the first place.

Yet every time Toscanini had to cue the strings, there was this one character, by name Licari, up to his games and sometimes so busy with them that he failed to come in on time.

Finally, Toscanini had had it. "You are a lazy scoundrel!" he cried. "You always prepare at the last moment, doing that minuet with your fiddle! I want to see the strings ready to play two measures before their entrance, do you understand that? Or next year you'll be playing in a music hall!"

Licari, feigning puzzlement, turned to the player next to him with "Whom is he talking to?"

"I'm talking to you," Toscanini shouted, "with your sleazy magician's tricks!"

"Well, so what?" Licari replied, provoking more vituperation from Toscanini, at which Licari packed up and left.

"Finally!" The conductor cried. "That fool has been irritating me for years!"

Licari then opened a legal objection, but as the judge seemed to feel Toscanini was justified in criticism for art's sake, Licari withdrew his complaint.

This necessitated a signature from Licari on the document of record, and as he took up the pen, Toscanini's lawyers' heads exploded as the conductor said, *What an idiot!*

Down With Everything!

After the wild success of *Salome* and *Elektra*, interest in Richard Strauss' next opera, *Der Rosenkavalier*, was keen, and La Scala mounted a production (in Italian) less than two months after the Dresden premiere. Tullio Serafin conducted, Lucrezia Bori sang Octavian, and Strauss was there, along with, among other boldface names, Giacomo Puccini and Arrigo Boito.

Also in the audience, in the topmost gallery, was a band of Italian futurists. This idiosyncratic movement, led by Filippo Marinetti and scarcely two years old, was clearer on what it was against than what it was for, as the futurists' many manifestos were vague even when specifying. (Sample title: "Let's Kill the Moonlight.")

But futurism knew what it liked, and it liked *Salome* and *Elektra* because their bloodthirsty action and unconventional harmonic palette was definitely *new*, and futurism, whatever else it was, was new as well.

However, *Der Rosenkavalier* was not new. Suddenly—to futurist thinking—Strauss was backsliding into burzhui kitsch, and though Act One passed amiably enough, Act Two, with its solemnly lovely Presentation Of the Rose, infuriated the gang in the gallery. They began shouting and whistling and even threw down copies of the latest manifesto, without which no committed futurist ever found himself.

And those waltzes! What is this, a ballet? When does Giselle come on?

The prelude to Act Three went well because—as Strauss himself noted in a letter—it was taken as some newfangled German thing and thus not anti-futurist. But once the curtain rose and the waltzes started up again, the shouting returned. There was noise until the Marschallin's entrance, when the futurists finally gave up. They let the final trio and duet proceed in silence, and the applause at the end was quite satisfactory.

Still, Strauss summed it up as "the battle royal of Milan."

Born To Be Mad

Toscanini was planning a production of *Lucia Di Lammermoor* with Toti dal Monte, whose plangent style made her a public favorite. She was also a little hyper, but then so is Lucia.

As usual, the conductor worked very hard with the singers, coaxing and badgering them through every line of their parts and staging the scenes meticulously. Still, only days before the premiere, he had not gotten to the Mad Scene, the high point of every *Lucia*.

"Maestro," Toti began—but carefully, now!—we haven't gone over the Mad Scene yet. How do you think it should go?"

"You've been crazy all your life, dal Monte," Toscanini replied. "Why do you have to rehearse it now?"

We Don't Need Your Help

After reopening in the post–World War II peacetime, La Scala grudgingly put on a *Wozzeck* in 1952, knowing it would sell poorly. The few people who did attend would hate it, and the house would have to hire specialists to sing it.

Atonal and expressionistic though it was, *Wozzeck* had all the same become a prestige point in the opera world: a house that couldn't produce it looked unskilled. Even the Metropolitan Opera, with its extremely conservative public, would put *Wozzeck* on, in the 1950s, and with a superb cast. So La Scala had to stage its own *Wozzeck*, bringing in Tito Gobbi for the title role and Dimitri Mitropoulos to conduct.

La Scala's chief conductor, Victor de Sabata, couldn't resist intruding on a rehearsal with a snooty air, walking around on stage in scornful supremacy and staring at Mitropoulos as if to unnerve him. The Greek conductor had nerves of steel, however, and simply ignored everything but the work at hand.

So finally de Sabata piped up with the suggestion that the cast and orchestra must be tired of work on this terribly demanding piece. It was time, he said, for everyone to go home and recover.

Whereupon Mitropoulos replied, "Thank you, Maestro, but none of us is tired, and we'll continue rehearsing. But perhaps you are tired? Yes? So we must not keep you. Arrivederci."

Cut to the quick at this dismissal—in his own theatre!—de Sabata scurried away. But Mitropoulos was never welcome at La Scala after that, and Gobbi himself felt that, ever after, he had to navigate his Italian career around rather than in La Scala.

A Hush Descends

The conservative *scaligeri* (as La Scala's audience regulars are called) had never heard *Wozzeck* before, but they knew that it was "modern," so, from the moment the curtain rose, the hissing, whistling, and catcalls began.

Suddenly, Mitropoulos stopped the orchestra and singers, and, turning to the public, asked for silence so that the company might concentrate on the difficult score.

"At the end," Mitropoulos told them, "you can tell us what you think of the music."

Incredibly, they accepted the offer, and quietly listened to the opera for all three acts.

And *then* the screaming began.

Bon Appetit

It frustrated the Scala management that it could present that tune-less German thing of a *Wozzeck* yet fail to do justice to the summum bonum of Italian music, Bellini's *Norma*. The house did occasionally program the work during the twentieth century, for instance with Maria Caniglia in 1950. She took on the part on behalf of national honor, admitting that she developed tricks to get around the intricate coloratura.

So it was a highly subtextual moment when Antonio Ghiringhelli, chief of La Scala, ran into Tullio Serafin, dining with Maria Callas and her husband, Giovanni Battista Meneghini,[1] at Biffi Scala, the tony restaurant hard by the opera house. Ghiringhelli knew nothing of opera—his was a political appointment, like many such in post-war Italy—and was as well a hypocrite and opportunist, given to boasting and evasions. Speaking metaphorically, one could say he was always looking over your shoulder into the opera world to see what important people he might talk to instead of you.

Serafin and Ghiringhelli hated each other; though the conductor led many of EMI's "La Scala" recordings, he refused to conduct live performances in the house as long as Ghiringhelli was running it. Still, protocol demanded that they greet each other with some measure of phony respect, though Ghiringhelli ignored the Meneghinis completely. But Serafin had a plan in mind: to bring the subject around to *Norma* and to indicate Callas as the Norma of choice,

---

1. Meneghini's given names are the Italian for John [the] Baptist. Also very popular in Italy, then and now, is Giovanni Maria (John Mary), so much so that, when filling out the certificate, if the parents choose Giovanni as their new son's first name, the clerk will then ask, "E Battista o Maria?"

thus to lead Ghiringhelli into engaging Callas to sing the opera at La Scala.

"Have you heard," Serafin began, "what a triumph we had with *Norma* in Argentina? Historic!"

Ghiringhelli wasn't glad, though he didn't say so. Not only was his Caniglia *Norma* more Caniglia than *Norma*, but it took Ghiringhelli three tenors to get through four performances. He knew that La Scala couldn't put on *Norma* without Callas. But he hated Callas and had sworn to bar his house to her.

"La Scala can raise up a splendid *Norma* at any time," Ghiringhelli boasted. "You will see."

"Will I?" Serafin replied, in a tone that promised that he wouldn't.

"La Scala is the greatest opera house in the world. And *Norma* is the greatest opera. They will go together beautifully, as all will agree."

"I am from Rottanova di Cavarzere," Serafin said, "a village in the Veneto, southwest of the lagoon. We are known for a famous rice dish. We call it 'Risotto alla pilota.' "

Ghiringhelli was doing his "looking over the shoulder" move to see if he could ditch this group for more exploitable quarry.

But Serafin, unperturbed, went on with "Do you know what you need to make Risotto alla pilota?"

Ghiringhelli gave Serafin a look. What do I want from this old has-been with his risotto and resentments, alfine? But he took the bait. "And what do you need," Ghiringhelli asked, "to make this rice dish?"

"The rice."

So Tall My Lady

Renata Tebaldi and Mario Del Monaco often sang together in the 1950s, and some must have thought it touching that, before their every performance, without fail, Del Monaco would visit Tebaldi in her dressing room. But it wasn't a good-luck call.

As Tebaldi often explained, "He was sensitive about being too short, and he would check up on me, to be certain I wasn't wearing high heels!"

Elvis Has Left the Building

Giuseppe di Stefano was another of those old-fashioned artists who wanted to come out on stage and sing, *netto*. Rehearsing was a waste of time to him, because he played every role in the same way. Yet here was that Luchino Visconti to direct Maria Callas and di Stefano in *La Traviata* and *fare il prepotente* (throwing his weight around) with his crazy ideas. *Ehi*, the chorus is not turning fast enough! That umbrella looks too modern!

Well, *ehi*, Visconti, they don't come to opera for the chorus and umbrellas. And of course he's building the whole production around Maria, because when it's a question of the great Callas, all must worship as if the Madonna had taken up Verdi on the stage of La Scala!

On opening night, conductor Carlo Maria Giulini broke the house rule and beckoned Callas on for a solo bow, and the house erupted in the biggest ovation ever heard in the place. Behind the curtain, di Stefano fumed impotently and then stormed out of the building and canceled his remaining Alfredos. Never again would he appear in a Visconti production, he vowed.

And never again would he share the stage with la Callas! Of course, he did change his mind about that. In fact, they became lovers.

Let us slip out of the chronology temporarily for a few stories about Margherita Wallmann, one of La Scala's greatest stage directors…

Bruno Walter ♡ Margherita I

A ballerina who gave up dancing after an accident and so turned to choreographing and then directing, Wallmann was especially noted for her handling of the extras in crowd scenes, creating superb stage pictures with subtle rhythms of chorus movement timed to the music. Thus, after a Salzburg *Orfeo ed Euridice*, when she congratulated Bruno Walter on how well he had led the orchestra, Walter replied, "I? Conduct? I completely forgot all about that because I was so busy looking at the stage!"

Bruno Walter ♡ Margherita II

When Wallmann directed Weber's *Oberon* at La Scala, Walter wanted her to use children as the elves in the first scene, set in fairyland. Wallmann said no, because, she felt, children are so amateurish that they throw everyone else off. Worse, they're so cute that the audience dotes on them and forgets to follow the action. So Walter had to settle for grownups.

But then, a bit later, at a summit meeting among the Salzburg bigwigs, during a discussion about reviving the *Oberon*, Walter leaned over to Wallmann and said, "Ma chère amie, this year I really want you to give me some children."

At which, the stuffy Salzburg Festival board members went deathly silent.

Wallmann then explained what Walter actually meant, and everyone heaved a sigh of relief. I think she should have left it where it was; stuffy meetings with stuffy suits need a teasing or two.

What?

Conductor Clemens Krauss telephoned Wallmann to say, "It's not very nice of you to refuse to collaborate with your old director of the [Vienna] State Opera."

Wallmann was dumbfounded. What collaboration?

Krauss explains: "Didn't I ask for you particularly for the Scala *Die Liebe Der Danaë* after our production at Salzburg, and didn't the Scala management say you refused because you're busy with the ballet?"

When Wallmann finally gets a word in after Krauss' lengthy spiel, she assures him that she knows nothing of this. In fact, she has been begging La Scala's Secretary General Luigi Oldani for a chance to direct an opera, but he keeps her locked up with the dancers.

So now Wallmann confronts Oldani, bursting into his office to demand to know why he didn't go along with Krauss' request to let her direct the Italian premiere of Strauss' last opera.

"My dear Margherita," Oldani begins, "you are a wonderful choreographer, and we don't want to lose you. But if we gave you the commission to direct the *Danaë*, you would have a disaster, and then we couldn't hire you for anything."

"And why would I have a disaster? I have already staged this opera with success."

"Yes, among the *forestieri* (foreigners) in Salzburg. Very chic, no doubt. But for a major new production at La Scala, the first theatre of Italy... well, the dancers would go on strike for a start. And as for the singers, my dear..."

"And why would that happen?"

"Because no one in Italy will take orders from a woman."

In the end, Wallmann did direct that *Danaë*, in 1952, as Krauss told Oldani he wouldn't conduct without her. The work was somewhat less than a hit, and a young Régine Crespin, hired to cover the title role and promised the last of the performances, never went on, as the run was ended after four nights. Still, Wallmann then became a fixture at La Scala as a director, so somebody got something out of *Danaë* after all.

Climb Every Mountain

One of Wallmann's assignments at La Scala was the world premiere of Poulenc's *Dialogues des Carmelites*, such a success in Wallmann's staging that she then directed the piece in London, Vienna, Lisbon, Monte Carlo, and all over Italy. This saga of the martyrdom of a convent during the French Revolution struck something in Wallmann so profoundly that her production was regarded as one of the don't-miss events of the music world.

Among those entranced by Wallmann's *Carmelites* was a group of nuns who saw it in Palermo. Visiting backstage after the show, the Mother Superior asked Wallmann, "But how were you able to make our sisters sing so well?"

"They aren't nuns, Reverend Mother," Wallmann answered. "They're opera singers wearing habits. Of course, we've tried to get them to act like sisters, for verisimilitude."

"It's not possible! I recognize them, because we have them, too—the mean one, the proud one, the lively little one with a playful side. Oh yes, they are brides of God, to be sure."

Rossini From the Bottom Up

In 1962, La Scala presented Joan Sutherland (and her co-star, Giulietta Simionato) with a grand production of *Semiramide*, under

Wallmann's direction and conducted by Gabriele Santini. At one early rehearsal, the staging required Joan to turn upstage, and Santini was not pleased. He thought the opera itself a grotesque old carnival of *aria fritta* (hot air), and Wallmann, to his mind, was just moving everyone around like chess pieces without a strategy.

And now here was Wallmann getting the queen of wherever this stupid opera was set to look away from the podium so she couldn't follow the beat.

"What do I see now?" he cried, rhetorically, thinking Joan couldn't speak Italian. "*Un culo inglese!*" (An English behind!)

Turning around and looking him spang in the eye, she corrected him with "*Australiano, maestro!*"

The Worst La Scala Scandal Ever

In 1982, La Scala revived the 1957 Visconti-Callas-Simionato-Raimondi-Rossi-Lemeni *Anna Bolena*, a historically imposing production. Montserrat Caballé and Yelyena Obraztsova were the new stars, along with the unknown tenor Antonio Savastano and the Met bass Paul Plishka—dependable but lacking in spark—under the high-strung conductor Giuseppe Patanè, guaranteed to fall to pieces at the slightest unease in the house.

At this time, the operating rules of opera were: One, Puccini sells out and Pfitzner doesn't; Two, You can cut the ballet, as it's always terrible, anyway; and, Three, On important occasions, Caballé will cancel.

So of course she did. Having studied at the Bette Davis School of Walking Out On a Work Of Music Theatre, Caballé looked at the menu and chose Stomach Chaos, leaving La Scala without a leading lady in a role that few sopranos know.

The *scaligero* management decided to admit the public to the opera's prima without letting anyone know that the uncelebrated Ruth Falcon would be taking the title role. With everyone in place, a voice on the loudspeaker announced the substitution. It would be an understatement to say that, directly after, hell broke loose.

That was not unexpected. What *was* unexpected was the intense participation of not just the *loggionisti* but everybody in the house, men and women, pit and boxes, young and old, near and far, sweet and cold.

Those who were there say they had never experienced anything like it. The storm was such that conductor Patanè didn't even attempt to start the music but simply fled the theatre. Then came a second announcement through the loudspeaker: the performance was now canceled.

Opera is always news in Italy, especially opera at La Scala, and headlines trumpeted reports that the entire run of *Bolena*s had been suspended. However, Caballé did show up for one performance, which was deeply, madly, truly booed, because there is a Fourth Rule: There is no excuse for canceling all the time.

Ruth Falcon did appear, but then even she canceled, and finally Cecilia Gasdia took over. Her voice is perhaps too lyric for the role, but she made a strong impression and earned a righteous success. Rule Five: It takes guts.

Expert to Expert

For a big magazine piece on La Scala, American Albert Innaurato was given a safe-conduct to wander through the life of the house in coaching sessions, full rehearsals, and performances. This was during the regime of Riccardo Muti, who, Innaurato revealed, knew everything about vocal production—"the diaphragm, the tongue, keeping the voice forward, helping with breath."

Where did Muti learn all that? Muti offered a wager. He would ask Innaurato a question, and if Innaurato could answer it, Muti would take him to lunch at Milan's fanciest restaurant. If Innaurato failed, he would lose his head—no, this is not *Turandot*. If he failed he had to give up one full day of following Muti around and getting statements for the magazine piece.

The question was: "Who was Maria Carbone?"

Only an expert would know, and Innaurato did: the first Desdemona in a complete *Otello* recording (in 78 days, with Nicola Fusati and Apollo Granforte), she was, Muti put in, the singers' singer, with occult knowledge on the physical foundations of voice production. She taught Muti what he knew—and now he threw out a second question: Who was Aureliano Pertile?

Innaurato responded with "The greatest purely Italian spinto tenor of the [twentieth] century."

A third question: What was his best recording?

This answer is inevitable; all lovers of Golden Age vocal art know it: "The Improvviso from *Chenier*."

Muti must have been stunned. An American knows this? Even Italians don't know this.

"Well, I hope you're hungry," Muti concluded. "I owe you two lunches."

Lucky Stiff

While Innaurato was taking this embed at La Scala, Muti pointed out photos of the famous conductors who dared the fury of the *loggionisti* in the topmost balcony—von Karajan, Abbado, Böhm, Carlos Kleiber, and others.

"All have been booed," Muti told Innaurato, "except this one."

He pointed out Toscanini's mentee Guido Cantelli, who was appointed principal conductor but then passed away in a plane crash.

"He was lucky," Muti observed. "He died."

This Evening's Performance Of *La Traviata* Will Be Accompanied On the Piano By Maestro Riccardo Muti

The cast was good enough: Tiziana Fabbricini, Ramón Vargas, and Juan Pons. But half an hour before curtain time La Scala's general manager, Carlo Fontana, told Muti that the orchestra was going to strike. The public was already seated when the announcement was made, and an infuriated house shouted imprecations and refused to leave. Enough of these strikes! We came to hear *La Traviata* and we're going to hear *La Traviata*!

Or else!

So Muti decided to give them the opera alone at the keyboard. Somebody located a baby grand somewhere and Muti had it moved onto the stage. However, the incline of the deck caused the instrument to roll toward the orchestra pit; the stagehands had to hammer wedges around the leg wheels to keep it steady. Luckily, the technicians weren't respecting the strike.

But the chorus was. To the last man and woman, they went home. Now Muti had to face the public and prepare them for Verdi with neither orchestra players nor chorus singers. As he appeared, noises of irritation rose up to greet him. Then, suddenly... nothing. They waited in wary silence to see what new surprise their marvelous La Scala had to offer.

But when Muti told them of his plan, everyone shouted, "Bravo!" It was On With the Show—and, as the ballet dancers remained loyal, they could fill out the two party scenes in place of the chorus. Of course, some of the opera had to be cut without the ensemble, but the big finale at Flora's soirée was included even so, sung by the principals alone as an octet.

At the end, the audience responded with immense enthusiasm, and the Scala press people alerted the RAI, the national airwave office, so television crews were on hand, and the event made global headlines. It was a victory snatched from the jaws of a scandal, but, in the end, Muti felt that everyone, from Verdi to the public, had been betrayed by the orchestra, and from then on his relations with them were never the same.

Blame Of Thrones

In 2006, Roberto Alagna was singing Radames and feeling that the *loggionisti* were out to get him. One night, his "Celeste Aida," nicely sung and crowned with a solid top B Flat, was being applauded when, as if on cue, the *loggionisti* cut in with thunderous boos.

Alagna made a rude gesture at them, moved vaguely toward stage left, and then turned around and defiantly marched off in the opposite direction. By then, however, the Amneris had made her entrance. Finding no one to sing to, she sang anyway. And then, improbably, Alagna's cover, Antonello Palombi, ran in in his street clothes and a wild mane of uncombed hair to take over Radames' music.

The Italian press sided against Alagna, calling him "un bambino capriccioso" (a wilful child). Still, one feels that the booing had nothing to do with anyone's singing. Rather, it was about the people who just enjoy making goons of themselves in temples of art.

To cap this section, let us consider the singer who was arguably the essential La Scala artist...

MARIA CALLAS

Born in Manhattan and spending her student years in Athens during World War II, Callas sang in many cities at first, all over Italy and in South America. However, as she became prominent, stories began to circulate turning her into a Warholian legend of who she "was" as much as for her singing itself. It made her too big for the provinces, and she concentrated on the cultural capitals of the West.

Venice was the first, very early on in 1949, for that is where she sang the *Walküre* Brünnhilde and—learning the music in just ten days to deputize for Margherita Carosio—Elvira in *I Puritani*: from dramatic soprano to lyric coloratura, a feat scarcely heard of since the nineteenth century.

It was so shocking it made headlines throughout Italy, and, as always with Callas, a story goes with it. She had dropped in on conductor Tullio Serafin, but he was out, and while waiting she sat at the piano, where the *Puritani* score was on the music rack. Playing through it and singing along, Callas struck Serafin's wife (herself an opera singer) as a potential Elvira, Brünnhilde or not. Callas had the notes, the passage work, even the Bellinian style. Stunned at a Valkyrie's persuasive vocalism in music long thought of as the property of canaries, Madame Serafin urged her husband to let Callas save the *Puritani*. And Serafin had to admit that it *sounded* right.

But "Surely there's someone else for this," Callas told him.

"We've tried every Elvira in Europe," he said. "They're all busy." Callas, ever suspicious of everything, wasn't certain, and Serafin concluded his pitch with "It's you or no one."

Thinking it over, Callas demanded twenty-four hours to have a look at the score and see if she could do it. And Serafin, the *Puritani* conductor, would coach her through it page by page. But she must have known that she could do it, even that she had to, because she was ready to abandon the Big Lady roles she had been specializing in for the archons of bel canto espressività—Lucia, Violetta, Norma. And Callas said yes.

Another place crucial to the Callas saga is Mexico City, where, just after the Venice *Puritani*, she began to try out Bellini, Donizetti, Verdi. Another story: the tenor in *Aida* was irritating her with his rush-hour exhibitionism, and, with the blessing of her other colleagues, Callas capped the Triumphal Scene with an interpolated high E Flat that remains one of the most famous notes in opera history.

Florence, too, figures importantly in Callas' career, as she gave that city a spectacular Elena in *I Vespri Siciliani* under Erich Kleiber that, broadcast throughout Italy, turned the nation's opinion-makers toward Callas and made it necessary for La Scala to invite her to join the company. In a way, that *Vespri* was the most important performance Callas ever gave.

There was America, too—Chicago, where a process server slipped past security (supposedly at the connivance of one of the higher-ups) to hit Callas with paper on a nuisance suit she had been dodging for years. Notoriously, Callas stalked behind the escaping legal messenger in agita fit for Medea, as a photographer preserved the moment. (Was he, too, enabled by whoever it was that had it in for the diva? She collected enemies the way robins find worms.)

Of course, New York was another central Callas port of call, where she set forth her Norma, Lucia, Violetta, and—her one concession to what she thought of as "pop music"—Tosca. After two seasons of complaining about the insipid quality of the Metropolitan's productions, she was to sing Verdi's Lady Macbeth in a new staging, but she stalled on signing the contract till (as we know) Rudolf Bing fired her. Dallas, too, was a Callas town, and it's where she was singing Medea when she learned that Bing had dropped her. Every time she looked at her Jason, the audience knew what she thought of Bing.

But above all there was Milan, because to a singer in the Italian repertory, La Scala was the zenith. There Callas appeared in her most famous stagings, built around her by Luchino Visconti and Margherita Wallmann. The former's specialty was unified productions in which the music seemed to "create" everything that happened onstage. Thus, the delicacy of Bellini inspired a *Sonnambula* in which Callas appeared as a nineteenth-century ballerina, bejeweled and moving in the mincing steps of a fragile dancer. Spontini's *La Vestale*, on the other hand, was Baroque in texture, everyone looking like figures in an antique print.

Adding to this was Callas' own identification with the characters, so that her *Sonnambula* Amina was Callas as she is: genius betrayed by everybody on false grounds. Or her Violetta, in Visconti's Scala *Traviata*, was likewise so treacherously used that, in the last act, she seemed dying not of consumption but a lack of appreciation—which really could be the pull quote for the Callas story itself.

Opera buffs traveled from afar if necessary to attend these performances. They couldn't delay, for Callas had only twelve good years, something like 1948 to 1960. After that, her voice, already weakened and badly supported at the top, began to unravel. Was it because she juxtaposed dramatic roles with lyric ones on an instrument that had not been securely placed from the start? Was it her famous weight loss, a costly glamour? Was it the intrusion into her life of Aristotle Onassis, who took her over by distracting her concentration on music?

Callas survived a terrible upbringing by a mother who made her feel worthless, which (in a typical irony of the paradigm of troubled artists) only drove her to become the most absolute of divas in the highest form of theatre, drama and music as one. Her destiny promised that others would deliver more beautiful art but none a more honest art. And her destiny warned her that she had to give up happiness to achieve this. But her destiny soothed her with, again, It's you or no one.

And Callas said yes.

That High E Flat In Aida

After hearing Callas and Giulietta Simionato rehearsing a Mexico City *Norma*, the company's interpreter contacted the intendant, Antonio Caraza-Campos, to say that Callas was the greatest dramatic-coloratura he had ever heard, including Rosa Ponselle. And what high notes!

Mexico City opera fans were wild for high notes, so Caraza-Campos hurried over, bearing the score of *I Puritani* and asking to hear Callas run through some music to sample her high E Flat.

But Callas does not audition. If he wants to hear her E Flat, he can sign her to sing *I Puritani* the following season.

Ah, but Caraza-Campos had another score in his library, an *Aida* that belonged to the nineteenth-century singer Angela Peralta, the "Mexican nightingale." In her score, Peralta had written in the high E Flat with which she capped the ensemble at the end of the Triumphal Scene. Caraza-Campos promised Callas a spectacular success if she, too, would sing this high E Flat in her *Aida*.

But it is not Verdian, Callas protested. It is ungainly, exhibitionistic. This kind of thing was common in the bel canto era but long gone by the time Verdi wrote *Aida*. And Callas would have to ask her colleagues how they felt about it. It is all so complicated and impossible.

But Simionato thought it would be fun. And then Callas had a tiff with tenor Kurt Baum at the dress rehearsal of *Norma*. Baum was to be Radames in *Aida* as well, and Callas wondered if perhaps a wild and crazy high E Flat in the Triumphal Scene would put him in his place.

With the other singers' assents, Callas did indeed give the Mexican public Peralta's high E Flat in *Aida*, and, as the archival recording attests, the audience went mad with joy. Only Kurt Baum was unhappy.

"You will never sing with me again!" he cried, as Callas was repeatedly called before the curtain for a solo bow. "I will bar the Metropolitan to you!"

As she went out to accept her ovation, Callas merely smiled and replied, "We will see about that."

There actually were two high E Flats in Callas' *Aida*, as she encored the stunt in Mexico City the following year. There is no record of her having done it anywhere else.

Dewey, Cheetam & Howe

Callas began in shame at her lack of physical appeal, but somehow or other (legendarily through the application of a tapeworm) she suddenly lost weight in the early 1950s, becoming so glamorous that singers she had performed with didn't recognize her.

So it made perfect sense that, in 1954, a pasta company, Pantanella Mills, advertised an encomium from Callas' doctor certifying that her nationally famous weight loss came from her use of Pantanella's macaroni.

It made perfect sense to Pantanella Mills, at least—because Callas didn't eat Pantanella's (or any) pasta, and the doctor wasn't her doctor in any real sense. Even if it had been true, she would never have sold her body (so to say) in this manner.

Callas initiated legal proceedings. Then it turned out that Pantanella's president was a twentieth-century version of that historical figure, the Pope's Nephew. Eons before, these nephews were thought to be the Holy Father's illegitimate offspring, favored professionally and highly influential under the traditional Italian belief that you can't trust anyone except your relatives.

In fifties Italy, to challenge one of these figures was a sort of treason. But Callas was determined to clear her name of calumny. Some call her "stubborn," others "resolute." In any case, she would not give in.

And then the Pope invited the Meneghinis to a private audience, during which he found a moment to express concern about the lawsuit against Pantanella.

Meneghini registered surprise that this utterly spiritual being, the very Vicar of Christ, should be so aware of mundane matters of law. To this, Pope Pius XII responded, "Nothing escapes me."

Hmm. Perhaps this was a glitch to consider. Meneghini now urged Callas to be reasonable—meaning, of course, serve as a tool of someone else's will. But Callas was Callas; one might as well ask Madame De Farge to skip the afternoon guillotining for a quilting bee. Callas held firm, at least until 1953, when the first court judgment found in her favor. The Pantanella people still tried to legal their way out of a retraction, but, as Meneghini saw it, Callas had won. And, after all, the Pope...

"All right," she said.

Then the Pope died, and new light began to shine in the eyes of Callas.

"Battista," she said, "telephone our lawyers. We're going back to court."

Still the case dragged on, and in 1959 Callas finally prevailed. But by then the Meneghinis were cruising on the yacht Christina with Aristotle Onassis, the man who would destroy Callas' marriage, career, and life.

A Wandering Minstrel He

In 1955, to test the truth of the legend of this wondrous Maria Callas, Rudolf Bing traveled to Chicago to hear what she was like in the theatre. The work on view was *Il Trovatore*, with Jussi Bjoerling as Manrico, and Bing noticed something unusual in this Big Star opera, so often the home of non-acting singers: as Bjoerling sang "Ah sì, ben mio" (Ah yes, my love) to Callas' Leonora, she seemed to turn the aria into a duet just by the way she was reacting to him.

As Bing later described it, "He didn't know what he was singing. But *she* knew."

Three For Tonight

La Scala was considering a super-special production of *The Tales Of Hoffmann*, with an all-star cast—perhaps Corelli or Del Monaco as the hero; Tito Gobbi, Ettore Bastianini, and Nicola Zaccaria sharing the villains; and Fiorenza Cossotto as Nicklausse, in a staging by Margherita Wallmann. And, as the three heroines, Maria Callas: a coloratura as Olympia, a drammatica as Giulietta, and a morbidezza as Antonia.

No sooner had the plans been set into motion than someone ran to Callas to tell her the news: "And they want you to sing the prima donna, three times!"

And Callas replied, "But will they pay me three times?"

Callas' White Paper On Tebaldi

Yes, there was a feud. It was complicated, because Tebaldi—tall, trim, and handsome, and blessed with a naturally beautiful voice evenly registered—had been a La Scala favorite for a time. But then Callas erupted onto the scene and supplanted her, and Callas—poorly favored by nature but possessed of the iron will to remake herself, from voice to looks—virtually hunted Tebaldi from La Scala, with the connivance of that saboteur Ghiringhelli. Further, Callas was vindictive while Tebaldi was sweet hearted (though she, too, had an iron will, hidden behind a smile that was at once radiant and a puff of smoke).

Feud, feud, the press was wild for it, and finally *Time* magazine got a quotation from Madam Callas on just why Madam Tebaldi could not compete with her. And note the sarcastic tone: "If the time comes when my dear friend Renata Tebaldi will sing...*Norma* or *Lucia* or *Anna Bolena* one night, then *La Traviata* or *Gioconda* or *Medea* the next—then, and only then, will we be rivals."

Angel Of Death

Callas was at the height of her fame and Renata Scotto just starting out when they met for a recording of Cherubini's *Medea*, under

Tullio Serafin. Callas would of course sing the Cretan virago and Scotto the role of Glauce, who has one aria early on and very little to do after that.

At the start of the sessions, Serafin announced that he wanted to cut a bit of Medea's establishing aria, "Dei tuoi figli" (Of your sons). After all, Callas had much to sing elsewhere in the opera (and was in poor voice for the recording, anyway), and this aria, so awkwardly placed in the middle of a dramatic scene, does slow up the action.

"No, maestro," said Callas. "It must not be. The aria shows Medea's fragility, her loving nature under the forgivable anger of a woman betrayed."

"But we must cut," said Serafin.

"Yes, I accept it," Callas replied. "But instead let's cut Glauce's aria."

Looking at Scotto, Callas added, "Completely."

Ifigenia In Grand Central Station

For Gluck's *Ifigenia in Tauride* (in the Italian version) at La Scala, director Visconti had his designer, Nicola Benois, create a unit set of a Baroque palace, full of stairs and arches. Callas was to appear as more of a queen than (as the story demands) a priest-ess, in a sumptuous gown of timeless grandeur, backed by a cape and topped with lines of pearls across her bodice and in her hair. Further, Visconti filled the stage with Ifigenia's handmaidens, now crowding around her and now drawing back in horror. (There is to be a human sacrifice—and the victim is her brother.) At one point, the women ranged themselves around Ifigenia on a huge staircase, their arms outstretched in supplication, an arrest-ing picture.

Callas never quite got the production concept. The story is ancient Greek in background, not Baroque, and the music, though dramatic, is somewhat austere in style, ceremonial rather than busy.

Years later, Alan Sievewright visited Callas to make plans for a tribute that never happened, but they did have an interesting chat about the Gluck opera. She recalled that Visconti wanted her running up and down a steep ramp, and, when she refused, he irately told her, "Any of my artists would do it."

"Then *let* one of your artists do it," Callas snapped back, walking out.

Visconti eased the ramp into a less forbidding staircase, and the show went over well, though Gluckiste tragédie lyrique tends to create the succès d'estime rather than the succès fou.

"Yes, yes, it was quite inspiring," Callas admitted. "But it's a story about only four characters. I never did understand why there were so many strange people popping in and out."

I'm With Her

Alfredo Kraus had been singing opera professionally for only two years when he was booked for an Alfredo Germont in Lisbon in 1958. His Violetta was Callas, so Kraus was a bit apprehensive; he had heard the stories.

It especially troubled him that the Lisbon audience, surprised at how good this unknown tenor was (he was especially passionate in his offstage interpolations in "Sempre libera") gave him a warm welcome. Would this turn her against him?

In fact, she was kindness itself. Perhaps he just had the right attitude. At the end, the stage staff held the curtains for her to take a solo bow, but she took his hand, saying, "You come with me, Kraus."

And out they went, together.

This was the series of performances whose broadcast created the famous "Lisbon *Traviata*," celebrated in Terrence McNally's black comedy.

The Visconti Touch

French actor's agent Georges Beaume would tell of a dinner party he gave at Maxim's in Paris for Luchino Visconti, Alain Delon (Beaume's client), Gian Carlo Menotti, and Callas. When Beaume invited her, she accepted, but nevertheless complained about Visconti. Yes, he gave her many successes at La Scala—but how vilely he treated her!

"There are times when I don't understand what he wants from me," she told Beaume. "He will say, 'Just do it!' And I look out into the auditorium where he is, into that darkness where who knows what is going on, and I call to him, 'Luchino, what do you want me to do? Can't you just tell me?' And you know what that scoundrel says then, Georges? With that smile of his—oh, which moves so sneakily from one side of his mouth to the other?"

She paused there. So Beaume prompted her with "What does he say then?"

And Callas replied, " 'Shut up and sing, you bitch!' "

Vade Retro Satanas

At one point in the finale of Bellini's *Il Pirata*, the heroine, knowing her lover is being executed, cries, "La…vedete…il palco funesto." In the context of the opera, the line means, "There…see…the scaffold of doom."

However, Callas' relationship with Antonio Ghiringhelli had gone from valid to rocky to ballistic over time, as Callas was too outspokenly independent to suit the Scala chief's domineering rule. In 1958, while singing in La Scala's *Il Pirata*, the singer decided to make the most of Felice Romani's libretto and give the public something to remember. When she got to the line in question, Callas unmistakably indicated the box that the Scala management always sat in. And it happens that *palco* means not only "scaffold" but ... "theatre box."

The theatre box of doom! Staring at Ghiringhelli (who sat with his features fixed in monumental fury), the audience went berserk as the curtain fell, and Ghiringhelli then ordered the house staff to cut short Callas' bows by lowering the fire curtain. Callas was not invited back to the house for two years, and even then just for one work, Donizetti's *Poliuto*, and only because so few other singers could handle the music.

And so ended Callas' reign as the queen of La Scala.

The Final Act

Riccardo Muti was off fulfilling an engagement in America when his phone rang. He heard a woman's voice, low and haunting—enchanting, even. An opera singer's voice.

"You don't know me, maestro," she said, "but I heard you are looking for me."

Of course, a conductor of international renown and numerous projects is always "looking" for various people, and it all fell into place when the speaker identified herself as Maria Callas.

Yes, Muti had been looking for her: to ask her to take part in a *Macbeth* he was putting together in Florence, as her Lady at La Scala in 1952 rang out through the years among all Verdians. Muti had consulted with someone at EMI Records who knew Callas—could he help bring her together with Muti? This phone call was the result.

But would Callas undertake the role, now, in the 1970s, years after she seemed to have given up singing entirely?

"I'm pleased that you thought of me," she told him. Then, using Violetta's words after she reads Alfredo's letter in the last act of *La Traviata*, Callas said, in the tragic delivery so especially reserved for that moment, "È tardi."

It's too late.

The Fat Lady Sings

Will You Come In, Mystery Challenger, and Sign In, Please?

Otto Klemperer was out walking in Zürich with an official of his record label, EMI; the official's name, as it happens, was Mendelssohn. They came to a music store and Mendelssohn thought they should drop in and see how well their star conductor was stocked.

But when they asked for "Beethoven's Fifth Symphony led by Otto Klemperer," the clerk said they had only von Karajan and Bruno Walter in that work.

Irritated, Klemperer drew himself up to his considerable height and announced that he *was* Otto Klemperer, and what a blot on this store it was! An insult to the art!

The clerk said, "Is that so? Otto Klemperer in our little music shop? And I suppose that's Beethoven with you, ja?"

"No," Klemperer replied. "That's Mendelssohn."

Cut To the Chase

In the early 1970s, the Dallas Opera suffered some financial embarrassment. So when Helga Dernesch got off the plane to rehearse her *Fidelio* with Jon Vickers under Charles Mackerras, her first words to the company rep who picked her up at the airport were "Where is check and where is bank?"

A Little Night Music

An all-star benefit concert in Carnegie Hall featured some of the biggest names in music, from Pavarotti to Fischer-Dieskau to Bernstein to Horowitz. To cap this vaudeville of immortals, assistants gathered everyone on stage, handed them scores of Handel's *Messiah*, and announced that there would be an impromptu finale of the Hallelujah Chorus. All together now...

Fischer-Dieskau later said, "I have never heard so many wrong notes." Indeed, on his way out, Fischer-Dieskau passed Bernstein on the stairs. They shared a look, and Bernstein said, "I know, I know."

Leontyne Price On the Quality Of Her Singing

"I'm *mad* about my voice."

Leontyne Price On Being Openly Boastful About Her Gifts

"You cannot be an opera singer and be humble."

The Führer Kiss'd Me When We Met

Baritone Herbert Janssen, who hated the Nazis, noticed that rival baritone Jaro Prohaska's wife, a Nazi enthusiast, was wearing on one hand a golden swastika that chained up her fingers.

When Janssen asked about it, Frau Prohaska replied, "That is where the Führer kissed me, so I have closed it up forever, in dedication to the Reich."

And Janssen said, "Too bad he didn't kiss you on the mouth."

The Lucine Amara Gala

A lyric soprano, Amara was versatile, singing everything from Pamina to Tatiana, and she spent her long career at the Met as one of Rudolf Bing's safeties, ready to step in whenever the expected singer was indisposed.

So those incorrigible Met standees invented a fictional Lucine Amara Gala, presenting one act each of her most constant roles—Liù in *Turandot*, Nedda in *Pagliacci*, and Donna Elvira in *Don Giovanni*. But Lucine wasn't scheduled to sing: she was covering the entire evening.

Frozen

Karl Böhm was talking with Wieland Wagner, who was known as something of an homme fatale, about Birgit Nilsson. This was in the 1950s, when she was just emerging as a major hoch-dramatische, destined to reign in Bayreuth as Isolde, Brünnhilde, and the like.

But Wieland wasn't so sure. "Yes, she's splendid," he agreed. "But so cold."

"Oh," said Böhm, "you'll find a way to warm her up."

Michele Molese's High C

Tenor Molese was the New York City Opera's go-to tenor in the Italian and French classics, your constant Faust or Pinkerton but never really a star…till the *New York Times'* music critic Harold Schonberg chastised Molese for "squeezing some high notes."

Schonberg never knew what he was hearing anyway, but Molese nevertheless sought to reeducate him during a performance of *Un Ballo In Maschera*. In the love duet in Act Two, he hit a tremendous open-throated high note, then spoke directly to the audience.

"That 'pinched' high C," Molese announced, "is for Mr. Schonberg."

It made local headlines, and intendant Julius Rudel had no choice but to fire Molese for unprofessional conduct. Still, the tenor was too useful to lose, so Rudel waited for the "scandal" to die down, then brought Molese back.

He sang his last City Opera performance in 1980, moved to Italy, and died relatively young. Sad to say, the only time Molese really made his mark was when he told Harold Schonberg off.

The Directa's Blurb Is Ready

During Mary Garden's reign in running the Chicago Opera, she was great copy for reporters, because she always had a quotable line on any subject.

One day, at a charity auction, a raggedy old man appeared out of nowhere and tried to attack her. The police intervened and arrested him, and when they asked why he wanted to assault Chicago's beloved Mary Garden, the guy answered, "She talks too much."

The next tale has been told and retold over the decades by Met opera buffs. Presumably apocryphal, it has enjoyed many changes of cast, but this is the version I heard most often…

High Holiday Fun

Early one autumn, Eleanor Steber ran into Regina Resnik somewhere in the house and asked what she was up to lately.

"Well," Resnik began, "this is the time of the Jewish holidays—Rosh Hashanah, which is the New Year, and Yom Kippur, the Day Of Atonement. There's quite a lot to do."

"How much do you have to atone for?" Steber asked.

"That depends on the individual. Mr. Bing would be quite busy that day, I believe."

The two exchanged playful smiles, and Steber then asked what happens in the New Year's celebration.

"Of course, we all go to the synagogue. And then we blow the *shofar*."

"My," said Steber, "you people certainly like to coddle the help."

Debussy On the Paris Opéra

A sometime music journalist, Debussy hated everything, especially the Opéra, where he had many a "painful experience." He didn't even like the building, otherwise regarded as an adornment of a beautiful city.

"A foreigner," Debussy wrote, "would assume it was a railroad station, and he would mistake the interior for a Turkish bath."

Callas' Master Classes

In 1971, Maria Callas undertook a series of pedagogical coaching sessions at the Juilliard School Of Music. Sitting at a table in a long dress, sensible heels, and no-nonsense eyeglasses, she started every-thing off with typical Callas bluntness: "Who wants to sing?"

Some of the students, such as Barbara Hendricks and Willard White, went on to major careers, but some others were not yet ready to demonstrate professional vocation. One mezzo sang the section reprising "Stride la vampa" in Azucena's second-act duet with Manrico, and came to grief on the high note after "Il figlio mio avea bruciato!" (I burned my infant son to death!)

Defending herself, the student suggested that dramatic verisi-militude gave her poetic license to fudge the high note. "It's a cry of despair," she explained.

"It's not a cry of despair," Callas fired back. "It's a B Flat."

Gay Divorce

Tamar Iveri, a lyric soprano from the former Soviet Georgia, was on the rise in the very early 2000s, appearing at major theatres, includ-ing La Scala and the Met. She was as well physically striking, with black hair and a trim physique.

However, in 2014, someone happened upon a post on Iveri's Facebook page in which she approved of a physical attack on a gay-liberation march in her hometown of Tbilisi. "Often, in certain cases," she wrote [as anonymously translated and used in all news-paper accounts], "it is necessary to break jaws.... Please, stop vigor-ous campaigns to bring West's 'fecal masses' in[to] the mentality of people by means of propaganda.... The Georgian people are aware of what fruits...to eat and what to discard. Just like my small dog guesses it."

In the ensuing controversy, Iveri apologized, blaming her hus-band for writing on her Facebook page in her name. However, the

Georgia gay organization Identoba noted that the offending post had actually been discovered a year before this, and Iveri said nothing then about her husband's alleged involvement.

Given the heavy concentration of gay people in the opera world on both sides of the footlights, posting so homophobically was an extremely reckless act. Iveri immediately lost a concert at the Paris Opéra and a *Ballo in Maschera* in Brussels. The Australian Opera, where she was to sing in *Otello*, tried to weasel out of making a stand till its commercial sponsors theatened to withdraw support and a popular boycott was brewing.

Moral: Be nice to gays or you'll be giving your Desdemona in Tbilisi for the rest of your life.

I'm Leading

Kathleen Battle showed up for a rehearsal for a concert feeling that her voice wasn't in its best shape. She suggested that the conductor and orchestra go through the music while she stood silently by, to make sure they were all in agreement about tempo, dynamics, and so on.

Good idea, and the maestro and his players were still on the first page when Battle called out, "Stop!"

They all did, and the conductor turned questioningly to Battle.

"You're not following me," she told him.

He Never Looked Lovelier

On the last night of the 2017 Bayreuth Festival, during a performance of *Götterdämmerung*, the Brünnhilde, Catherine Foster, injured her leg. So the assistant director, Andreas Rosar, donned the valkyrie's gold-lamé dress and a wig and enacted the role silently for Acts Two and Three while Foster sang her lines in a wheelchair at the side of the stage.

Rosar, a handsome fellow, made a distracting Brünnhilde, but the audience cheered, anyway. And, after all, as Siegfried observes when he first encounters Brünnhilde in the preceding *Ring* opera, "Das ist kein Mann!" (That is no man!)

Wo Ist Brunnhild'?: a mystery for my readers

Speaking of *Götterdämmerung*, Decca's John Culshaw was so proud of his recording—the opera's first complete commercial release—that he sent a special disc of the Immolation Scene to his Brünnhilde, Birgit Nilsson, but she listened to it in a fury. She was inaudible, or so she said—and what if she now refused to record *Die Walküre*, which Culshaw had saved for the last shot of his *Ring* cycle?

Culshaw tried to get Nilsson to come hear the same music on better equipment than she was no doubt using, but she seemed to enjoy being irate. Celebrities love getting mad about things. Nilsson wouldn't budge from *I can't be heard on this record and don't try to play me your substitute la-di-da disc in your control room to confuse me!*

What to do? Culshaw finally produced a trim little battery-powered portable player and urged Nilsson to try the disc on it. No control room, no cajoling Decca engineers. And she would see at last that there was nothing wrong with the way she sounded on Decca's *Götterdämmerung*. Sure enough, Nilsson now loved what she heard.

But what had gone wrong in the first place? A low-quality record player would give poor reproduction, but it couldn't diminish the volume of the voice without the diminishing the volume of the orchestra. So what could have happened? Reader, can you guess?

The answer: Culshaw's opera sets exploited stereo technology for sound effects unavailable in the theatre, to heighten the experience for the home listener. One of these effects was movement on the singers' microphone platform, so they might be heard to pass from one speaker to another and back. Nilsson must have been using a player with one of its speakers out (or the separation knob turned all the way to the right or left), so that, at certain times, the orchestra could be heard but Nilsson's voice would have moved from the working speaker to the dead one, where her voice would sound faint. Incidentally, this story's title is the first line Wotan utters when he strides onstage in *Die Walküre*'s third act, as angry at Brünnhilde as Nilsson was at Decca. And, to put a happy ending on our tale, Decca let Nilsson keep the little portable player, which thrilled her no end. Celebrities love getting things for free.

The Queen and I

In Chicago singing Verdi's *Don Carlo* with a very glamorous singer from Down Under, Neil Rosenshein took a moment to recall the summer when she was starring in Santa Fe and Rosenshein was one of the company apprentices.

"I have to tell you this," he said to her. "I really, *really* wanted you."

With a playful smile, she replied, "And you could have had me."

Your Genial Host

Rossini's soirées during his retirement were famous as much for the stingy refreshment menu as for the glittering guests. "Smoke and lounge as you please," Rossini would urge his guests. "Pretend you're in a café."

"If this is a café," someone once muttered, "why doesn't he give us something to drink?"

But the company truly was impressive. The great contralto Marietta Alboni was present one night, when Prince Poniatowski asked her to favor them all with "Ah! quel giorno" from *Semiramide*.

Alboni was willing, but Rossini, seated at the piano, said he doubted he could recall the whole thing. "The cavatina, perhaps, he mused. "But the rest...and there's the recitativo. I wouldn't get past the first line!"

A guest suggested he pull out the score, but Rossini didn't have one, neither in manuscript nor as published. Of course, the others were flabbergasted, to which Rossini asked, "Do you keep your empty matchboxes? Or your worn-out slippers?"

In the ensuing silence, Rossini pensively told Alboni, "Va bene, let's attempt it, but who knows what will come forth from me? As for the recitativo, don't wait for me. You forge ahead and somehow I'll follow. If only we were trying the *Barber*–I know entire pages of that one! But coraggio. The devil take it if I can't sneak through the cavatina, at least. As for the cabaletta..."

But the piece went off wonderfully, and Alboni, in superb voice, drew tears from many an eye. For here was no ordinary aria. Manuel Garcia himself said that if all the great vocal scenes of old were to be swept away, this one alone would revive the lost art of bel canto.

Then the clock struck ten and Madame Rossini sternly ushered everyone to the door while the composer embraced Alboni with

"Buona sera, l'ultima diva del mio cuore." (Good evening to the last of my favorite singers.)

In a way, it was more or less the end of an era.

Goodbye, My Dears

Lisa della Casa, inarguably the greatest Arabella of her day, had to deal with a personal problem: her daughter was undergoing convalescence after a serious operation and needed constant care.

Della Casa asked her husband if they could afford her leaving the opera world; he said yes. So, one night, on the stage of the Vienna Staatsoper, della Casa made her farewell. There was no announcement: she simply canceled her outstanding engagements and went on for one last Arabella.

But something happened when she came to the line "Dann fahr ich fort von euch auf Nimmerwiedersehn" (Then I will go away from all of you, never to see you again), very notable words, as Strauss set it to jump up to a sustained and very exposed high B Flat. Della Casa unmistakably sang that phrase directly to the audience instead of the baritone she was sharing the stage with at that point. Then she went back into character, finished the performance, took her calls, and went home to her daughter.

And that was the farewell of Lisa della Casa.

More Apocrypha?

Pauline Viardot-Garcia wanted to sing only the noblest roles in opera—Orphée (in Berlioz's version of 1859); Beethoven's Leonore; Meyerbeer's Valentine and Fidès (which she created); even one act of Isolde—the "love" act, between the "potion" act and the "death" act—in a private performance in which Wagner sang Tristan.

One part eluded her, for Viardot was a mezzo-soprano, and perhaps the noblest role of all was more than she could manage.

But we are told that, on her deathbed, the last thing she said was... "Norma."

Renata Looks Back On Her Life

Interviewing Renata Tebaldi after her retirement, Albert Innaurato caught this strange and marvelous outpouring of ideas from the soprano: "My voice, it was from God.... But you know, God makes us pay for His gifts. I have paid Him a lot, and I praise Him. But sometimes, I pray, please, I would like to stop paying.... And my bill is walking in the graveyard.... My friends are buried there, and my enemies.... But opera is buried there, too."

> Now for our last story, told by Arrigo Boito to his friends and spread among others till all the leadership class of Italy had heard it. Giulio Gatti-Casazza, who was to take charge of La Scala shortly thereafter, recounted it in his memoirs in too short a version. This tale needs room in which to expand...

A Puff Of a Cool Breeze

By the time Verdi wrote his final opera, *Falstaff*, he had become more than a national treasure: an icon of Western art, like Shakespeare or Goethe. Although Verdi treated Boito as an equal and though Boito was himself a luminary in Italy's literary world as well as a composer of no small account himself, he always felt intimidated.

So when Verdi played and sang through *Falstaff*'s Act Two, Scene Two—set in the Ford household—and asked Boito what he thought, the librettist answered with thoroughgoing praise. And yet...all the same...*no*. No, this is Verdi, virtually the soul and history of Italy come to life. One cannot criticize.

"Come, come, Boito, why this reticence?" said Verdi lightly. "Would I ask for your opinion if I didn't want to hear it?"

Boito had to concede that point, for Verdi never bluffed. And so: "Very well, Maestro," Boito sighed. "That arietta Falstaff sings, 'Quand' ero paggio.' (When I was but a page.) This is my personal opinion, you understand, such as you have asked for. But the music of this little song seems to me...perhaps a touch...too facile. Too delicate and simple at the end of such a sophisticated scene, with its arresting changes of mood. I am sorry, Maestro. But you did ask me to be honest."

"Hmm, I wonder," Verdi replied. He went back to the piano to sing and play the little piece—it lasts barely a minute—once and then again.

"Alas, mio caro Boito," Verdi concluded, "I cannot agree. This tiny thing is necessary to break away from the big duet of Falstaff and Mistress Ford, like a puff of a cool breeze on a warm day. And the little hopping melody sits very well on your verses. If it sounds facile...well, it needs to be so. Have patience, now, for I will leave the scene as it is."

The next year, when the opera was finished, Verdi played through it in its entirety. And Boito, overwhelmed to hear his words so imaginatively set in so free and fluid a musical style, still felt that...Let's let him say it: "That little canzonetta is too cold, Maestro. It weakens the duet." Feeling he was too arrogant, Boito added, "Or am I wrong?"

Without replying, Verdi played and sang through "Quand' ero paggio" once more. Shaking his head with a smile, he said, "Caro Boito, I still feel as I did before. We must leave our little opera as it is, to seek its fortune in the world."

At *Falstaff*'s premiere, in 1893 at La Scala, when the Falstaff, Victor Maurel, sang this arietta, he was greeted with such vociferous cries of "Bis!" that he had to repeat it three times. And thus it seemed that Verdi had created just the right music at just the right moment in the story.

Backstage, at the end of the act, Verdi walked over to Boito and said, "Well, there it stands, my friend. Was the old man right—this time, at least?"

Humbled at this proof of Verdi's lack of ego aggression and, especially, his acumen as a genius of theatre and music, all music, the world's music, Boito replied, with touching sincerity, "Yes, Maestro, you were right this time. And you have always been right. And you will always be right forever."

INDEX

INDEX